CW01072780

People grow old by deserting their ideals.
Years may wrinkle the skin,
but to give up interest wrinkles the soul;
You are as young as your faith,
as old as your doubt;
As young as your self confidence,
as old as your fears;
As young as your hope,
as old as your despair.

Douglas MacArthur

ABOUT THE AUTHOR

Ian Hamilton was born in Southport, England
and was involved in show business for many years;
managing and promoting a range of entertainers.
He came to Australia in 1972 and became involved
in the tourism industry on the Gold Coast throughout
the 70s.
Returning there after numerous business ventures in
Sydney he commenced his own publishing business,
producing a range of colour magazines during the
late 80s and early 90s
A marriage to Fay and a new life establishing the
holiday retreat, Possum Creek Lodge in the Byron
Hinterland, brought a wider dimension to his life.
Ian has always had a passion for travel, good food,
hard work and exciting challenges.
A free lance travel journalist, this is his first book.

COVER ART AND DESIGN

Sydney based artist Bronwyn Woodley has extensively
studied the oil painting techniques of the Old Masters.
She specialises in figuartive portrait, still life and
contempory landscapes and welcomes commission work.
She is owner and resident artist of Balmain Art Gallery
& Studio. Studio 2, 332 Darling St., Balmain NSW 2041
Tel 02 9818 8998.

ILLUSTRATIONS

Illustrations by Susie Dureau
Tel (61) 0403 810 760 Email dureau@aol.com.
or sdureau@hotmail.com

TRANSPORTATION

Our choice of travel was an Australian-made
Sunliner Motorhome

Beaches
Bush Roads
and Bull Ants

Ian

Hamilton

OPTIC

PUBLISHING

First published 2003 by Optic Publishing
Copyright © Ian Hamilton.
All rights reserved
Editor Fay Hamilton
Printed by Mc Phersons Printing Group

ISBN 0-646-42390-8

National Library of Australia

Disclaimer
This book is sold subject to the condition that it is taken in the spirit it was
intended. Certain names and identities have been changed to protect the
privacy of those concerned and also to save thousands of dollars in litigation

All correspondence and mail orders to

Optic Pty Ltd,
PO Box 125,
Suffolk Park,
NSW 2481
Tel 02 6685 3374
Email look@bbbullants.com

TO

My dearest wife
Fay
Whose encouragement, assistance and support
made this mountain a whole lot easier to climb.

and

TO

My two sons
Scotty and Brett

May they one day have the opportunity and desire
to tread in our footsteps, in a world that will
hopefully see minimal changes.

This book has been written to entertain, to amuse and to
educate, but more importantly to encourage people of any age
and from all parts of the world to reach out and discover our
captivating country

ARAFURA SEA

CORAL SEA

m LAND

GULF OF CARPENTARIA

CAPE YORK PENINSULA

COOKTOWN

GREAT BARRIER REEF

ATHERTON TABLELANDS

CAIRNS

KARUMBA

NORMANTON

TOWNSVILLE

WHITSUNDAY ISLANDS

TENNANT CREEK

MT. ISA

CHARTERS TOWERS

MACKAY

PACIFIC OCEAN

USTRALIA

ROCKHAMPTON

FRASER ISLAND

BRISBANE

BYRON BAY

AIN

FLINDERS RANGES

THE HUNTER VALLEY

EYRE PENINSULA

MUDGEE

SYDNEY

ADELAIDE

MILDURA

CANBERRA

MELBOURNE

BASS STRAIT

HOBART

vii

FIVE STAR BUSH DINING

RECIPES

CONTENTS

ACKNOWLEDGEMENTS

I recently read a novel by an Internationally acclaimed author who individually thanked over 80 associates, whose love and support had never failed to inspire him.

They had all contributed in one way or another; areas of research, editing, publishing, and generally assisting him in producing his best seller.

In this repect I would like to singualarly thank my wife Fay, aka the co-driver, my little wife or 'her outdoors' , who crossed all my T's, dotted my I's and proved to be an editor of remarkable patience.

She also provided unlimited amounts of tea and pulled the odd cork whenever needed.

In addition I would to like to especially acknowledge the generous help of the following friends who contributed in one way or another.

Simon and Guy Beaven who generously gave me technical guidance with the lay out of the book. Dennis Gilham and Jan Dawkins who spent hours proof reading while Richard Schmidt assisted with his culinary contributions.

PROLOGUE

**'It is in moments of decision
That your destiny is shaped'**

I awoke to another perfect Byron Bay morning. The golden sun ball was finely balanced, only for seconds, on the distant contours of the Pacific Ocean, before its ascent into the peerless blue sky.

Overlooking the crashing waves from our beachfront cottage, I lay quite still trying to absorb the decisions of the previous night.

My wife Fay and I had finally bitten the bullet and cemented our decision to take a year out, freewheeling around the Australian continent. She lay next to me, peculiar little noises emanating from her sleeping form and a look of contentment on her half-smiling face as though she had already started our adventure.

After a lifetime of corporate-style living and running our various business ventures, we felt the time perfect for a 'sea change'. Ever the inquisitive types, we were looking for an investigative adventure into an Australia we had only heard or read about.

Visions of deserted beaches, wide-open spaces, out of the ordinary destinations, and a closeness with nature filled our fertile minds. We also looked forward to seeking out offbeat characters, meeting travellers with similar ideals and immersing ourselves in the history and culture of this vastly diversified country.

Always inclined towards the funny side of life, and with an awareness of the futility of unnecessary trepidation, we intended to attack our life on the road with a degree of lighthearted ambivalence. "Don't sweat the small stuff" was to become our favourite saying.

Our journey started long before we actually departed. The preceding weeks were filled with a flurry of preparations. Major decisions were to be made pertaining to our mode of transport, departure date and the actual route we would travel.

1

We wanted to be free as larks, unrestricted by the need to stay in commercial caravan parks unless absolutely necessary. Our vision was more attuned to awakening to the sound of nearby rolling surf, or the view from a deserted cliff top, or perhaps bird calls around the banks of a quietly running stream. To do this we would need to be completely self contained, small enough to be easily maneuverable but large enough to cater to our hedonistic side with a reasonable degree of style and comfort.

A new seven-metre Sunliner motorhome was decided upon after reviewing the appearance and performance of literally dozens of likely contenders. We preferred the concept of the one-piece vehicle that realistically is a home on your back, compared with having to tow a trailer or caravan with the various restrictions involved. It's a personal choice and one we would debate with fellow travellers over the coming year.

To convert normal everyday living conditions to one of substantially reduced dimensions was an initial challenge. Given that cooking is one of our great pleasures, surpassed possibly by dining on the results of our efforts, the stocking of the pantry, which fortunately was quite accommodating, was of prime importance. Once again there were decisions to be made – choosing various herbs and spices and which oils, vinegars and condiments just had to be included. One thing was certain, there would be no canned spag on toast or burnt bangers on the barbie for this pair of gourmet travellers. We were looking forward to the challenge of creating interesting recipes under these more limited circumstances and the pleasure of sharing them with our friends.

In the meantime, Fay managed to condense her extensive wardrobe to a miniature 'something for every occasion and just a few frivolities'. I was happy with the basic T-shirts, shorts and togs and had to be coerced into packing extra things 'just in case it was cold' or 'just in case we went out to a smart restaurant'. Then came the crockery, the pots & pans, the games and the books. The chattels seemed to grow daily but somehow all found a place in the surprisingly commodious storage spaces.

The departure date was set for January 3rd, and the fact that it was the 'Year of the Outback' seemed to give our odyssey a degree of significance. Long hours were spent pouring over maps often in the company of friends who had already made similar trips. We dutifully noted all their advice.

"Make sure you travel anti-clockwise because the headwinds across the Nullarbor are a nightmare".

"The Northern Territory has to be explored during July to September because of the mossies and heat in the wet season".

"The heat in the Flinders is unbearable in summer", and so they went on.

But the most important one of all was,

"Don't set a timetable on your travels, and let your agenda be flexible".

The concept of being able to uproot our home and move around in an unshackled sort of way had always appealed to the gypsy in me. How exhilarating it would be to turn the ignition key and move to the next destination whenever the weather changed or the urge for time on a new piece of real estate presented itself.

Friends came to visit with good cheer and messages of farewell. I saw in the eyes of some, a look of longing as they surveyed our new lifestyle. They spoke as though a time would arrive when their desire for a free and unplugged life would eventuate. The appeal of an unfettered existence is never far away from the majority of our fellow Australians. Not that they wish to go anywhere in particular, but to break free from government bureaucracy, social restraints and the hum drum of everyday life and just go.

We spared a brief thought for the unadventurous; those who stay at home until they are too old to appreciate such journeys. It is only in adventure that some people succeed in finding themselves and perhaps liking what they find.

A journey like this can often be compared to a marriage. Unbridled pleasure in the expectations, the hopes and planning. The fulfillment and joy of the occasion eventuating and proceeding to plan. And ultimately the ongoing challenges and satisfactions that a new lifestyle can bring.

The rough but flexible plan was finally formed; we would head south to Newcastle, straight across NSW, down to South Australia and from there circumnavigate the continent in a clockwise direction. We hoped to encompass most of the extreme geographical points, deviating inland whenever our fancy took us.

The days on the calendar were ticked off and went by very quickly. A few memorable goodbye dinners, drinks at our local and seemingly endless final arrangements filled our days.

A sense of anticipation was mounting !

CHAPTER ONE

SCREW IT—LET'S DO IT

Suddenly, ready or not, the designated departure day arrived. We nonchalantly threw in a few last minute 'essentials' and hit the road with a sense of almost subdued excitement.

Good friends and neighbours Lynne and Richard, bearing a suspicious looking farewell package were waiting kerbside to wave us off. Their gift, covered in its strange looking hessian bag, was a camp oven and they claimed we could not be leaving on a trip such as this without one. Instructions and suggested recipes were hastily provided as they sang the praises of this formidable piece of cooking equipment. It subsequently became a treasured and well-used provider of a wide range of delectable dishes.

A bit further down the road, Susie, Dennis and family were gathered holding high a boxed bottle of Moet with accompanying glasses. "Keep it for a very special occasion" our more than generous friends suggested. We did, and it was eventually opened in the most romantic fashion.

With the good-byes, hugs, kisses, hand shakes and last little bits of advice behind us we drove off through the verdant hills of Byron Shire. South we headed and the big adventure was just beginning.

Our new Sunliner was not just a means of transport and a home away from home. In the weeks of trialing it pre departure, the vehicle took on its own character, became part of the family and had to be given a name. It's just like christening a new-born. Suggestions were drawn up, tossed around and one by one deleted. Finally the list was reduced to just a couple of names. A decision had to be made. Comedy often surrounds us in our lives and it is never far away in this book, so the name had to create a smile if only to ourselves. We had a few weird and wonderful ideas such as RV Norman, which Jerry Harvey would no doubt have enjoyed sponsoring. There was Priscilla, Queen of the Desert and Willie Who? in honour of Willie Nelson's 'On the Road Again'. But none seemed to fit the bill.

Finally Morrison 'The Van' was chosen. The name, which was blazoned across the bonnet, brought vacant looks to some faces but it did bring smiles to many that shared both our dry sense of humour and our enjoyment of the Irish entertainer Van Morrison, universally known as 'The Van'. His music was regularly heard streaming out from our on-board sound system. There is one character that we befriended in Darwin who is still scratching his head and cannot relate to the fact that our surname is Hamilton and not Morrison.

With our journey still very much in its infancy, it dawned upon us that we were now an integral part of the burgeoning business of motorised holidays. One of the fastest growing industries satisfying the needs and pleasures of the baby boomer brigade. The grey nomads as the media christened us. One newspaper even classified us all as Geriatric Gypsies'. As we wound our way around the continent, it was a revelation to see so many young couples, families with small kids and early retirees heading off to experience their own unique adventure.

There is a distinct difference between a holiday and an adventure. A holiday is generally finite in its destination, schedules and date of return. An adventure is more loosely planned, there are normally minimal time restraints and freedom is maximised. It is possible to stay in any particular place as long as your heart desires, or move on at a mere whim. An adventure is unique in its entity and there is individuality to each one.

Aussies have inherited a tendency to be mobile, continually searching for greener pastures. A pioneering restless spirit is in the genes of most of us and there are few that don't appreciate the smell and feel of the great outdoors. This is a country that encourages and exemplifies such actions. People who have emigrated here over the decades have been travellers and adventurers and their stories abound in Australian folklore.

The spirit of Robbie Burns is alive and well in the quaint NSW Northern Rivers town of Maclean, known as The Scottish Town in Australia. It is only a short afternoon drive from Byron Bay so we decided not to exert ourselves too much on day one and had arranged to meet friends there. As the town was holding its annual rodeo it seemed a good idea to spend some time checking the place out.

Nestled along the banks of the expansive and picturesque Clarence River, it is a few kilometres off the main Pacific Highway with most travellers bypassing it, in their quest to reach their destination. As we drove into town, our attention was immediately caught by the power poles, over 150 of them were clad in various tartan drapes. There were also colourful signs of Celtic history suspended from roadside structures and the shop windows offer an insight into a community with strong ties to a faraway land. The MacSwans, MacGregors, MacPhersons and Wallaces gathered here in the mid 1800s and the place has attracted many thousands more from the highlands over the years. They have Highland Games each Easter with caber tossing, throwing the hammer and other unusual Scottish activities, while the town band struts around in their kilts, bagpipes at the ready, playing stirring highland tunes. Tartan Day remembers the time when the Poms banned their northerly neighbours from wearing the kilt and sporran. During our stay there, I must say that I didn't see a single swirling kilt, nor were there any haggis or Scottish delicacies included on the menus of the rather limited eating spots. It would seem that our Scottish friends had things more Australian on their minds at the evening's twilight rodeo.

I am certainly a sucker for the rodeo. The dusty country atmosphere of the occasion mixed with the smell of the horses and cattle. The abundance of oversized bush hats, boots and jeans on the characters that are drawn in from the bush and the blaring music, 'Another one bites the dust', as yet another beast and its rider are released from the holding chutes.

Events such as bareback bronco riding, breakaway roping, steer wrestling, and the ultimate wild bull riding by kamikaze cowboys highlighted the evening. A couple of gaudily painted clowns stole the show with their agility, escaping serious injury by centimetres as the frustrated bulls horned down on them. The audience erupted when 'Woolly Bully' an automated bull on wheels, reared up to the fence and started spraying the nearby crowd from its nether regions with gallons of mysterious liquid.

Around the bar the accents were broad and slurred and everyone seemed to be talking like Billy Connolly. And they didn't mind the 'mickey' being taken out of them when it came to Scottish humour. How about one of their workmates wanting severance pay after a vasectomy. Then there was a local perv called Jock who had been arrested for reversing the charges while making obscene telephone calls. A couple of old mates met up after 15 years and suggested renewing old times with a few cold ales. "Aye" said the bearded one, "and it's your shout Mac".

All by himself at the other end of the bar, a young guy wearing an 'I belong to Glasgow' T-shirt looked really lonely, even though it transpired that he was on his honeymoon.

" Where's your new wife then"? I asked him.

"Oh, she's been to Maclean before" he dryly replied.

The Celtic spirit is truly alive and well in this laidback little town.

We camped right on the riverbank and in the morning were rewarded with an exhilarating sight. Within metres of our breakfast table, a procession of dolphins travelling in pairs cavorted along the river. Their apparently carefree existence seemed indicative of the days ahead of us.

Our friends, Felicity and Bruce also love to cavort but in the most unusual places. They were travelling north, so we arranged to meet where our paths would cross which happened to be Maclean. They are what could be called a 'sexually-embracing' couple, only recently married, and like many lovers infatuated with the delights of a new relationship. The banks of the Clarence appealed to Felicity's enthusiasm for 'trying it' in different places, and after lunch, which included a few lubricating drinks they stumbled through the adjacent trees. Fay and I had clear memories of our wedding day, when this very same couple were overcome by the emotion of the ceremony, and vanished into the laundry to consummate our marriage on top of the washing machine. The motions of that particular utility have never quite been the same.

Screams filled the air as a half-naked Felicity plunged towards us through the undergrowth, clutching a piece of miniscule underwear and using language normally attributable to a two-pot screamer.

It appeared that at the very height of their passion, her exposed nether regions came into contact with a bull ant nest and all hell broke loose. Large red itchy lumps appeared, hysteria set in and although the cursing mellowed, an urgent drive to the nearest doctor was needed.

"Goodness Gracious Me" the Indian medico cried, as he found it difficult to believe her story that she had simply sat on this large mound crawling with ants. Closer inspection found she was allergic to the big black fellas, and an ever-concerned Bruce enthusiastically rubbed the prescribed quantities of cortisone cream on to the effected parts. This is one little lady who certainly does not adhere to the old adage 'Once bitten, Twice shy.'

It was the peak holiday period and traffic along the Pacific Highway was akin to the aforementioned bull ants on the march. With this in mind, consideration had to be given to our ongoing route. Roadside signs advocating the delights of tourist trails and countless beach destinations competed for our attention but we ignored the ocean's tempting call and headed up the ranges to quieter pastures. We cut through vast areas of sugar cane fields, banana plantations, broad expansive rivers and exhilarating mountain ranges of greens and blues as we headed south.

The rustling of fresh green leaves on the grape-laden vines, bees buzzing around the bordering roses, a bird chorus in the background combine to create the summer song of The Hunter. This would be the first of many wine district visits and the last of our protracted farewells. A merry band of close friends from Sydney gathered at Lomas Lodge, the country farm retreat of Fay's long time friend, Helen. The group, individually and collectively, love their culinary pursuits. We were sure they believed that we would not see another decent meal for the duration of the trip, so it was a week-end of feasting combined with visits to the many friendly wineries for the mandatory wine tasting rituals.

The smell of smoke was in the air. Bush fires were rampant throughout much of New South Wales. Our decision was made to beat a fast track across New South Wales in the general direction of South Australia. It had always been our intention to give a wide berth to populated areas and explore destinations that were of a more natural beauty. Mudgee happened to be a combination of both.

After a goodly drive through diversified countryside we arrived just after sundown in need of a spot to settle down for the night. A large area of vacant land fortuitously appeared on the left-hand side of the road just before entering the town. This seemed to be the perfect place to set up camp.

After plucking a good bottle of red from Morrison's wine bin, I thought a tasty beef dish would be the order of the day. Like most Australians we love our beef and are always looking for different ways of appreciating it.

For those who like their meat red and rare, this one is a winner. It was not difficult to put together given our late arrival time, and proved to be clean, fresh and succulent.

10

True Blue Carpaccio of Beef

Mix together cracked black pepper, coriander (seeds are preferred), fresh or dried rosemary, salt (preferably sea) and if you want it a little spicier, some Cajun seasoning.
Blend well and rub into a 1kg fillet of beef, making sure it is well bedded in.
Cook in very hot frying pan, griddle or on a barbecue plate with olive oil until well browned & crisp.
Turning regularly, this should take only about five minutes. Set aside for ten minutes.
The meat should be quite rare inside.
Mix baby spinach leaves or mesclun, asparagus spears, semi dried tomatoes, shavings of Parmesan cheese or any other suitable combinations. Slice beef thinly and dress salad.
A horseradish dressing goes well.
A little olive oil, ½ cup of sour cream, a table spoon of white wine vinegar, horseradish to taste, sprinkle of white pepper and mix into smooth paste. Blotch on salad, top with the rare beef and enjoy.

Imagine our surprise at five o'clock the next morning when the thundering of hooves awoke us from a sleep heavily induced by copious amounts of red wine.

We were adjacent to the town's racetrack and the crack-of-dawn training sessions had begun for the weekend's race day. The unblinkered horses had not seen anything quite like Morrison before, and as he was only metres from the adjoining fence, their concentration became quite disrupted. Apart from an irate jockey giving us a one-fingered salute we were enjoying our front row seats until a charming young lady arrived in an official car. She kindly explained that Mudgee horses are a sensitive mob and are not used to strange looking vehicles spying on them. At her smiling request, we retreated to a safe distance and planned our day's activities.

The main attraction for travellers to the Mudgee area is the burgeoning wine industry that covers abundant areas of barren looking land. Over 20 wineries open their doors and take great pleasure in offering a taste of their current vintages. We would not miss this opportunity to do some comparisons with their neighbour, The Hunter.

Cycling the wineries has a number of advantages. Besides the exercise to be gained travelling between these establishments, there is the advantage of arriving at the next one in a greater state of sobriety. The disadvantage of course is that carrying cartons of your purchases around in a backpack can be quite cumbersome. We therefore cycled, tasted, ordered and returned later with Morrison to collect our liquid pleasures.

Mudgee has come of age in terms of producing wines that are becoming competitive with other areas. One vineyard owner with a distinctive Dutch accent informed us that there are more vines being planted there than all of the Hunter Valley. The aboriginal meaning of Mudgee is 'Nest in the Hills' and the place is a fine example of an old country town with a number of lovely heritage buildings. It comes alive every September when wine buffs and those who just appreciate knocking back varying quantities of the local produce, pack the place for the highly successful Wine Festival.

Morrison's springs gave a little groan as we loaded a few more cartons aboard and we were on the road again.

The Australian movie 'The Dish' was probably one of the most forgettable movies I have seen in many years. The massive CSIRO Radio Telescope on which the film was based, happens to be located about 20 kilometres north of the pleasant country town of Parkes. This is one of the worlds great research instruments and after 40 years of use has notched up some notable achievements. The first moon walks, assistance in rescuing Apollo 13, and collected data from Halley's Comet and other astronomical happenings have all been relayed from here. We stood dwarfed under the massive 64 metre steel paraboloid, elegantly balanced atop a three story concrete tower. The rumbling of the machinery and sibilant whining of the huge electric motors are occasionally heard by the groups of onlookers who gather with craned necks as the Dish probes into deepest space.

Rick who manages the adjacent visitor centre reckoned that since the release of the movie, visitor numbers have doubled, which must be great for the economy of the town.

The short diversion proved rewarding while the town exuded an atmosphere of a bygone era when gold was the big word. The place was named after a great statesman and Sir Henry visited here a few times during his tenure as Prime Minister.

Walking around the broad streets and grand old buildings, some of the folk appeared to be 'ring-ins' of characters from the movie, while others did not appear to have altered much from those halcyon-days of the late 1800s. The town had a fresh, cared-for look about it and they were proud of their place; something that was noticed in many of the country towns we passed through.

We pressed on to the Victorian border with mallee scrub, forgettable scenery and occasional sightings of wild life peppering the long drive.

Mildura, which is a bustling, attractive oasis town, is nestled along the banks of the mighty Murray. At 2700 kilometres in length, it is the world's third-longest navigable river. These days the numerous paddle steamers serve the tourism industry yet at the turn of last century they were the main means of transport, providing supplies to the town and remote stations. This is one of the country's richest agricultural areas, thanks to the Chaffey brothers who came from Canada in the 1880s and created an irrigation system that still operates today.

Morrison found a lovely place to settle, facing right onto the banks of the Murray at the Buronga Riverside Tourist Park and we unwound and absorbed this fascinating change of scenery. Strange looking birds joined us for nibbles, ducks lazily floated past and the paddle steamers headed into the setting sun for their last trip of the day. This was our first taste of living in an organised caravan park. It had been recommended to us and with its natural setting and the easy going 'park anywhere' rules, it was a far cry from the more regimented establishments we saw along the way.

Late arrivals to the park, Vicky & Bob, busied themselves setting up tents and their kitchen a stone's throw down the river from us. It appeared they were quite new to this camping game and were showing the big outdoors to their teenage son, Joe and his mate. Knackered after a day's hiking, the two young fellas retired early to their respective one-man tents while we oldies got together and chewed the fat over a drink or three.

Mum eventually decided to give her little darling a goodnight cuddle and in the twilight of the evening she got the tents mixed up. Imagine the surprise on the teenage friend's face, when in the darkened confines around his sleeping bag an intoxicated lady was making strange advances.

"Goodnight Mrs G" he mumbled, as she realised her mistake and embarrassingly fled back to hubby, who thought the whole episode hilarious. There were a few wry smiles around the breakfast table next morning with the young fella enquiring about padlocks for his front zipper. I presumed he meant for his tent.

Our newfound friends continued north while we headed towards the South Australian border through what is termed Sunset Country. It was pretty average scenery during the time the sun was high in the sky, and we saw no reason to hang around until it disappeared behind the trees, regardless of the advertising blurb on the place.

Through Renmark and we discovered the pretty township of Berri and as luck would have it we stumbled upon a deserted riverbank at Katarapko in the Murray River National Park.

With the sun's rays reflecting on the mirror-like waters, disturbed only by the landing of the water birds, it was time to crack a Mudgee red and think about cooking up some Murray Cod that we had picked up in Mildura. And what better way to do it than wrapped in the vine leaves we had collected along the way.

Mighty Murray Cod in Vine Leaves

The wine leaves we had picked were put to good use with this innovative fish dish. If you're not in a vine growing area, preserved vine leaves are often available at local delicatessens. Dip the leaves into boiling water for a minute, making them pliable and easy to work with.
The good looking Murray Cod, was big enough for the two of us, but other fish with firm flesh can be substituted.
Mix some butter, oil, lemon juice and seasoning and spread over both sides of fish. If available add some coriander or dill on top.
Wrap the whole fish in the vine leaves ensuring it is fully encased. Cook on hot coals or on a covered barbecue for about 20-30 minutes depending on heat.
Eat with or without the leaves, but either way the fish will be sensational.

After dinner a smile emerged on my little wife's face as she completed reading a study on longevity. Contrary to most peoples thoughts about having to slog it out at the gym, worry about cholesterol and blood pressure, minimise drinking and smoking etc, there is another answer. 'The Australian Doctor' reported that people with a 'positive outlook' to long life are the big winners. They grow old seven and a half years later than those with a less positive attitude. Fay had always thought that she might one-day hit the big double '0' and taking into account her extremely positive attitude, she calculated that she was seven and a half years closer to reaching that goal. I reminded her that there were other contributing factors. But life on the road, away from the stresses of everyday living, was indeed a major one.

A few days by the banks of the Murray, in an idealic setting with not another soul around gave us both a big dose of anti-stress. This was one of many places we would enjoy and wish we could linger longer. We were beginning to realise the importance of the first lesson of living on the road. Forget how to spell the word schedule.

Treat pre-made plans lightly, taking every day as it comes, and disappointments will be minimalised. Australia is a vast continent, and even though we had given ourselves a year on this trip, only an infinitesimal part would be visited. This sat well with one of 'her outdoor's' pet theories 'It is always good to leave a little bit for later'.

During the months of travelling together I came up with up a number of nicknames for my little wife and 'her outdoors', seemed rather appropriate.

We had been long-time lovers of the British evergreen TV series The Minder and like most viewers noticed that Aurther Daley's wife, known as 'her indoors', rarely made an appearance. Fay in total contrast is all about and hates to miss out on anything that is happening.

And so it was time to move on. It was one of those mornings when the air was motionless, the birds were even having a day off and the heat from the early morning sun was already filtering through the gum trees surrounding the campsite. We decided on some lazy morning activities in the nearby town.

My co driver wished to have a few hours doing what women universally enjoy, luxuriating in a beauty salon. A time to be pampered by young spunky things who are trained in the art of making you feel and look far better than when you walked in. It always works well for her and the money is well spent as she bounces around full of the joys of spring after one of these sessions of 'secret women's business'. She always seems to come out with some humorous piece of women's talk that girls like to impart on such occasions. The one for that day was about a well-known local client who maintained that she had a certificate in the three 'F's' of marriage - first she faked chastity, then she faked orgasm and is now successfully faking fidelity. Makes we mere men wonder, doesn't it?

While all this was taking place, I decided to amuse myself in the local courthouse, which is always good for a laugh. Perched in the back row, scanning the various characters lined up for their moment of truth, I found a different perspective of life here compared to larger towns and cities.

A bedraggled old soul who obviously couldn't claim to any particular success in life was first up before the beak. He looked like he had been sleeping in a hay barn in his only suit and with greasy unkempt hair flowing down his back, looked a sorry sight.

"Ever been cross examined before?" the magistrate asked glowering down upon him

"I'm a married man your Honour, so the answer is yes" he slowly mumbled.

"How long have you been married?" countered the Judge. There was a pregnant silence before the almost inaudible reply of ,

"Incessantly" your worship.

It seems he was defending himself against accusations of receiving quantities of stolen grog and the police were having difficulty in substantiating their evidence.

"Case dismissed due to lack of evidence" the bewigged one eventually thundered.

"Does that mean I can keep the grog then Milord, your Honour?" the pathetic defendant retorted.

The morning's proceedings were unexpectantly discontinued for a well-deserved coffee break, and I sauntered out into the morning heat to find Fay and enjoy the exchange of stories as we headed off for the Clare Valley. Time to check out a few more wineries and soak up the reputed atmosphere of this boutique wine area.

The Clare Valley is Australia's Riesling Mecca, but it is the old stone buildings, the gentle green valleys and the softness in the air, which initially strikes you. The pioneering heritage is everywhere and it is like suddenly stepping back in time. Exquisite villages, many trapped in their own veritable time warp are cushioned in a kaleidoscope of rolling hills, meandering streams and verdant blankets of vineyards.

Back in the 1800s, Pommies and Poles in their thousands came here to find their fortune in copper and other minerals, but it was the Jesuits who planted the first grapes. They had escaped an Austrian life of religious and political persecution and their original objective was to make wine for sacramental and religious use.

Nestled in this marvellous countryside at Sevenhill next to their church St Aloysius, they have continued their winemaking operations uninterrupted since settlement. Wine is now produced for more pleasurable reasons, with their highly drinkable Verdelho and a range of other whites and reds maintaining popularity. Their sacramental drops are not the winners they used to be and we didn't confuse our palates by even trying them.

The underground cellar is where it all began back in 1851 and is still used for storage of liquor fortifieds. Many sandalled feet have walked these flagstones over the last 150 years with plenty of tales told by candlelight during those testing early times. From those early days of pressing a formidable load of four buckets of grapes at a time, they now yield an annual crush of 350 tonnes, which results in about 20000 cases.

We fell in love with the State Heritage Town of Mintaro and decided to base ourselves there for a couple of days. Nearly all the buildings date back to pioneering days. Chapels and churches, schools, coach houses and settler's cottages abound, with wonderful country gardens and small vineyards providing colour and warmth. Mintaro has certainly lost none of its charm during its journey into the 21st century.

We found a sports ground surrounded by magnificent shade-providing weeping willows, which looked to be yet another perfect camp site. Within minutes of our arrival, an elderly gentleman appeared and by his look of authority we feared he was about to move us on. We had no need to be worried, he was merely welcoming us, indicating where water and toilets were located and offering to leave lights on if required. What hospitality this was and it set the seal for a memorable few days.

The traditional village pub called 'The Magpie and Stump' serves excellent cooling ales. This pleasant watering hole was particularly welcome after a long cycle ride around the dusty lanes, taking in all the wonderful buildings and equally stunning gardens. It seemed so right using a non automated means of transport in this old world setting.

Our fellow drinkers were charming folk, a couple of whom looked as though they could well have been there at the opening 150 years ago. Conversation was limited, as they weren't aware of anything that happened outside the village, except of course, 'sport' which perpetually diverted their gaze to a ceiling television. But they made us feel very welcome and even gave up watching the television to learn how we had come to be in their neck of the woods.

Around the village, National Trust Buildings have been converted in to B&B's, and quirky eating spots in ancient stone buildings combine to make Mintaro a place that will show little change as time marches on.

The Clare Valley was first discovered as a foodie's retreat back in the early 80s and the wines of the area, like their makers, are intense but unpretentious. That noble white variety, the Riesling, has been partly responsible for the success of wine sales here. It is such a great drop that we wonder how this wine-style fell out of favour for a while before making its recent reemergence. The formidable 'cattle king', Sir Sidney Kidman lived at nearby Kapunda for many years, but over the last few decades, it is the grape itself that has become king in this area.

There is a 27 kilometre Riesling Trail which winds its way through the unspoiled bush valley, cushioned by rolling hills and ever-changing landscape. Fresh air enthusiasts are encouraged to walk or cycle from village to village, calling in at the numerous places to imbibe as they go. Stamina and timing are the essence as the heat of the sun can easily take its toll on those who appreciate their daytime lubrications.

We said goodbye to the grand old houses that proudly stand today as testimony to the heyday of yesteryear's pastoralists. For those wanting to escape a world hell bent on self-destruction, The Clare Valley could well be their Utopia.

CHAPTER TWO

UNPLUGGED UNDER
STAR STUDDED SKIES

The rock strewn, pitted creek bed was our road, as it twisted and turned through narrow steep-sided gorge walls, water lapping Morrison's tyres as we occasionally crossed a floodway. Leading us through this dramatic drive, and only a few metres ahead were a handful of emus, striding out in convoy as if to show us the way. They repeatedly looked back at us, their inquisitive but know-all expressions unconcerned at our close proximity, and seemingly proud to be natures own tourist guides. This Brachina Gorge geological drive through the heart of the Flinders Range National Park was the stuff of dreams.

The road opened up to reveal stark, craggy masses of rock rearing half a mile into the air, creating amazing colour patterns of exquisite purples and blues on the distant slopes. Winding creek beds bordered with massive, gnarled river gums, scrubbed clean with time, were home to the shy yellow-foot rock wallaby and hill kangaroo. Multitudinous galahs, their pinks and whites flashing in the dappled sunlight, swooped and shrieked in delight through the branches of the trees. The internationally acclaimed painter Sir Hans Heyson was so inspired with this quiet, exhilarating countryside that he spent a third of his working life painting this icon of Australian scenery. The acclaimed Heyson Trail is accepted by avid walkers as the world's longest and most scenic walk. His famous quotation 'The bones of nature laid bare' perfectly describe the dramatic hills, slopes and peaks that combine to make the area a very special part of this dear old land.

As twilight arrived, the eerie silence was highlighted by the striking light-show of stars that sparkled in the heavens in unprecedented glory. A feeling of spiritual ecstasy enveloped us. If ever there was a single evening to christen our camp oven, this was it. The pungent smell and the noisy crackling of the open fire in our first National Park camp gave us a feeling of being 'at one with nature'. Although there were numerous other creek-side camping sites all with their rustic fireplaces and raw stone seats, we had the place to ourselves on this occasion. With the sun long vanished, the growing shadows created a surreal atmosphere. Conversation was totally unnecessary as the dancing flames mesmerised us. Furry bush creatures peeped out from the nearby gums and even more stars flooded the sky like diamonds.

The camp oven was tentatively submerged into the glowing embers and our roast lamb dinner was only an hour away.

Swaggies Camp Oven Lamb

The early day swaggies from these parts would have probably stolen their beast but we went the conventional way and bought a leg from the local butcher.
As we became accustomed to using the camp oven, this proved to be one of our favourites and it is so easy to make. Lamb is perfect for cooking by this method and only takes around an hour.

*Cut into the leg of lamb around the bone and insert a mixture
of rosemary, garlic and olive oil.*

*At the bottom of the oven place some sprigs of fresh rosemary
and then rub into the skin some cracked black pepper, salt and
a little oil and place into camp oven.*

*The heat should spread around the oven and after a short while
move it along the side the fire and fill the lid with coals so as to
provide more even cooking.*

*About 20 minutes later add some seasoned onions, potatoes,
pumpkin and spread around the joint.*

*The taste of both the meat and vegetables is quite different to
any prepared by conventional cooking methods.*

Camping should not be a forfeiture of standards but a gratification of natural living, and sitting around the dying embers, we both felt that life could not get much better than this.

A soaring wedge-tailed eagle, breakfast in sight, welcomed us to a new day while the sun's early morning rays created warming colours on the surrounding mountain walls. Squawking rainbow-coloured rosellas brought a feeling of urgency to this otherwise peaceful setting. Over-indulgence in solid and liquid substances, without an equal measure of exercise on my behalf, were becoming obvious to Fay's well-trained eye. The belt was in need of another hole and the mountain bikes had not seen action for weeks. I therefore decided to cycle ahead leaving my trimmer partner to complete her various household duties, eventually catching up with me around an hour later. A completely different perspective of this ancient landscape is gained by two wheel travelling. The smells and closeness to the passing flora and fauna provided an awareness not fully appreciated within the confines of our vehicle. The jarring pitted road provided numerous potential mishaps winding past scabrous red gums, across dry creek beds and through soaring gorge walls. The resident wild life watched with amusement as I sweated away under a flawless summer sky, wondering where the hell my bloody wife was. Dragon lizards lazily sunning themselves on the smooth rocks motionlessly gazed at me, while I stopped for a much-needed breather. This was nature on a grand scale and uniquely Australian.

She eventually arrived, driving at a pace which was fractionally quicker than that managed by me on my trusty bike, obviously aware that time was not of the essence when it came to my daily exercises.

We soon arrived at a spot not far from where Hans Heyson erected his easel to paint some of his more famous works. The old homestead where he spent much of his time created images of a quite different world and was well worth the rough uphill climb to its crumbling ruins.

A middle-aged couple were striding ahead of us, along a path to an advantage point which overlooked the surrounding countryside. The man initially appeared to be carrying what looked like a young child, until we got a little closer and realised that no child could be that hideous. It was in fact a fair dinkum garden-variety gnome that he held in his arms, and without a doubt the ugliest figure I had ever seen. A bright red bulbous nose that any inebriate would be ashamed of, cauliflower ears of great proportions and a supercilious leer like a dromedary. Twisted stumpy legs supported his potbelly and he had a really badly faded paint job. If Moses had seen this unsightly figure, there may well have been another Commandment.

Graham and Maureen were travelling round the country with their little friend who we immediately christened Horace the Horrible. Maureen asked me to take a family pic of this unusual threesome and promptly perched Horrace on the adjacent stone fence while the dutiful parents lined up on each side of him. As they all three leered into the camera I suspected that there was more to this than met the eye so asked Graham

"What's with the gnome".

"It's a long story" he said "and it all began back home in Bendigo when my next door neighbour and I had a bit of a barney over our dividing fence. It nearly got to fisticuffs so early on the morning we left, I nicked his favourite garden gnome and decided to take him with us".

Maureen chirped up "and now we are getting our own back by sending him a photo with the message 'great fence, wish you were here', from every place we visit".

They strolled off to their caravan, happily swinging Horace between them obviously feeling very pleased with themselves.

Wilpena Pound is one of the most striking scenic features of these ranges and we spent a day hiking around this natural amphitheatre. Our approach was past the much-photographed Rawnsleys Bluff with the great rugged purple mass of rock becoming larger by the minute. On the southern part of this enormous wall a clear profile of a massive dogs head can be seen; a sort of canine sphinx, dramatically welcoming us to this wild, imperious part of the world. The Pound can only be accessed past soaring steep-sided walls, up to 500 metres high, and through a narrow gap which provides passage for the Wilpena Creek. Once inside this astonishing 80 square kilometre arena, we realised that it was indeed a natural fortress. Surrounded by towering red-brown crenellated ramparts, fingers of stone point to the sky, interwoven with rugged peaks in a truly memorable display of nature. It has been home to vast numbers of sheep, cattle and wild horses since it was discovered back in the mid 1800s.

Apparently Wilpena means 'place of bent fingers', which could signify the cold that freezes the fingers in the stark winters, but more logical is the explanation of a partly clenched fist with the digits being the surrounding saw-tooth peaks.

We climbed the Wangarra Lookout, a rewarding seven-kilometre hike that provided breathtaking panoramic views of the Pound. It was hard to imagine the carcasses of 20,000 sheep once littered the billiard flat expanse before us, in a time long ago when like the current drought situation, rain was as rare as rocking horse poo. Whoever quoted the words 'Without adventure, civilisation would be in full decay' would have felt very much at home, sitting as we were on this rocky outcrop

The journey south provided reminders of the great sheep and cattle runs of the 18th century together with the ensuing productive copper mining industry. Crumbling, roofless homesteads and graves of the brave and sometimes foolish pioneers scatter the barren countryside. The scars of past failures and heartaches slowly eroding into the arid earth.

The ruins of the once substantial Kanyaka Homestead warrant time to look around and immerse ones-self into the daily lives of the early settlers and their workers. Over 70 families were once supported by the Homestead's various activities indicating the importance and size of the operation. This harsh uncompromising land took no prisoners and the hardships of those itinerant adventurers are eternally carved in stone across this once magnificent complex. Tragedy took the life of the young man who founded Kanyaka when he was swept from his horse and drowned in a flooded creek. Hugh Proby was only 24 years old when he was the first of many to be dug into the hard earth of the ranges. It was 40 years later that his sister, accompanied by her husband, Lord Hamilton, made the arduous voyage from England to visit her brother's grave outside Quorn. As somewhat of a coincidence, my families' home in England was in Quorn, and that's where the similarity ends.

This dusty little town of Quorn, with lots of old stone and fibro cottages claims to be the capital of the Flinders but held little appeal for us. The old style shop front verandahs that have not been touched since erection and the four ancient country pubs standing side by side could have come right out of a movie set.

Surprisingly the place did provide a little humour, which occurred down at the local supermarket. It doubles as an internet café and while Fay was feverishly catching up with a multitude of messages from our time in the outback, where connections are few and far between, I scoured the community notice board for items of interest.

'Thought for the day' one said. 'There is more money spent on breast implants and Viagra than Alzheimers resarch. In the next 10 years a large elderly population should have oversized boobs and huge erections with absolutely no recollection of how to benefit from them'.

At this point, I was happy to find that Fay had finished her Internet business and with the fresh sea air of the Eyre Peninsular beckoning, Morrison put his head down for the run through to Port Augusta.

CHAPTER THREE

FREEWHEELING IN FLINDER'S WAKE

Most travellers traversing the continent from South Australia to the West have little alternative but to pass through Port Augusta. It is a miserable place. Better to do whatever brought you here and quickly move on. Morrison surveyed the street activity watching a few locals falling about as they staggered out of the pubs and he was suitably unimpressed. At the supermarket Beryl's corrugated face had a vague resemblance to a bulldog and her studded dog collar and bark added to the image as she squatted behind the cash register, wanting our money but not our presence. She eyed me suspiciously as I stood there grinning. Little did she realise that I was trying to imagine what kind of 'animal' her husband might be. The bottle shop and the butcher were hardly an improvement, as unsmilingly and without any recognition that I was in fact a customer, they counted away the minutes till closing time. This was not a happy town I told myself and concluded that the inhabitants had a serious attitude-adjustment problem. I needed no urging to hit the accelerator and head off in the direction of Whyalla.

Set against the deep orange twilight sky, the industrial stacks looked like an architectural drawing. They disappeared into the inky black waters of the Spencer Gulf, providing a dramatic finality to another day. We set up camp not far from the waters edge, as the cooling offshore breezes welcomed us to our first night on the Eyre Peninsula.

Whyalla is a big industrial town, and even if it didn't fit into our preferred criteria of places to stay, at least visitors are made welcome here. The locals offer genuine smiles, don't mind a chat with a stranger, and generally give the impression they are happy with their lot.

We had no preconceived ideas as to what this south westerly part of the South Australian coastline would have to offer. The State Tourist Commission produces an excellent range of tourism publications aptly entitled 'Secrets'. The very comprehensive one on the Eyre Peninsula really whet our appetite and seemed to offer everything we were looking for, particularly as our intended route hugged what appeared to be a very dramatic coastline for nearly 1000 kilometres.

As we travelled around this area, we became convinced that it was indeed a well kept secret. Even though it was February, with blue skies every day, we had the place pretty much to ourselves. Deserted beaches, solitary fishermen on isolated rocky outcrops, just a handful of people in the natural bush camps and only the occasional car on the long country roads.

The next day proved to be a winner. I had not swung a golf club in weeks and the local course boasted the fact that their greens had been voted the fourth best in Australia. Those readers who have the slightest bit of interest in this absorbing but totally frustrating game, will agree that greens with such a reputation are quite irresistible. And they were sensational. Unfortunately it was summer time and the fairways, that were as dry as camel's dung, consisted of mongrel scrub which made the game a little more than challenging.

My playing partner was Rick, a strapping chap of 50 plus years. He had a vice-like handshake and hit the ball a million miles.

Unfortunately for him, most of them went on to other fairways. He loved a chat and was proud of the fact that he had been employed in the local steel works all his working life. "Thinking of retiring in five years to do what you're doing, travel around Australia and all that stuff" he jovially confided as we strode off down the first fairway. Rick was not exactly what you would call the adventurous type, given that he and his family had spent their annual holidays in the same small seaside town of Port Neil for the last 16 years. You meet all kinds of people travelling the countryside, but this hardworking family man was the epitome of monotonous stability. He will work out his last few years, earn just a few more dollars, and hope for enough time left to fulfill his dreams.

What the hell! If Rick can go to Port Neil for 16 consecutive years, we thought we should at least take a look.

A couple of hours easy drive found us in this pleasant little seaside fishing township, where everybody goes about their business nice and slowly. Just out of town we found the perfect place to camp, an isolated rock face overlooking a vast expanse of breaking surf. And it was only a short cycle ride to the local watering hole for a refreshing drink.

When a stranger walks into these quiet small town pubs, there's every chance they'll get more than a passing look or even prolonged stares from the regular drinkers at the bar. Even more so when you've got a blonde wife like mine who loves an opportunity to dress up and would talk to the flies on the wall if there was nobody else available. The pub at Port Neil is one where conversation is easily struck.

George was a huge man with hands that made his beer glass look like a thimble. His full bushy beard, glinting eyes and eagerness to talk to we strangers, made him a fascinating drinking companion. Fishing, farming, tourism and sport were all covered over a few glasses of the amber stuff although he showed a total disdain for anything political.

An educated man, he was intrigued by our round Oz adventure and proffered some thought provoking observations.

"It is only the limit of your imagination that stops you moving on to greater things" he confided. Great attitude, I inwardly thought and countered with the frivolous,

"It's a wonderful world; you're lucky if you get out of it alive" which bought a wry smile to his earnest demeanor.

At the far end of the bar, a couple of two-pot screamers were having a domestic, disrupting our concentration on George's more thought-provoking observations. Fay tuned in to the conversation when she gleaned that they were arguing about his lack of interest in matrimony. We had to smother our laughter when he heatedly declared that there are three rings involved in this marriage stuff – the engagement ring, the wedding ring and the suffering! At this point we decided to jump on our bikes and return to Morrison for a bit of dinner.

Another unusual golfing opportunity presented itself at Port Neil. The course is apparently the only one in the world where every single tee plus all the greens have ocean views. The views were great and that's about all it had going for it. The fairways were miserable, parched, uneven scrubland whilst little areas where you are supposed to 'putt' the ball in the little hole were covered with uneven black shale. Throughout all this, a mighty 50-knot gale blew in off the ocean, tossing my little white balls in exactly the opposite direction to which they were intended. However at $3 to play all day it was certainly a bargain compared with some of its well-manicured counterparts in other parts of the country.

Spending a couple of days in Port Neil was perfect, but we were left scratching our heads wondering what Rick could do for a month every year for 16 years. Rick, there's a big world out there mate, get your arse into gear and see a bit of it.

We travelled on down the East Coast of the Eyre Peninsular through fields of golden wheat as far as the eye could see. Always in the background that formidable awesome coastline which seems to get more dramatic with every turn. We pulled into quaint seaside towns such as Tumby Bay where there is a curious rotunda, painted with scenes from yesteryear and a lovely old pub with $5 Dinner specials. Too good to miss we stayed the night, once again right on the beach, and joined the locals who were out in full force to enjoy the weekly special.

An old dilapidated corner store had a large sign declaring 'BEWARE OF THE DOG'. The very aged mongrel appeared on its last legs and seemed too knackered to be of any use as a guard dog. Sleeping inconveniently across the doorway it was totally oblivious to anyone who happened to be entering the shop.

"What's with the 'Beware of the Dog' sign"? I asked of the old weather-beaten couple lurking around at the back of the shop "He looks about as dangerous as a stuffed rabbit".

The old man, who looked about as worn out as his dog retorted, "The sign is there so stupid customers like you don't trip over 'im".

I apologised and wished them well at the town's forthcoming fancy dress ball, where their appearance in the nude may well have won them first prize as a 'dried-fruit arrangement'.

An early morning walk along a totally deserted, blindingly white beach with another flawless blue sky above us and we were on the road again. Only a short drive and 'The Welcome to Port Lincoln' sign, indicated that we had just about reached the civilised southern tip of the Peninsular.

Best known as a thriving fishing port, this bustling town is also now a major education hub for aquaculture and is fast adding gourmet cuisine to its list of attractions. It has a perfect location overlooking a bright blue harbour and the modern tuna fleet is a big earner for the community.

Seahorses hold a fascination for young and old and hidden away in a shed behind Lane Cove Marina, there are aquariums full of them. Tracy Warland has held a lifelong passion for these defenseless, prehistoric-looking creatures that have long prompted mythical and artistic interpretations. This dedicated mother to broods of these tiny fish with toothless snouts, prehensile tails and extraordinary fragile looking fins, operates one of only four places in the world that breed the species.

We stood spellbound as Tracy described her aquaculture venture, explaining how 20 million of these fascinating creatures are taken from the wild each year to support the herbal medicine trade and aquarium and curio markets. We even hand fed the little fellas with microscopic brine shrimp, which she breeds on site as well.

The big attraction here is The Port Lincoln National Park, which covers the southernmost extremities of the peninsular, and its exhilarating coastline makes it a mandatory visit for any traveller. The long dusty winding road brought us past glistening salt lakes, sweeping bays with translucent azure waters and rocky inlets scattered with remarkable limestone shapes. Families of emus and roos cautiously eyed us as we slowly drove by and there was an inordinate amount of bird activity in the trees.

Captain Matthew Flinders and his crew would have been equally moved in 1802, when they discovered this remarkable corner of our continent in their leaking old tub 'The Investigator'. His name is entrenched in the annals of history in these parts, with towns, capes, bays, rivers and even mountains named after his crew, friends and family. Port Lincoln was named after his native Lincolnshire. Little has changed along much of this narcotically beautiful coastline that he successfully charted over 200 years ago.

We camped in an isolated spot overlooking the ocean; dusk came and went with the sun a golden ball dropping into the sea. The blackness of a moonless night had settled around us when Fay suddenly stiffened. A car engine disturbed the silence and even worse it was approaching towards what we had determined was our own little private patch for the night. The vehicle came to a halt only 30 metres away, its outline barely recognisable in the night. A lone figure was scuffling about, moving mysterious objects, occasionally tripping in the darkness.

Thoughts were going through our minds that did not augur well for a sound night's sleep. Even though our little home was locked each night, there were occasionally those unnerving incidents that set the imagination off on a tangent, especially when a stranger arrives at such a late hour.

Morning allayed any such misconceptions, as our visitor turned out to be a delightful and attractive Swiss lady looking for the comfort and safety of an overnight stop not too far from other campers.

Elaine was visiting Australia by herself for the second time. She had been renting the old banger she was driving but decided in WA that for $1500 she would buy it from the rent-a-bomb company, traverse the Nullarbor and explore the East Coast for six months. Her little one-person tent, cooker and sleeping bag were about her only possessions but she was loving every moment of the experience. "So very different from Zurich, so few people and so much animal life" she exuded in her strong European accent. Looking south to Cape Catastrophe along this 'one of a kind' coastline it was easy to appreciate her love for our continent. The stark beauty gave no clue to anything catastrophic, past or present.

"I would like to make some good Aussie friends, yes", she confided. She had an affectionate habit of putting her hand on Fay's arm each time she spoke, looking directly into her eyes, ignoring me as if I didn't exist. I wondered what kind of friend she was looking for, and if I was invited to the party. "It would be quite impossible to have a holiday like this anywhere in Europe" she breathlessly whispered as though trying to keep the whole episode very private. Fay exchanged some travel tips with her, as we were heading in opposite directions. Her possessions were packed in minutes and the good sort with the very butch haircut from Zurich was on her way, looking for that very special Australian experience which I am sure she would find before too long.

There had been little summer in South Australia that year and the waters were still cool. The fishermen were complaining all along the peninsular that fishing was at its worst for years. ' When there is a drought on the land, there is a drought at sea' was a saying I would hear many times over the coming months. Consequently our catches had been somewhat limited until now, with only a few fair sized squid worth mentioning.

Back in the 60s and 70s, Australia's calamari and octopus consumption was amongst the lowest in the world; a national antipathy towards munching on little tentacles prevailed.

By the mid 80s, European food styles, particularly those of the Greeks, had put these unfortunate looking cephalopods on to the menus of many eating houses and they were suddenly in vogue. Aversion towards certain strange looking foods had been overcome and now there was a hearty appreciation of the flavoursome calamari.

They are still used for bait by many and unappreciated by some, but I love preparing, cooking and eating squid. I must admit they are a bit of a bastard to clean, but once they are marinated for half an hour or so they become quite tender.

Try these ideas, when next you're cooking this delicacy.

Ridgy Didge Squid

This was the 'real thing', straight from the water into the frying pan.

Squid alternatively known as Calamari, there being only a slight difference between the two, are easily caught with a jig off jetties and rocks.

Separate the head (ink sack) from the tube, wash well under water and skin with sharp knife.

Slice pieces into good-sized rectangular shapes and make a criss-cross pattern on the inside of each one.

The secret to lip-smacking calamari is in the preparation. Depending on what is available, I try to cover with paw paw or kiwi fruit skins for half an hour (the acidity tenderises the flesh). Otherwise try milk with a squirt of lemon/lime juice and let sit for an hour.

Mix some flour, sea salt, black pepper and if you want an extra bite, a sprinkling of chilli..

Coat mixture onto dry calamari and drop into hot olive oil for only a few minutes until brown. Don't overcook or it may become a tad chewy. Serve with wedges of lemon, accompanied with salad, chips or whatever your little heart desires.

Freshly caught squid are a delight and we enjoyed numerous meals featuring this underrated and quite unattractive mollusc.

Tuna in this part of the world is a big industry and on the way back into Port Lincoln we pulled into a substantial tuna processing operation. All manner of marinated and smoked tunas, octopus, mussels and prawns were available in the little shop and we stocked up with a bit of everything until the freezer was bulging. My eagle-eyed wife spied some large spider crabs at the last minute and my mind went immediately into culinary mode, determining the best way to prepare them for dinner.

Whalers Way is a wild, spectacular headland covering around 30 square kilometres, and juts out into the ocean at the south western end of the Eyre Peninsula. The 24 hours spent there were certainly one of the highlights of our visit to South Australia. Once inside the gated entrance, to which we were given the keys, a winding road through sandhills and scrub took us on a 12 kilometre route of awesome discoveries. We were literally gobsmacked by the rugged visual impact of the cliff faces, spellbinding rock formations, gaping blowholes, contoured caves, minute sandy beaches, and rock swimming pools. Bird, animal and mammal life was omnipresent with the highlight being families of fur seals basking on the rocks below us. This was one of nature's most environmentally protected retreats offering some of the best visually dramatic scenery we had experienced. And as an extra bonus, it was virtually deserted the day we were there giving us a sense of ownership as we clambered around the various beauty spots.

The visit also presented the unexpected. There was a brief but ferocious storm during the night and on our drive out the following morning, we found that it had caused a serious sand drift, blocking our departure road with metres of sand. With not a soul around, my days exercise had been involuntarily determined and with much digging, sweating and grunting, and, needless to say, encouragement and instructions from the forewoman, the road was cleared and we were on our way. My old mate Richard had stuck a long handled spade in my hand prior to our departure saying, "Guaranteed you'll need this pal" and wasn't he right?

Around the tip and a little way up the West Coast is Coffin Bay. Named after one of Flinder's seafaring officers, and not as most people think after the number of unfortunate people who end up in coffins, subsequent to being mutilated or eaten by the Great White Pointers which are regularly sighted in the area. The place is a refreshing surprise and one of the few 'out of the way' townships that boast lots of new and rather substantial, well presented houses. Things are a-changing here, albeit against the old-timers wishes, and with a new hotel, reasonable eating spots, improved facilities, and a reputation second to none for fine fishing, Coffin Bay is anything but dead and buried. As one old timer at the post office succinctly put it "Change is inevitable.....except from a vending machine son". It is one of those getaway spots that we felt we would love to return to one day, and spend a few quality weeks soaking it all up, instead of the 48 hours we allowed ourselves. There's just something about the feel, the ambience; a laid-back place with a touch of style. And friendly too. Jackie, who hails from Liverpool and with an accent like any one of the Fab Four, runs the store in town and tells you exactly what you want to know about anything "From tha Mursey ta Coffin Bay...can yu believe it?" she joyously informed us......her infectious spirit really gave us a lift and we found ourselves laughing out loud as we left her shop. Who could argue that a move from gloomy Liverpool to this paradise would excite most Liverpudlians.

Coffin Bay oysters are a big deal here and if you ask around you can find the right places back o' town where a fresh dozen costs you around $4. We shucked a few at the jetty, washed them down with a cool beer, threw a line in, and a few more memoirs were deposited into our memory banks.

All along this wild imperious coast there were moments of sheer magic. To see the large schools of salmon from the clifftops churning vast pools of water below us was something very special. And always the rugged cliffs, golden sands and crystal blue waters were competing for our attention. In the balmy evenings we sat around beach campfires watching the sun drop into the ocean; ever a captivating sight for those of us who spend the majority of our lives on the eastern seaboard.

Locks Well is a name which you often hear bandied about along this coast when talking with people who enjoy fishing for salmon. This place is the Mecca of ocean salmon fishing. It's a short drive from the town of Elliston and the local council has spent millions of dollars building a road, car parks and an amazing staircase down the cliff face, to accommodate the growing band of fishermen. The steep winding approach road to the car park was breathtaking. Morrison was having palpitations as I pressured the brakes down the three in one incline, while Fay was hypnotised by the huge surf crashing on to the beach, way down below us. There are exactly 286 near-vertical timber steps down to the sand, which doesn't sound much, but try the return trip armed with the days catch and all your tackle. It is enough to knacker the fittest fanatic, so the sensible way is to make a couple of trips, if you are lucky with the rod.

On the day we visited Locks Well, the salmon were being hauled in left, right and centre. I was fishing between two locals who had cottoned on to the right holes and were pulling them out with monotonous regularity. Peter was a study in concentration with long hair wafting in the morning breeze and a chin that hadn't seen a razor in years. He was friendly enough, even offered me a bit of local knowledge, but I was happy that I didn't have to carry the 19 he pulled in, up the dreaded staircase.

These salmon require bleeding as soon as they are caught, and the easiest way is to cut them open between head and body and bury them upside down in the soft sand with just their tails exposed. This simple method totally confuses the hoards of waiting seagulls, drains the blood into the sand and keeps them cool. Peter's catch was lined up like soldiers, while the number of patient birds, waiting for breakfast steadily grew. Out on the far breaker, a white pointer was eyeing the school of salmon thinking of his own dinner, while the head of a young sea lion, only a few metres from shore kept resurfacing to check us out. All this action was quite off putting for Fay who was dying to cool off in the enticing waters.

There was lots of activity and varying degrees of success along the beach all day. Klaus and his bride Hannah were on their honeymoon from Germany. He had been growing totally frustrated over the past weeks with his inability to catch one single fish. With help and instruction from the rest of us he managed to pull in a few beauties. This pleased Hannah immensely and she confided to Fay as they sat chatting, that she was pleased that he could now concentrate on his conjugal duties which had been pretty 'schizenhausen' due to his frustrations in the fishing department.

The salmon we caught were to provide us with many wonderful meals and they filled every spare space in the freezer. A couple of them were smoked over sawdust in the barbecue, a sort of curry was also conceived, while some Thai style fish cakes were winners. That night overlooking the heaving surf rolling in below us, we devoured the freshest of salmon, cooked in a simple but interesting sort of way.

Murdoch Salmon in Newspaper

It is great to eat fish that you have just pulled out of the ocean and know that it is indeed fresh.

I bled these ocean salmon on the beach as instructed by the locals and they needed it as they had a pretty strong taste.

I found it easier to cook them on our inbuilt gas barbecue with the cover on to maintain the heat.

Get half a dozen pages of newspaper from the likes of the Australian : sports, business, world affairs, whatever turns you on and wet them.

In the good old days, the fish would have been placed on page 3, where there may have been a good-looking sort ready to be rolled. Today, a closer awareness of health issues requires us to have a piece of baking paper between the fish and the printed material.

Cut some slices into the flesh and smear a mixture of butter, lemon juice, a drop of white wine, a sprinkling of cumin, salt and parsley on the outside and inside of the fish.

Roll paper tightly keeping all the juices inside and flap down the page edges so that the weight is lying on them.

It should only take about 20-30 minutes and the result will be magnificent

The essence is simplicity – the excitement is the possibility of the newspaper catching fire so don't forget to wet it thoroughly.

The euphoria of the previous day was lost next morning when we were invaded by a swarm of wasps. After battling with them over breakfast, we decided it was a good time to move on before they planned a major assault. Morrison agreed.

It was Valentine's day. The bottle of Moet was chilling in the fridge. Fay was hell bent on finding somewhere 'romantic' to have our Valentine's Day Dinner preceded by the bottle of bubbly that we had carted half way across the country. Venus Bay had the right sort of ring to it and suddenly popped up out of nowhere.

The desolate grave-like approach was initially disappointing as were the lines of fishermen's fibro and besser block shacks, most in seemingly unloved condition. Out of towners have built here, holidaying a few weeks a year, leaving the place pretty dead for the rest of the time. That's except for the 20 residents who actually make up the permanent population.

But the town's redeeming feature was the magnificent bay surrounded by rugged cliffs. Here we perched high above a long line of crenellated rocks, overlooking the ocean with sheer drops to the crashing surf 50 metres below. We were well pleased with our dinner setting as our table was prepared just metres from the cliff face.

The last of the seafood extravaganza had disappeared. A million stars twinkled, the moon was bright, while an occasional lightening strike hit the dark distant sky giving us an unexpected bonus of a floorshow. Bedtime called an end to a perfect evening or so we thought.

Lying there in a contented foetal position after doing what comes naturally on Valentine's night, we were suddenly rudely awakened with the violent rocking of Morrison and the howling of gale force winds. It was early hours of the morning and a huge storm had hit our precarious little love nest. The immediate thought of being hurled over the too close cliff face threw us into a frenzy of activity. Our two nude bodies dived through the doorway, bracing ourselves against Mother Nature's onslaught as we hurriedly grabbed the chairs, table and other items that had been part of the evening's celebrations. The savage wind was coming straight off the Southern Ocean with unimaginable ferocity and our uncovered bodies were uncompromisingly fragile against the challenging conditions.

Without delay and still totally naked we steered the terrified Morrison off the cliff and slowly drove down the main street of town, endeavoring to find a less windy spot to spend the rest of St Valentines night.

The next morning was warm and sunny with no hint of the dramas of the previous night. It was still quite early in the day and I felt contented and relaxed, fishing all by myself on the town jetty that was supposed to have a top reputation for those who like to cast a line. Meanwhile, Fay was making up for lost sleep.

It was deathly quiet, meditation magic, and from nowhere an old-timer's gravel-like voice startled me out of my reverie.

"You're wasting your time son" he drawled over my shoulder.

Edgar is one of the few residents who has been living here for decades, and just loves a chat with anyone, anytime anywhere. His faithful Jack Russell was busy ferreting about, sniffing anything and everything, oblivious to the problems of the fisherman's world.

"Fishing's getting worse here every year" he lamented. "10 or 20 years ago you could be a mug fisherman and still take home enough fish to feed you for a week. Today it's all getting fished out with those big commercial boats, peculiar weather patterns and more people from the cities buying up in the place".

And so he droned on about the comings and goings around town, while lack of sleep and the soothing sun put me in grave danger of dozing off and falling into the water below.

One comment that struck my fuzzy fancy was

"Young man, I intend to live forever and so far so good!"

Finally he said it was time to go and slowly levered himself into his old Suzuki, followed at a far greater speed by his four legged faithful. Edgar was off looking for another chat. By the look of the deserted main street, he'd have to be pretty lucky. Salt of the earth and a delightful old fella who just loves Venus Bay and the few things it has to offer. His bright blue eyes would have popped out of his balding head if he had been up and about on the nearby cliff face in the early hours of the morning when we were dashing about like a pair of idiots.

Edgar or in fact anyone else who might have witnessed this Fawlty Towers type escapade, and had the foresight to video these hilarious proceedings, would no doubt be guaranteed finals status on 'The Worlds Funniest Home Video' show.

For the very few readers interested, a block of land in Venus Bay, with glorious water views can be snapped up for a mere $50.000. Unfortunately only the occasional one becomes available, but if you do happen to choose to invest in this backwater paradise, Edgar will be around for years to come, to assist with a bit of local knowledge.

We headed further north, through dramatically dry countryside that gave us the impression we were on another planet and eventually arrived at the quaint fishing township of Streaky Bay, well known for its high achieving, award winning pub overlooking a lovely foreshore. Flinders gave it the name Streaky Bay back in 1802, due to the bands of colour in the water that are actually created by oil being discarded by the kelp.

A stunning coastal drive brought us to Smokey Bay where they take their oyster farming and fishing very seriously. Old, dilapidated, mostly rusty tractors that have seen decades of farmwork are now utilised for other purposes. They adorn the driveways and front gardens of the majority of the fishermen's homes and are used to transport their fishing craft into the briny at a moment's notice. Fishing is their life. They eat it and live it, while the atmosphere down at the pub can be somewhat sombre if the fish are not 'on the bite'.

At this point, we had virtually circumnavigated the Eyre Peninsula. In less than two weeks we had travelled 1000 kilometres providing some of the most memorable scenery imaginable.

The Peninsula was named after the young British explorer John Eyre and we had read quite a bit about this respected pioneer. The challenges that he encountered in those long-ago days are quite unimaginable to today's traveller. No roads, no communication, no facilities and the additional hardship of encountering aggressive aboriginal tribes.

He built a reputation for peacefully resolving any issue instead of opening fire like many of his quick-tempered fellow voyagers. A tall athletic youth, son of a Yorkshire vicar, he arrived in Sydney at the tender age of 17 and within a few years proceeded to make his mark as one of this countries true adventurers.

Somebody once wrote that 'no country can become great, without great pioneers'. This Englishman with the 'never say die' attitude certainly epitomised that select and brave bunch of heroic achievers who discovered vast tracts across the length and breadth of this huge continent.

And as for our impession of the Eyre Peninsula – yes, it still is one of Australia's best-kept secrets.

CHAPTER FOUR

A BITE AT THE GREAT OZ MYTH

After time spent drifting from one small fishing community to another, our arrival into Ceduna was a refreshing change. There was a good selection of shops, a choice of service stations with smiling attendants and friendly coffee houses where a long overdue Cappuccino was well appreciated. An ATM stood proud outside a bank, which was quite significant, as we hadn't come across one in ages. When out on the road for extended periods of time, life often revolves around access to these indispensable providers of the folding stuff.

Ceduna claims to be 'the beginning' or 'the end' of the Nullarbor, depending on which way you are travelling and everyone that 'drives the drive' calls in to check it out. Fellow travellers had warned us to be careful of the little black fellas who have a penchant for permanently borrowing things. Free camping should not even be considered we were told. "You really need the security of a caravan park," said one old Victorian couple who looked as though they had spent their life on the road. We took their advice, but during our five day stay we never gave a second thought to the racial problems which occasionally erupt. On the days we were there, the 1960s hit song, Ebony and Ivory could well have been written with this place in mind. The age-old problems between different colours, on the surface, did not appear to warrant any concern. Kids of all ages and colours were playing together and the same with the adults, who were fishing, drinking and socialising harmoniously.

However, we were not in town on a Thursday, which is supposed to be a big day if you're looking for a bit of entertainment in the pubs. It is dole collection morning and the liquid amber flows non stop; a recipe for trouble and strife.

Certainly not what we were looking for, so we hopped over to Shelley Beach Tourist Park, about three kilometres out of town. It is right on the beach and came recommended to us by our friends back in Byron, Dennis and Heather who had an extended stay there a few years ago. Given the minimal amount of nights we spend in commercial caravan parks, it still wasn't difficult to make some interesting comparisons between this one and others we had come across. The little 'freebies', the warm hospitality, and the extensive facilities offered by the young owners were certainly impressive. How many Caravan Park owners would offer the free use of crabbing pots to guests, facilities to cook their catch in a sizable crab cooker, and point them in the direction of the garden where a sign stated 'please help yourself to grapes, figs etc.' which grew in gay profusion. The substantial walk-through fruit and vegetable garden was totally screened against any insect invasion and the generous offer was duly accepted on more than one occasion.

Lynton and Anna Brown bought their 55 acre oceanfront dream a few years ago, when the original Caravan Park had become extremely run down. A new image was definitely needed and a few dollars had to be spent. Coming from the gold drilling business in Kalgoorlie, this young energetic couple had imagination and the conviction of their dreams. Their life savings went on improvements and today they have established a wonderful retreat in which to relax and unwind.

Like most of the coastal places we had visited, the strong winds come in off the Southern Ocean each afternoon. The day's social activities often take this factor into consideration, especially if fishing is on the agenda. Crabbing from the various jetties was certainly to be a high priority as we joined the jolly band of kids energetically pulling up their baskets from the ocean below. Getting a second opinion on the size of some borderline crabs from their little mates appeared quite important in differentiating between right and wrong. More often than not they were thrown back in, to spend a few more months growing an extra couple of centimeters before they would be hauled in again.

Some of these children were really cute and one little fella just loved having a chat. He had a smile like a slice of watermelon, mischievous eyes and tight black curly hair, the colour of coal. He cheekily asked Fay how old she was, and quick as a flash she replied "I have been young a very long time my boy". He look perplexed at the reply, stared at us long and hard as he thought about this astounding revelation, and suddenly ran off giggling to tell his mates about this strange lady.

In only a couple of hours we pulled up enough Blue Swimmers to feed the two of us for the next few days. Back at the Tourist Park they were quickly thrown into Brownie's cooker and a few minutes later emerged ready for preparation.

Eating fresh crabs under the stars accompanied by the sound of nearby surf and with a brave little Chardonnay on the table is one of life's more pleasurable experiences.

Ceduna Blue Swimers - Iti Style

Years and years ago, Fay remembers spending time with the Italian communities in Southern California who had a crab specialty which was as fiery as their personalities.

This recipe is based on her recollections of those memorable culinary moments.

Cut the blue swimmers into pieces, and after debraining and cleaning them, set aside in a cool place.

Mix a large chopped onion, red capsicum and some celery with a teaspoon (or two) of chillies and brown in hot oil. Add a tin of tomatoes with juice, strong Italian tomato paste, sugar, a healthy pinch of cumin and turmeric, lemon juice and stock (fish or chicken) and cook for an hour on a low heat.

Cook sufficient pasta, we prefer fettucine, in a separate pot and add pepper, butter and coriander.

Into a wok of hot olive oil, add some garlic and finely chopped ginger. Toss the crab pieces in this mixture for a few minutes until heated and well coated.

Pile crabs on top of a generous serve of pasta and pour lashings of tomato/chilli sauce over the lot. Best to have plenty of paper towels available as the eating process is messy.

Attack with a good appetite and wash down with a cold beer or near freezing white.

The remainder of the catch provided us with another dinner and a few sandwiches, which was not a bad return for a few hours hanging around on the end of a jetty making conversation with the locals.

We were lucky enough to be in Ceduna for a weekend of celebrations. The Tall Ships were in town, commencing their voyage along the South Australian coastline in memory and celebration of Captain Matthew Flinders, who surveyed this area 200 years ago. Hundreds of people congregated on the foreshore to enjoy water sports, live music and dancing. There was also a significant amount of lubrication for the revelers, a couple of these well oiled fellas being very persuasive in deciding that Fay should be their dancing partner.

One particularly bold chappy suggested they might try the Camel Dance. When Fay asked what kind of dance that might be, he replied "Twice around the dance floor and a hump out the back". We decided it was time to move on.

Viewing the magnificent vessels from the wharf gave us a deeper insight into how tough life would have been back in the 1800s when voyages lasted for months at a time. As locals disembarked from half and full day trips around the bay, we noticed the mixed looks on their faces, obviously appreciating the difficult and arduous traumas of yesteryear's seagoing travel. How times have changed we thought, as we prepared for our somewhat less grueling trip across the Nullarbor.

Friends with experience in such matters had warned us that the Nullarbor in February would be unbearably hot. The strong winds against us would make the trip uncomfortable and slow. It would be long, boring and monotonous. We would need to take lots of water and various items to helpwhile away the long hours. What a lot of crap.

Not one of these warnings came to fruition, particularly the weather. Someone up there must have been waving a magic weather vane as the days were pleasantly cool, the evenings crisp and the mild winds only came up in the afternoons. And it was anything but boring. Conditions were certainly unusual for that time of the year, but it was only symbolic of ongoing climatic changes around the world.

Just before Penong, only an hour's drive out of Ceduna, we hung a left and took a side trip down to Cactus Beach. As we passed crystal white salt lakes of great dimensions, overlooked by massive sand dunes that had an amazing similarity to a meringue pie topping, we knew we were in for something very special. It is sometimes possible to get a good feeling about a place before actually getting there. This was one of those places. Cactus Beach is not named after that prickly Mexican succulent, but after one of the three perfect surfing breaks that are found here. Cactus and Castles for the uninitiated, are both left handers while the third Caves, is a powerful right hand break. Oh well, life is a continual learning experience.

The magic pull of this beach is well known in the surfing fraternity and the surfing conditions are regarded as quite unique. The matchless length and shape of the waves bring fanatics from around the world to match their wits against the relentless rollers.

Tucked into the sand dunes along the borders of the beach we found dozens of camping sites that were individually private, but part of a community of campers. Circular stone facilities had been roughly built providing semi open showers, toilets and some barbecue areas where visitors congregated around the fires at dusk. The combination of scrubby grass, sand and rough rock could hardly be called beautiful but the place had a special sunburnt appeal and provided a great foreground for the brilliance of the beaches and the nightly sunsets that never failed to enthrall us.

Each evening a battered rust bucket of unbelievably dilapidated proportions appeared out of the sand dunes like a mirage on wheels, and rumbled around the camping areas with garbage bins bouncing around on the back tray. A figure would emerge; dressed in stained white overalls and with long, flowing, grayish bleached hair sticking out from underneath a battered rag hat. Comparisons with the Strawman in 'The Wizard of Oz' immediately came to mind.

Bill Gates (no relationship to his famous namesake) is a truly lovable eccentric. He enjoys his round of the campsites, having a chat, telling stories, replacing firewood, emptying garbage and more importantly, collecting his rents. This long time surfing fanatic bought his parcel of 600 hectares nearly 20 years ago and lives here overlooking the ocean always ready to 'hang five'. Forever environmentally conscious, Bill is very protective of his patch and deals harshly with anyone who doesn't respect it. In fact he's been known to 'kick em out' if the rules aren't adhered to. I suppose he could be called a true greenie, except there is an almost non-existence of that particular colour around there.

The magnificent swimming beach with it's pure white sand goes on for kilometres and was our reward after clambering over a jutting headland not far from the camp. We were somewhat upset to actually find another couple skinny dipping a few hundred metres away. They too may have thought that they had exclusive rights to this little piece of isolated paradise. Footprints on the sand are a rarity out here, as most visitors have nothing but surfing on their minds and head straight out to sea from the headland. Soaking up the sun, we gazed out at the amazing rock formations and lazily watched the efforts of a couple of frustrated rock fishermen and the bobbing lines of distant surfers waiting for the perfect wave.

The lone white pointer prowling the deeper waters was casually mentioned in a most matter of fact way later that evening around the campfire. The young International set were discussing their individual experiences as they discovered some of Australia's unique and hidden surfing locations. I asked about their attitudes towards surfing in waters where the 'big white' is known to hang out, and was quite surprised by their replies. This real-life everyday scenario, which would scare the living daylights out of any ordinary landlubber, was not even considered as a serious concern by most of them. "Its all part of the adrenaline of the sport" a bleached blond 20 year old from Scandinavia commented with a beautiful broken English accent, while a seemingly worldly American teenager thought-provokingly interjected "There is a greater chance of getting knocked down in a busy street than being taken by a shark". Personally, I would much prefer the former. At least there is a better chance of survival with medical assistance hopefully not too far away.

The following day we were shown the spot where a young honeymooner was taken by a white pointer last year. His bride of only a few days watched horrified, as the love of her life vanished in an eruption of churning bloodied water, just 100 metres from shore. It is all part of the sport but unfortunately her memories will linger for an eternity.

Back in Penong we felt that the Nullarbor was really about to start. And this is where everyone fills their tanks to capacity at the local service station. For some unexplainable reason this one outlet offers petrol at around 30 cents a litre cheaper than any other station for the next 1000 kilometres. This little gem of economy is well known by the travelling fraternity and passed on from one motorist to another. Penong is known as the town of 100 windmills and Fay, needing a bit of mental stimulation, did a 'mill count' and found them to be correct.

As we filled up and gave Morrison a last check over, we were once again made aware of the accomplishments of John Eyre. Back in 1861 at the age of 25 he tracked over 1500 kilometres of previously unexplored land from Albany in Western Australia to Fowlers Bay in South Australia. His necessity to search for water and food over 18 months has put him into the annals of history as one of Australia's hardiest and most resourceful explorers. The young Eyre was fascinated by the ingenious methods the Aborigines had of living off the land. He completed the journey with only one Aboriginal companion whose capable procurement of wallabies, goannas and even rats kept them alive during some perilous months in the harsh mallee scrub. Records show that he later became a magistrate and protector of the indigenous peoples and after returning to England, subsequently became Lieutenant Governor of New Zealand.

Today the journey is very easy by comparison. The infamous Eyre Highway has been upgraded and bitumened, reaching completion in 1976, but many distinguishing features remain to intrigue the first time traveller. The first section traverses the world's largest treeless plain. Then there's a 90 kilometre section, which claims to be the longest straight road ever built. And so it goes on.

There are two distinctly different ways that motorists tackle the journey. There are the white-line wizards that chew up the kilometres in as little time as possible, or the relaxed easy-going voyagers who enjoy the many points of interest along the way. The latter was definitely our choice so we decided to find out what this supposedly notorious and challenging crossing had to offer. We were not disappointed.

The road signs are immediately intriguing. It is the only place in the world where there are warnings that camels, emus, wombats or kangaroos might cause concern by suddenly crossing the road. To see them altogether in procession could be construed as some sort of hallucination and would definitely stretch anyone's vivid imagination. Much to our disappointment, not a single roadside camel or wombat were sighted over the next couple of days, but there were emus and roos by the dozens. The Royal Flying Doctor Service made us aware of a more mechanical 'animal' that could block the highway from time to time when they needed to make emergency landings.

Fay wondered at the organization that would be needed to bring to a halt the massive road trains hurtling down this highway at frightening speeds.

Yalata comes up fairly quickly and is a vast Aboriginal reservation with warnings that this is private land and must be respected. No alcohol is allowed on the property and as the local community operates the Service Station, it is probably a good thing. About 100 kilometres after Yalata there is a sign for the 'Head of Bight'. Just a few minutes off the highway and there before us, in all its panoramic glory was the vast 'Great Australian Bight'.

From May to October each year, 100 or more Southern Right Whales choose this corner of the continent to spend their annual vacations. The viewing platforms, studded into the sheer limestone ramparts, provide a real life close-up of their activities, as these 80 tonne protected monsters of the ocean, court, mate and give birth. It was February and there wasn't a whale in sight but it wasn't difficult to imagine the blowing, breaching, and tail dancing that happens here during the right time of the year. Whales or no whales, the view of the sheer cliffs being mercilessly smashed away by endless ocean swells was extraordinary, and certainly worth the small diversion off the main highway.

Another 50 kilometres and we were standing gobsmacked on the breathtaking Bunda Cliffs, which is the first viewing point of the Great Australian Bight Marine National Park. Gatherings of intrepid travellers were gawking, pointing and shooting away with cameras and videos while making inevitable comparisons with the Great Ocean Road. Maybe it was the impact of the moment but I had to agree that the view along this unforgettable coastline was as spectacular as anywhere I could think of.

Equally in awe were a middle aged couple who joined us for a chat and before long we knew more about them than some of our relatives. George was typical of what I might call a pen-pusher. He had spent his life in cramped offices pouring over debits and credits, the deep furrows in his forehead clearly showing the anxieties that he had suffered.

The stresses and pressures of life in the city eventuated in him seeing his doctor on a weekly basis, and for years he was a sad pill-popping case.

One day, quite uncharacteristically his wife recalled, he said "Stuff this, I've got to get a life before its all too late". To the amazement of his family and friends he bought a caravan, told his boss to find another idiot to do his job, bundled up his dumbfounded wife and hit the highways. Myrtle, who looked as though she had been a bit of a pen-pusher too, couldn't believe the change and confided that since they left home over a year ago, he hadn't taken a single pill and hopefully those rorting doctors were a thing of the past.

George seemed to be a walking talking advertisement for the de-stressing qualities of life on the road.

The much-commercialised saying 'But wait there's more' was very much our catch phrase over the next 150 kilometres of coastline. There were numerous options to turn off the highway, gaze in awe, or even stay the night overlooking these dramatic cliff faces.

I cannot remember smuggling a single thing in my life. Why then, did I get an uneasy sense of guilt as we approached the Border Quarantine Station? Had we cleared the fridge properly? Was there some nasty piece of fresh produce lurking at the back of one of our cupboards? The 'border police' were here to check that we had 'done the right thing' and they were looking for certain types of fruits, vegetables and any nuts or honey that we may have mistakenly overlooked.

Clare should have been in public relations. With one of the friendliest faces and dispositions imaginable, she gave the impression she was doing us a favour in relieving us of a half jar of honey and a bunch of wilting wild flowers from our dashboard vase. Fay had made a habit of collecting and regularly refreshing her windscreen presentations, which had day after day, amazingly endured the ongoing heat inside the windscreen. She did not realise that they were definitely not allowed to travel into West Australia and had to reluctantly part with them.

We were reminded to adjust our watches, gaining an hour and a half, and realised that this was only the first of two time adjustments along this highway. That in itself emphasized the enormous dimensions of this tract of land we were traversing.

Clare suggested that Eucla, her home base just down the highway, was a place to check out. "There's a great little bar which can be fun, depending on who's drinking there at the time" she enthused "and the Old Telegraph Station is not to be missed". She obviously enjoyed her job and hoped her little bit of advice may help the economy of Eucla that night.

Giving the bar a miss, we drove down to the beach and inspected the ruins of the Old Telegraph Station. It had originally been built far too close to the imposing sand dunes, and is now roofless with the sands of time realistically but slowly filling each room. Established in the late 1800s it only served for a short period as a communication centre between the East and West Coasts. More thought in the actual location might well have seen the building utilised for many more than just a few years.

Those were the days when linesmen riding camels made occasional inspections to what is now just a sad reflection of bygone times. Majestic sculptured white sand dunes reaching great heights surrounded us and as the sun dropped, the sight of half a dozen wild camels striding out in procession with their peculiar gate along the skyline, was almost surreal. We had visions of the old camel trains trekking across the vast Sahara Desert and felt as if we were in some exotic location rather than on the good old Nullarbor Plain. Nothing stirred or moved in our immediate vicinity as we set up camp, providing a kind of spooky feeling.

As wanderers traversing the Nullarbor inevitably lose most of their fresh fruit and vegetables at the Quarantine Station, it is good to ensure a decent feed by stocking up on tinned food, along with some frozen meat.

The embers of the fire changed from oranges to deep reds as the camp oven was lowered in to cook an age old standby that can easily be concocted with items from the cupboard.

Cobbers Chilli Con Carne

We cooked up a fair amount, just in case any other cobbers called by and had not had the foresight to have sufficient non-confiscatable food available for dinner.

Heat the camp oven and add 4 tablespoons of peanut oil, then 6 chopped onions, stirring until golden brown. Add 2 kg of minced or finely chopped beef or lamb and stir till well browned. Add 2 tablespoons of minced garlic, 1 each of cumin, chilli powder and basil. When all mixed up add 3 cans of chopped tomatoes, 2 of drained red kidney beans and 3 cups of water. Take camp oven away from heat so dish is just simmering and stir regularly for an hour or so, ensuring it doesn't stick to the bottom. It may well need some salt and pepper so season to taste. If any cobbers don't join you, then there is plenty left to warm up for the next day or two.

We awoke to an unimaginably clear morning, the sky a brilliant blue as we headed down the highway. Everything seemed perfect until it happened. Within minutes the air was thick with a plague of locusts, smashing against the windscreen in their hundreds, and darkening the sky as if dusk had arrived early. It seemed like a moment from Biblical times and although we slowed, eventually stopped and waited, the little critters had enmeshed themselves into every one of Morrison's front end crevices. Travelling is all about experiences, but this one was not a real lot of fun, as we stayed cocooned in our home, surrounded by this mad insect frenzy. The real fun started later that day, as I tried to scrape and clean off the seemingly endless mutilated little terrestrial bodies, that had become embedded wherever I looked. There are few parts of Australia that provide such experiences, but the Nullarbor is so vast and uncompromising that any freak of nature is possible.

We were nearly caught short one night with the setting sun blinding us and seemingly a million kangaroos on the road. For some peculiar reason certain parts of this highway attract large numbers of suicidal skippys.

Truckies mentioned seeing mobs of up to 30 congregating in small groups on the bitumen just waiting to be struck.We slowed to an amble, meandered around the unconcerned creatures and grabbed the first available off road camping spot which was nothing more than a tin lean-to with a water tank.

Next day we sped through Mundrabilla, Madura, and Cocklebiddy, all Roadhouse settlements and decided on a new challenge. We needed a stretch, some exercise and what better than some 'do it yourself' cave exploring. Entering the depths of the earth without a guide is not everyone's cup of tea, but Fay loves all that disappearing under the ground stuff, so what the hell.

Cocklebiddy Caves are hard to find. Mainly because the highway signs, for some reason get regularly stolen. Ten kilometres out of Cocklebiddy there's a track on the right of the highway, in fact a track that leads to lots of tracks. It was not one of Morrisons happier mornings as the stones tore viciously at his tyres and the overloaded springs groaned in anguish. The 20-minute bone jarring trip must have seemed an eternity to him. It certainly was for us. We found eventually that all these pitted and stony tracks across monotonous scrub actually led to 'the cave'. A vehicle stuck in the middle of nowhere, like shag on a rock, gave us a clue, otherwise we could have driven around in ever-decreasing circles never to find these mysterious caves that burrowed into the flat landscape.

Sarah and Joe, a young adventuristic couple from the UK were just emerging from the deep and were dusting themselves down. "Yes, it really was worth the effort" Sarah enthused in her delightful Surrey brogue, her bright blue eyes rapidly blinking in the bright sunlight.

"Its pitch black once you get to the bottom and without a torch it's not even worth thinking about". As she got into her rented 4WD with her apparently nonplussed boyfriend, who hadn't spoken a word, she shouted a farewell "be careful on the way down and watch out for the snake". Joe looked like he was still in a state of shock as they drove off and we wondered whether he had actually experienced a reptilian encounter.

Descending the 20-rung vertical ladder, Fay looked at me with a degree of trepidation as the darkness loomed upon us. Apparently at the end of this foreboding hole in the ground, there is one of Australia's largest underground lakes which some explorers have estimated to be over 200 metres long. The way down was more difficult than the return journey. Finding a footing on boulders and stones of every size was a serious challenge, particularly if the torch was not pointing in the right direction. Eventually we were at waters edge, mesmerised at the smoothness of the rocks, the vastness of the cavern above us, and the clarity and reflections of the deep water in front of us. It was pitch black and deathly quiet. Behind us and very high up was a tiny speck of light which was our direction out of this amplitudinous hole. Not everyone's dream of an afternoon's entertainment, but an experience that we found immensely exciting. And to think that the snake was just lying there under a rock, waiting and watching .

Another surprise awaited us on our return to Morrison. Unknown to us on the bone shaking drive out, a ten kilo container of water had lost its top and shed its contents all over the storage bin. What a mess! The sun overhead was hot and the wind off the desert even hotter; what better place to fix our problem. So with everything pulled out to dry, we set up our picnic table for lunch in one of our more unusual settings. The land was as flat as a billiard table as far as the eye could see and apart from a few wizened shrubs there was not another living thing in sight. Not a fly, not a bird and certainly none of our furry native friends. It didn't take much imagination to envisage that some dreaded disaster had happened and we were the last people on earth. An intense feeling of togetherness enveloped us.

Road kill is a distressing fact of life along this highway of renown and consequently, each morning, hordes of fat black crows, vultures and the occasional eagle are to be seen breakfasting on the fresh meat, gorging themselves on the many roadside carcasses. There always appeared to be one crow that put its stomach before its life and let vehicles hurtle past while continuing its indulgences without apparent fear.

Our closest convergence with the resident animal life happened out of the blue, as such encounters often do. With around a 100 on the clock, and a similar number of metres in front of us, a large emu emerged from nowhere, looked right, then left, and cautiously strode out into the road. The brakes screeched, Morrison moaned, and our two-legged friend survived, not realising how close he had been to becoming a large feather duster. A fatalistic encounter with a roo would have been bad enough, but an emu would have been highly embarrassing.

We spent a little time getting to know the ways of the truckies who live uncomplicated and quite singular existences. Their families are often thousands of kilometres away while they traverse the nation's highways carrying all kinds of goods and produce. They are a breed unto themselves, talking in small groups, and the ones we struck up a conversation with were friendly and easy to get along with. Being avid radio listeners they knew the pulse of the nation as they cruised from one state to another without being part of anywhere. Enquiring into their knowledge of the local countryside was a waste of time as they were dedicated to their mission. Delivering their loads, they just passed through places, were on tight schedules and knew only the various truck stops and roadhouses. We admired their enormous output of energy in the hours they drove, their constant vigilance for possible emergencies and the long time away from their loved ones.

Caiguna roadhouse flashed by, we gained another 45 minutes in a second, as West Australian time made us realise the backbone of the trip had been broken, and within a couple of hours Balladonia arrived. Only 200 kilometres now to Norseman and a suggested celebratory cooling drink at the pub sounded just right. We ended the journey with a great sense of achievement and fulfillment, knowing that The Nullarbor would always harbour fond memories for us. The interest -packed three days seemed to occupy a much greater space in time.

Norseman is the gateway to West Australia and the beginning or end of the Eyre highway, once again depending on which way you are travelling. An old gold town, it is a good place to stock up, fill the tanks, take a stretch and move on. Apparently the town became a target for gold settlers back in the late 1800s when a horse was tethered outside a watering hole and scraped a gold nugget out of the ground with one of his front hooves. Its population has dramatically increased and declined a few times since that event, but it is still the home to the country's longest active mine production company.

There is an old fashioned type supermarket in the main street which sells just about everything and as my co-driver was 'working the net', I sauntered around the aisles with my delapidated trolley.

My attention was caught by an old fella who shuffled in wearing a raincoat, which was most unusual for that time of the year. He had a tartan ratter hat pulled down over his ears and he was spending an inordinate amount of time perusing items for sale in the women's section. After much reading of labels and product comparison he took a packet of brightly packaged tampons to the counter and requested the purchase.

"They would be for your wife then" the mousy girl behind the counter whispered.

"No for myself" he quietly confided, not realising I was standing right next to him.

"Really!" the mousy one exclaimed

"Well yes - it says on the instructions that if you use these, you can swim, scuba dive, parachute jump and play sports, and I can't do any of those things", he mumbled on. I was dumbfounded and not sure if the little battler was for real, just a little retarded or taking the sales girl for a ride.

With Esperance and the South Coast of Western Australia in our sights, we were ready to shake off the Nullarbor dust in the cooling blue waters of the Southern Ocean.

CHAPTER FIVE

DAYS OF WINE AND BEACHES

The last person we expected to meet along the engaging southern coastline of West Australia was the Queen of Denmark. This attractive young lady, in fact, was not royalty but quite the opposite. We chatted to the wild, rocking, Joplin-like singer after her brief guest appearance at a local Hotel. Tracee Morrison hailed from Denmark, down along the coast a bit, and she was interrupting her successful Perth season to visit her birthplace. We learned that while there she would perform as a 'crowd warmer' at an under the stars concert heralding the inaugural Festival of Denmark, scheduled to be an annual event. Whilst we were amused at her title, we could see why her warm infectious personality, would endear her to the locals and earn her the nickname of 'The Queen of Denmark'. The big draw card at the concert would be the main performer, John Williamson. We are long time fans of John's simple Australian music and love to sing along as we play his albums travelling through the places that are dear to him.

With the concert scheduled for two weeks hence, we immediately secured tickets and adjusted our travel plans to be there on time. As we waved good-bye to Tracee outside the pub, she was equally amused that our van was named Morrison even if it was in honour of 'The Van' and not herself.

From the foreshores of Esperance, visitors are immediately struck by the numerous islands of all shapes and sizes, which are dotted all along this unforgetable coastline, known as the Bay of Isles. This picturesque historical town is the site of the first settlement in WA, originally discovered by the French in the 1700s. Many of the bays, cliffs, rivers and parks are named after these early French Seamen. Due to the all encompassing business of the French Revolution, their government of the day never got around to laying claim to this part of the world, leaving us with an interesting hypothetical.

What would Australia be really like today, if the French and not the British had transported their thousands of convicts and soldiers here? Would our French friends have produced the dauntless pioneers that have made Australia the great nation it is today? Meanwhile, frogs legs, snails, baguettes and casoulet would have become everyday tucker while poodles would be poncing and pooing everywhere. Our world beating cricket team would be non-existent, golf courses few and far between, while our rugby union and soccer teams would be unbeatable. Two wineglass screamers would replace the two pot variety, pub life would be non-existent and g'day mate would be replaced by bonjour with a few ooh la la's thrown in. Condoms might well have been called English letters and Morrison would probably be a Citroen automobile called Maurice. So thank God for the French Revolution, without which we could well have been overrun by the fumes of gauloise cigarettes, an over abundance of garlic, and men thinking of nothing else but l'amour'.

"And what is wrong with that" says my little wife.

Our long drive over the mainly arid Nullarbor had given us a thirst for some lazy secluded beach days, a chance to soak up the sun and do absolutely nothing. The nice people at the Visitor Centre, and also several fellow travellers, highly recommended Cape le

Grand National Park, which was just a short 40 minute drive eastward along the coast. Words defy description of the beauty of the place. Superlatives are something that we quickly ran out of so we will leave it to our readers to picture blinding white beaches, contrasting with glass-like turquoise waters, framed by spectacular and unusual rock formations all watched over by spectacular mountains covered with flowering native trees and shrubbery.

The fish were biting the next morning at a deserted little bay called Rossiter, where we had spent the first night in total isolation. While Fay enjoyed a bit of skinny dipping in the crystal clear water, I threw in a line from the nearby rocks, pulling in a fair sized Mulloway along with a handful of herring, garfish and a very aggrieved rock cod. Gutted and scaled, the herring were quickly dispatched to the freezer while the big fella was destined to be eaten that night.

Namatjira Blackened Fish

This recipe is based on spicy tastes I picked up while spending time in New Orleans, and I saw no reason why one of Australia's most famous indigenous artists shouldn't have a dish named after him . I have always found it an easy and rewarding way of cooking fish when you're looking for that little bit of a bite, and it is perfect for most kinds that have firm white flesh.
Make a mixture of 1 tablespoon of salt, 1.5 teaspoon of garlic powder and black pepper, 1 teaspoon each of white pepper, onion powder and cumin along with half teaspoons of cayenne and paprika...shake up real well. Melt butter and oil in heavy-based pan, pat mixture firmly into each side of the fish cook quickly in the very hot butter & oil. Serve with a green salad

One day while I was out fishing, Fay encountered some locals decked out in wet suits, who had just returned from diving for abalone at their favourite hole. Although they complained that their patch had been 'pirated' a few days before and the catch was poor, they rewarded her total fascination with their haul by pulling out an absolute beauty and presenting it to her. Now that was a touch of generosity and typical of the friendliness of many of the locals who live around here. They even went to the trouble of filleting the meat leaving the shell as a trophy. Apparently, abalone meat sells at Perth airport for $200 a kilo so we wasted no time preparing our treasure for lunch. The succulent morsel was frying in the pan within minutes of our newfound friend's departure. With a touch of garlic and a dab of butter it was delicious and easy to see why people pay an arm and a leg for this delicacy. The shell is used regularly as an olive dish and always brings back memories of that reclusive hideaway.

Our seclusion was interrupted when a rather futuristic Motorhome pulled up close by. A smart looking couple emerged and within minutes the conversation had turned from fishing, to drinking and generally having a good time. Paul was a Burt Reynolds looking type of guy whose face I could have sworn I had seen on TV sports shows. He suggested we take a couple of rods to the nearby rocks and try our luck. I presumed he meant at fishing. Debbie was drop dead gorgeous, quite a few years younger than her partner and with her itsy bitsy bikini and islander tan, could have walked right off a Vogue front page. Her plastic surgeon had obviously excelled himself with his various procedures on her person. The fish weren't biting and anyway Paul was keen to return to base to open his first cold one. It's often easy to determine the difference between a new relationship and an old one. Its not just the body language, but when a couple vanish inside their Motorhome and draw the curtains in the middle of the day, then it's a 'laid down mizere' that the friendship isn't exactly stale. It wasn't just the springs in the mattress that got a working out, but the whole suspension system was tested, highlighted with muffled moans and yes yes yes!! This can be very distracting if you happen to be within cooee and concentrating on some important reading material. The advantages are that these activities can also be quite infectious and so; 'When in Rome'.

Trekking through the coastal heath it was surprising to find an abundance of wildflowers, which apparently are quite unusual at this time of the year. The bright yellow flowers of the Christmas Bush were prolific, dispelling the theory that this variety of banksia only blossoms in December. Brightly coloured birds shrieked and squawked, flying with an aerial grace from one favourite eating spot to another. A protected bird sanctuary only 100 metres away, provided a close up of the tree-top antics performed by these vociferous creatures of fluff and feathers. Hiking up the rough-hewn headlands, climbing over time-worn smooth rock, shared with tiny sun-baking goannas and admiring the surrounding 360 degree ocean vistas, were moments that will last in our memories until Alzheimers sets in. Granite monuments of time, some pyramid shaped like the Frenchman's Peak, dramatically rise above undulating heath. This peak's rocky beret-shaped top, protruding over a gaping 'eye' hole, through which the blue sky appears at certain angles, makes it easy to see how it got its name.

After four days of sublime weather, driving rain suddenly arrived out of nowhere.It was the first inclement weather we had experienced so far, so it was a good time to point Morrison back to civilisation. Esperance's oceanfront caravan park seemed a likely place to seek shelter, and even though it did rain cats and dogs for 24 hours, there were a few interesting distractions. Watching some of the transients setting up camp was pure entertainment in itself. I found it more than enjoyable sitting down with a cup of tea, watching the manoeuverings of various newcomers. One elderly gentleman concentrating at the wheel, was cursing away as his highly excitable wife gesticulated and shouted while running up and down each side excitedly waving and signaling. 'Just a few centimetres forward' or 'a bit more to the right darling' as the van went backwards and forwards until positioning was exactly right. Overhead branches, sufficient shade, level ground are all considerations, and new owners of vans who haven't quite got it right are often heard to use language they wouldn't dream of uttering in front of the children. I often feel like offering a round of applause on the completion of these Herculean tasks but realise that the whole procedure is often a great challenge to any relationship. Better to let the dust settle so to speak. However, the whole performance did serve to cement our resolve to seek the privacy of our special little off road spots that we had developed the happy knack of finding, or alternatively head into the more natural National Parks Camp Sites.

Esperance has a range of interesting attractions and with the weather changing for the better, we decided to check them out. Fay was clearly intrigued with the Pink Lake, which appeared to be one of the town's major drawcards. We looked at it from one side, and then drove around to the other and for a moment, thought we had the wrong lake. Maybe the colour was a pale shade of mushroom if we really tried to push our imaginations, but indubitably not pink and positively a huge disappointment. It must sometimes be, or at some stage must have been pink, as businesses of all descriptions; a country club, a motel, shops and a major road all have 'pink' names and some are even painted a nauseating shade of lolly pink. A wrinkled little shopkeeper who had obviously been the target of Pink Lake fanatics on untold occasions, told us it really is sometimes, occasionally, sporadically, sort of pink, but you've got to be here on the right day and at the right time. 'Try again tomorrow' he cheerfully called as we packed away the unused video camera. He could have made a fortune selling rose-coloured glasses !

On the west side of town there is a wonderful circular tourist route of some 38 kilometres incorporating the 'awesome' Great Ocean Drive. A descriptive word regularly used in respect of memorable sights by numerous Yanks that we met on our travels. It really is comparable with some of those great touring routes on the Italian coastline where a stop on any corner is ill considered, due to the seemingly ever-present long line of impatient drivers behind. Fay was turning her head faster than a spectator at a Davis Cup final and with every turn in the road was running short on expletives. Spectacular certainly would be an understatement.

We pulled into one viewing area overlooking the ocean, and decided to stay the night right alongside a spellbinding beach. The only other vehicle was an older style camper van driven by an engaging young couple from Venice. This was Luigi and Lisa's third trip around Australia and they were obviously smitten with the country. They import Indonesian products into Italy and it made a lot of sense for them to hop over to Darwin whenever they were in Indonesia and could spare the time. "Six a weeks from ze Northern Territory through Western Australia and zen all ze way back up ze middle is not nearly enough time" he pronounced in his broken English. "Zere is nowhere in ze world that has ze beauty and how you say, solitude that Australia offers" he enthused.

He was out on his boogie board riding the small waves at sparrows the next morning in what could be described as extremely parky conditions, and he was in 'eaven.

I often think how lucky we are being so far away from the heavily populated centres of Europe and America. Our isolation, environment and natural attractions would dramatically suffer if we were in a closer vicinity to that travelling mass of humanity north of the equator.

Back on the road again and another dream, or in some peoples eyes a nightmare, was being kept alive. From a distance she could have been a Willie Nelson lookalike, with gaudy bandana wrapped around her head and scuffed leather jacket. Vivienne stood out like a lighthouse in the desert in her multi coloured leggings, astride an inharmoniously vividly decorated bicycle, which towed a two-wheeled mini trailer. This eccentric lady of the road was not your every day cyclist, regardless of her idiosyncratic appearance. She told us that for the last two years she had been on the road raising money for Amnesty, Greenpeace and a few other worthwhile charitable organisations. She had cycled from The Gulf of Carpenteria, down the Queensland coast, across New South Wales and through South Australia to Esperance. During this epic journey, she had peddled her way, raising thousands of dollars for her chosen charities. Of course we could not resist a donation and she gave us a receipt from her multitude of receipt books and was off to the bank with her weekly takings.

As companions she takes along her two faithful dogs, who mostly walk but when the occasion arises, take it in turn to rest on a pack atop the trailer. She claims they regularly walk up to 75 kilometres a day and offer companionship as well as protection. "I only had the black one when I was in Queensland but another type of mongrel stole my computer and belongings, so Freddie over there is now my protector". Freddie was outside a Hungry Jacks, gazing enviously at the comings and goings of customers. It could have been a while since he had devoured a good feed but staying mean and lean on the road with Vivienne was all part of this dog's life. "Beware anyone who approaches suspiciously." She confided, "he's like a canine Jeckyl and Hyde".

Her life's belongings were just a few items bagged up in her trailer and she hadn't yet decided on where or when to call it a day. With thousands of kilometres behind her and God knows how many in front, Vivienne's dream is somewhat bizarre but at least she is keeping it alive. We had a strange feeling that our paths would cross again as she was heading in the same directions as us, albeit a little slower.

The South Coast of West Australia appeared to have a tendency to offer unpredictable and varied weather conditions. Late February, early March were supposed to be the pick of the months, but like the rest of Australia that year, anything could and did happen. We found days of heaven with the bluest of skies, a slight breeze and perfect swimming conditions. Then came the winds, which are part of life around here. With them the temperature dropped more than a few degrees, and it was bloody freezing. Linking the sunny days with time spent on the beach can be a fine art, especially when you are on a schedule. With this in mind, we made a decision to hit the road and move westward along the coast towards the highly recommended Fitzgerald National Park.

How many girls are lucky enough to have an orgasmatron on hand whenever the need calls? In fact, how many know what an orgasmatron actually is? My little wife couldn't do without hers knowing that at a moment's notice it will send shivers down her spine, and promote goosebump-breakouts on certain body parts. Her hair has been known to stand on end on the rare occasion, while the overall feeling of drifting off into a state of pure bliss is quite common. To suggest that it performs in a similar manner to a vibrator is somewhat exaggerated, but with a deft hand this ultimate wire head massager can still create a state of euphoria.

She was totally enmeshed in this state as we arrived at Stokes Bay and suddenly emerging into a new world of awareness she screamed, "Bloody hell! Look! Snow!" Indeed, a most unusual sight that initially defied comprehension. Piled high on each side of the road appeared to be mounds of dirty snow, drifting across our approach in waves and rivulets. Upon closer inspection this mirage was found to be wind induced quantities of foam, blown in from the nearby inlet. It was a photographers delight with the feathery candy floss substance flying all around our lunchtime barbecue area.

We drove alongside vast pastoral holdings, many with large impressive homes of grand character and accessed by long avenues of tall trees. The coastal road to Hopetown, which we had been told was in quite good condition, was a real shocker. A Centurion tank may well have found it smooth going but Morrison's cries of anguish, as his springs were tested to the full were heard with every pothole we encountered. It was too late to turn back. . Even at ten kilometres an hour he was not enjoying this part of the trip at all. The pitted and corrugated road went on forever and when Hopetown was eventually reached, a well-earned refreshing drink or two in the lovely old ocean-front pub was nothing short of an absolute necessity.

Only a ten-minute drive away and out of the dwindling twilight a perfect camping spot suddenly emerged. Within a stone's throw of the picturesque Barren Beach and in the shadow of the formidable East Mount Barren, this was a little piece of paradise. Within minutes of pulling a cork out of a brave little Margaret River Sauvignon Blanc, a Fitzgerald River National Park ranger arrived out of nowhere, his timing immaculate. Dressed in his voluntary ranger's outfit with ruddy complexion and warm smile, Brian was not your typical ex Melbournian. He was on his way driving around the continent for a year or two, when he fell in love with this part of the world and became a volunteer ranger for a few months. His Motorhome was parked beside his newly provided cabin, a 4WD truck thrown in for good measure, ensuring that he and his wife enjoyed every minute of their new temporary lifestyle.

He obviously appreciated an evening chat accompanied by a glass or three, and the ensuing conversation in the gathering shadows covered the many enjoyable aspects of life on the road. We sat there watching the sun slowly vanish behind the hills, leaving behind a golden hue, dappled through the wispy clouds.

'Her outdoors' loves walking and climbing and if the two go together, then it is hours well spent. There's plenty of that in this vast National Park, so I tagged along for the exercise on a two-hour climb to the top of East Mount Barren. The heart pumping climb eventually brought us to the summit, providing dramatic 360-degree views of this immense park and its commanding coastline. From the very uppermost ledge we looked down to see the singular outline of Morrison, a lonely speck in the car park below, like a minute white beetle on the bright red soil.

The wildflower season is normally at its height in the spring, not February, yet there was a profuse array of bright reds, mauves and yellows amongst the varying greens of the bush. The fresh summer foliage was intermingled with satiny knots of colour. Wild flowers are such delicate things, threads of life to be appreciated and left untouched by human hand.

Fitzgerald River National Park appears luckier than many we have visited when it comes to the Dieback problem. Dieback is a plant disease caused by a fungus carried in the soil. This slow acting microscopic fungus, which was introduced from Asia in the late 1800s, is killing hundreds of species of flowering plants, shrubs and trees by rotting their roots. Unable to take up water, large numbers of plants and trees are dying of thirst. The problem seriously reflects on the bird, insect and mammal life and we had seen some devastated areas on our travels. Some parks have installed footwear-cleaning stations to control the spread, but unfortunately once an area becomes infected, the disease will be ever present, as no cure has yet been found.

Morrison was ready to put distance under his wheels hence we headed towards Albany, passing thousands of acres of cultured tree farms. Christmas trees of all shades of green flashed by, quite delightful in their various stages of life and presenting us with a new picture of this diversified part of the great South Coast.

Approaching any city does not inspire me, having spent most of my working life in one or another. Albany, which was recognised as a city only a couple of years ago, initially presented the same preconceived feelings. All that changed dramatically as we viewed the harbour and adjacent National Parks from the top of Mount Clarence. The city is steeped in history from the time convict settlers arrived here in 1826 and subsequently through the challenging eras of whaling and sealing. It was also the departure point where our gallant soldiers gathered and left for Gallipoli and the Far East at the start of World War 1. Like many of the places we visited along this remarkable coastline, Albany certainly deserved much more time than the short visit we paid it.

The afternoon was spent in the adjacent Torndirrup National Park where we picked up some fascinating data about the dramatic cliff faces that were once connected to the Antarctic, when we were part of the Supercontinent Gondwana, over 50 million years ago. Sheer drops of fractured cliffs plunged 30 metres to the merciless waves below. We were standing on one of the extreme boundaries of the southern world.

At the tip of the peninsular lies Whaleworld, one of Albany's leading tourist attractions. Guided tours take visitors around the old whaling station. Sadly these massive mammals were still being slaughtered until operations ceased in 1976.

The average thinking traveller to WA must be intrigued as to why there are so many towns and villages that finish with the letters 'up'. Manjimup, Kojonup,Yalingup,Kendenup, Normalup,the list goes on and on. Obviously we have some historical indigenous connotations here, but the response we got from the locals was somewhat varied.

'A meeting place with a watering hole' with the 'up' part meaning 'place of' seemed the general consensus. Not totally satisfied with the explanations, we pulled up alongside a couple of colourful indigenous characters and endevoured to have a 'deep and meaningful' on this important subject. Enjoying a midday kerbside lubrication, they were confused with our interpretation of 'a watering hole'and produced gleeful giggles on finding it to be licensed premises. Not a lot of sense was gleamed from this mainly one-way conversation and further blank looks understandably appeared when Fay suggested that Billy Joel may well have found inspiration for his 'Up Town Girl' hit recording from these parts.

The village of Denmark was only 50 kilometres away and claims to be 'The Jewel in the Crown' of the South Coast. We were immediately enveloped in the ambience, style and culture of the place. Forests of majestic karri trees spread down to the water's edge, with lakes and ponds in abundance, while homes and rural properties indicated a degree of affluence and flair. The atmospheric setting has inspired the residents into throwing themselves into the world of arts and crafts.

The attractions that nature provides are quite extraordinary. Nearby beaches have wonderfully sculptured smooth rocks of all shapes and sizes, creating natural swimming pools that would be the envy of any 5 star resort. Elephant Rocks rise out of the translucent waters like some long lost mystical herd wading in from Africa. At Madfish Beach a crystal waterfall cascades on to a pristine beach while across a shallow channel, dozens of saltwater falls run into miniature rivulets and pools on a rocky deserted island. The rushing inward tide creating a spectacular show of nature with crescendos of water crashing onto the rocks.

Cycling along the town's heritage trail brought some interesting encounters. A group of birdos were busily in pursuit of their favourite hobby. With walking sticks in hand, binoculars and cameras at the ready, they were a world unto themsleves with their brows creased in concentration under their distinctive bird watching hats. As they scurried to their chosen hide, the recognisable face of Keith Potger, local resident and original member of the evergreen group the Seekers, cycled by, waving nonchallently. He was gearing up for the evening's concert, which he partly organised and was scheduled to be one of the comperes.

The night was crisp and clear as a few thousand John Williamson fans settled down on chairs or blankets, picnic hampers at the ready, and drinks in hand. The Queen of Denmark burst on to the stage like a whirlwind, perpetal motion for an hour, performing breathtaking memories from yesteryear. Warm the crowd up? Yes she certainly did.

On stage after the interval, simple trappings awaited the man himself; a campfire, a chair and a 40-gallon drum. He did not disappoint and drew the crowd to him like a magnet. We agreed that our slightly hurried trip to Denmark was well worthwhile, as he breezed through some new songs and lots of old favourites.

The next day we regretfully said goodbye to Denmark and headed off to Parry's Beach where the salmon were being netted. This is a lot of fun to watch and we happened to be there at the right time.

'Spotters', their eyes straining through binoculars, sit for hours in their huts and 4WD's waiting for the schools to arrive. When the unsuspecting fish cruise into the bay, the siren goes off and there's a hive of activity which involves everyone within earshot. Speedboats power out into the surf, the nets are cast and excited people run down the beach to await the catch. Helping with the nets is a local pastime and our assistance earned us a lovely fish to take back to Morrison. While only a couple of tonnes were pulled in that day, previous hauls had recorded up to 40 tonne catches. I found it somewhat thought provoking that a fair percentage of these quite handsome fish do not end up on the dinner table but in cray pots as bait. Obviously the cray market is much more lucrative.

As the crowd dispersed, a particularly fit young lady wearing a tiny orange bikini was hauling in a big one from the surf with her rod. It was a tough 20-minute fight, which drew a small crowd of watchers, some of whom were pretty free with advice. With considerable patience and effort she eventually pulled in what we were told was a good six to seven pounder. Her expression of relief and delight were apparent, while her boyfriend instantaneously bled it by going straight for the jugular with experienced fingers. When the young lady caught her breath she told us it was the first salmon she had ever landed.

There was a time in these parts, decades ago, when parking a car right inside a hollowed out tree used to be a bit of giggle and was obviously a photographers delight. These days 'The Valley of the Giants' which is just out of Walpole, has become a protected and environmentally sensitive area. The nearest you will now get your vehicle to one of these beauties is in the nicely graveled car park near the entrance. I had certain preconceived visions of massive trees but had underestimated the effect that these 300-year-old monsters would have on me. The tingle trees are unique to this area and leave a mark that stays with you.

Their height, approaching 80 metres, and girths of up to 15 metres make them impossible to successfully paint or photograph in their entirety. Many of them have burnt out hollows at the base which could accommodate a large family or in previous days, the family car. These black, cave-like hollows are often surrounded by distorted trunks bearing lumps and scars which take on the appearance of human faces. Decades of fire, fungi and insect attacks have been the main causes.

Their unbelievable stature commands silence and awe, while admirers, minute against their might, are cast under a spell of wonder and respect. The Valley of the Giants is now one of the south coast's most popular and best loved tourist attractions welcoming vast numbers of people every year. Large sums of money have been spent on conservation for future generations and the cash has been invested wisely.

It was as though we were walking on air as we traversed the 40 metres high 'air walk'. These walks, consisting of six lightweight spans each 60 metres long supported by guyed pylons and steel trusses, allowed us wonderful views of the treetops and the terrain below as it falls to a deep valley.

Tingles have very shallow root systems and the decades of visitors trampling around their bases caused irreparable damage and the destruction of many. The newly created spans and walking paths now enable them to breath and regenerate, while visitors appreciate, learn and understand the environmental needs of the forest though the numerous signs posted along the way.

Later that evening we drove a short distance to an isolated camping spot deep in the forest. There were tingles, jarrahs, karri and marri, many of awesome proportions, which proffered a church-like dome overhead. The sun sets early in these dense parts and the nights seem a little longer. Our campfire was lit, the temperature dropped by many degrees and we were surrounded by an eerie blackness. A couple of stars peeping through high above seemed our only companions. It was a remote feeling and as the fire crackled away and we smelt the perfume of the burning wood, I wondered whether an enclosed environment such as this might be a little claustrophobic for some people.

Next morning we drove for over 100 kilometres through endless forests on both sides of the road. I had never seen such a continuous density of trees before and wondered how the prevention of fires had been handled over the years. The Diamond Tree Lookout provided an explanation.

Just south of Manjimup at the side of the South Western Highway is a parking and rest area that makes for a grand lunch stop. At the back of the driveway a karri tree of immense girth and height has a precarious looking spiral ladder, rungs embedded into the massive trunk, that winds itself around and around to the disappearing top. Sitting at 50 plus metres, above the highest canopy is a wooden cabin, which until modern technology was introduced, was effectively used as a fire lookout. For over 30 years until 1974, local volunteers sat for days on end in this and similar lookout trees, watching for the dreaded smoke signals, relaying any signs to waiting messengers on the ground below. Today, spotter planes perform the job, leaving this stairway to the heavens as a challenge to the general public.

We watched admiringly as a devoted father, looking as though he was on holiday from one of our neighbouring Asian countries, attentively took his young son slowly up the rungs. Foot by foot, step by step, they slowly became smaller and smaller until they disappeared into the treetop hideaway. His daughter who looked around eight years old was very cute with her shiny black hair and big smile. She looked cross at being left behind and decided to go it alone. We watched with some concern as she made it up to about ten metres looking like a little doll against the mighty trunk. Just as we were wondering what we should do, her mother appeared from their motor vehicle and together we gently persuaded her down. The little one looked quite non-plussed and wondered what all the fuss was about.

We continued westward towards the expansive Indian Ocean.and soon arrived at the popular little holiday town of Margaret River, well know as the centre for some of Australia's best boutique wineries. In addition, the district has all the artistic trappings that draw hordes of visitors from around the world. Stylish shops, innovative restaurants, trendy coffee houses, a myriad of accommodation choices, fine surf and swimming beaches and wonderful special events provide something for all tastes. Cottage industries abound with city escapees suddenly finding they have varying talents in the world of pottery, painting and hobby farming.

Locally grown produce is important here.The word organic is often seen and appreciated. Jams, pickles, vinegars, relishes and ranges of new culinary accompaniments are proudly displayed in striking, imaginative packaging.

But the wine industry is the pulse of the place. It is by far the area's greatest money spinner and the locals have a claim that stirs the adrenalin that flows through the veins of the community. They vigorously maintain that this district leads the world in quality wines and who would want to argue with them.

Over 60 wineries advertise their wares and facilities, presenting the problem of how many and which ones to visit.. I have spent a fair percentage of my life extracting corks from bottles and there are obviously some wines which revived past memories. Some proven wineries were put right at the top of our list but there were plenty of others that had been recommended and warranted a visit. Confusing the taste buds with too much tasting can defeat the object of the exercise. We thought that a couple of morning visitations, lunch at a special favourite and then two more in the afternoon would give us a chance to be a little discerning in our opinions.

The dramatic coastline stretches from Yallingup in the North, through the quaint hamlets of Graceville and Prevelly Beach down to Augusta in the south. World class surfing conditions are normal here, and it is about the only area in the state that offers consistent quality breaks.

A smattering of people gathered on the headland at Prevelly Beach as black afternoon clouds, bringing threatening lightning storms in from the ocean, slashed the sharp blue skies. Monstrous, intimidating waves were being challenged by groups of intrepid hardened surfers who indulge their hobby from sunup till dark. A couple of mongrel dogs sat transfixed on the ocean seemingly not blinking an eye in case they lost sight of their masters out on the waves. To the joy of the waiting canines, the storm soon forced the last of the dripping boardies to shore. More people arrived as the word got out that the storm combined with the half blue/half black sky was about to produce a spectacular sunset. Of all the sunsets, on all the beaches, that we had seen or were to see, this one was unparalleled.

Autumn proved to be a good time to be here; warm days, fresh evenings, temperate sea and not too many people about. Our last evening was spent high on the cliff face, overlooking the ocean at Graceville. Pleasure and fishing boats bobbed in harmony in the little bay reflected by the bright full moon and the world seemed very much at peace. Dinner required something delicious and delicate and I came up with the following.

Arty Farty Risotto w Mushrooms and Semi Dried Tomatoes

We called it this for two reasons. Firstly, a couple of boring old farts from England astounded us by saying that each night they went out and bought take-away Fish and Chips. In this region of plenty, it was hard to comprehend.
Secondly the wonderful arty selection of available foodstuffs from the specialty stores in the Margaret River area made this dish a little different from others we had been cooking. To be truly successful, risotto is one of those dishes that can't be left. So staying with it and ensuring the rice doesn't stick is essential. Finely chop an onion and some sliced celery and brown in olive oil in a deep pan for a few minutes. Add a couple of cloves of finely sliced garlic, more if you want, then add a cup of aborio rice while the temperature is still hot and stir in. Stir and cook until rice mix is crackling, then add ½ cup of dry white wine and let soak into the rice. Turn down the heat and keep stirring. While all this is going on, separately cook some sliced button mushrooms in oil, and add about half of them along with some garlic and thyme to the risotto. Add some more white wine, a little salt and adjust heat, ensuring boiling doesn't take place. Start adding some previously heated stock, and the rest of the mushrooms. Keep adding stock and stirring until rice is cooked and the risotto is a smooth texture. Add the semi dried tomatoes and small pieces of pickled artichoke at the end, sufficiently to warm them.

We said goodbye to the rolling hills, tree-lined country lanes, innumerable Bed and Breakfast signs and headed north, our bin laden with a few chosen drops of the fermented stuff.

Crabbing has always had a certain appeal to me, highlighted by thoughts of actually eating these aggressive little creatures that remind me something out of an extraterrestrial horror movie.

On the way to Perth there was a weekend house party with friends Barry & Suzanne. Barry suggested a few early morning hours on his runabout, putting his ten new pots to good use, leaving the girls uninterrupted in their quest to cover every imaginable topic in the shortest period of time.

Peel Inlet is normally the picture of serenity at six in the morning but as we raced from one net to another, pulling, emptying the catch and dropping the pot in again, the scene was one of frenzied activity. Not counting the dozens that were measured and thrown back, we took home over 20 legal-size crustaceans for Suzanne's chilli crab dinner that night. Funnily enough on the dot of ten o' clock the crabs suddenly lost their appetite, disappeared and we didn't catch another one. We sped home pondering this unusual occurrence and sorry for the hopefuls who were just arriving, pots at the ready.

We were soon back in the land of traffic lights, zebra crossings, suburbia and the hustle and bustle of commercial life. Fay with tongue in cheek shouted, "look, traffic lights" as though we had been off the planet for months. We estimated that with the exception of Esperance and Albany it had been over a month since we had encountered such everyday normalities of city life.

Perth was one city I would not be able to persuade Fay to bypass. An old hunting ground of hers where she had spent many years and made close friendships; it captured us for a couple of fun weeks. Morrison was tethered as we did the round of lunches and dinners. As the inclusion of cities and areas of suburban sprawl defeats the object of this yarn, I will not elaborate further.

CHAPTER SIX

A DILLYBAG FULL OF SURPRISES

Morrison was as frisky as a colt at the Spring Derby as preparations were made for our departure from Perth. Although we were sad that it might be some time before we saw our Perth friends again, we too were champing at the bit to get back on the road to a life that had become second nature to us.

With the exception of a couple of days in Esperance, the capital had provided us with the only inclement weather of our trip so far. Not bad considering we had been on the road for a few months, traversing the continent from east to west.

Perth's outlying northern suburbs quickly passed us by. In the rear vision mirror I could still see the increasingly smaller outline of the city's last high rise buildings, barely distinguishable in the soup-like skies. We were heading north towards warmer climes, open roads and a coastline that would provide us with quite a few surprises.

It was cold and miserable as the winds and driving rains bent the roadside trees. It took just over an hour to reach the city's outermost limits and the last of those demon traffic lights.

The Swan Valley welcomed us with open countryside, vineyards and a greenness that was doing its best to counteract the greyness of the day. Cluttered houses and neatly laid out estates were replaced by spacious farmsteads, surrounded by rows of swaying trees providing privacy and peace. Vehicles were becoming few and far between, as the near empty roads brought us back in touch with nature again. Mares and their young foals peacefully grazed in the lush verdant fields, raising their inquisitive heads as we passed by.

Our substantial wine supplies purchased in the Margaret River, which had given Morrison's springs so much anguish, had unsurprisingly become somewhat depleted due to our lunch and dinner excesses in Perth. With this small problem foremost in our minds we headed towards the picturesque little township of Gin Gin and a small winery called Cheriton, whose Chardonnay came highly recommended by a friend who takes his imbibing quite seriously.

The winding, tree-lined lanes as we approached Gin Gin were very English. I immediately felt at home when we arrived at the large commodious country house set in a thousand acres of rolling hills. Lovingly built of local stone by craftsmen of days long gone who obviously took immense pride in their work, the property now operates as a successful five star bed and breakfast, as well as a busy little winery.

A fresh looking young country lass with a strong Irish brogue and the smile of an angel warmly greeted us, insisting that she show us around. Shirley and her husband sort of inherited the100 year old property that has seen extensive renovations over the last few decades. There is something about a Celtic accent that really turns me on, and the pride and warmth in her welcome made her the perfect host. They've had some grand functions here, and from the large photographs on the walls of the dining room, she appeared to throw herself into the job with gusto. I could imagine no better setting for a wedding or banquet, with marquees set on the lawns, superbly presented tables settings, performers staged in the background and the sounds of music enveloping the surrounding hills and valleys.

Making our acquaintance with young Shirley was no less enjoyable than making friends with her remarkable little Scotch Terrier. Endeavoring to concentrate on the tastings of some brave little Chardonnay and Shiraz, the little canine took great pleasure in diverting our attention to his presentation of doggy tricks. However, the main purpose of the visit was to stock up with the juice of the grape and after an extended sampling session, we loaded up and bade our farewells.

I love the Irish sense of humour. It can often be quite subtle, not necessarily so in this case as Shirley shouted 'Whiskey, Whiskey, Whiskey', as four furry stumps chased us down the driveway

There were many days when we had no real idea of where we would be staying that night, until it happened. The immediate road ahead was loosely defined and we had a 'take it as it comes' attitude. John Lennon once wrote: 'Life is what happens to you while you're busy making other plans' and we tended to agree with that philosophy. Quite spontaneously we would divert from our planned route to some interesting sounding place and 99 percent of the time we would gleefully claim it to be 'just perfect'. We were becoming increasingly spoilt and loath to accept anything less.

It had been a long day's drive and our various diversions found us approaching darkness without a place of abode. Entering the township of New Norcia on this black, windswept, rainy evening was a little disconcerting. Every single building, and there were some unusually large and important looking ones, was in complete darkness. There was no sign of life and an unusual stillness hung over the place. It was the perfect example of what we imagined a ghost town to be. Settling down for the night at the back of a large field, we poured over our brochures, which gave us the information we were looking for. It was, in fact, a monastic town with 16 Benedictine monks making up the permanent population.

We were woken early next morning by the chiming of the 150-year-old bells atop the nearby Chapel, while the heavy ethereal mist that enveloped the whole town added to the spooky feeling we had experienced the previous evening.

New Norcia has a fascinating history and was conceived by Dom Rosendo Salvado, a Spanish Priest, who was sent out by the Vatican in the 1840s to build a mission. The original task was to provide learning and assistance for the disadvantaged aboriginal children of the area, but it remains a mystery as to how the wise old men in Rome had even heard about our early indigenous problems. Over the following 40 years the good Dom amassed a workforce, substantial funding, and a big helping of spiritual assistance in building this riverside township. Today it is one of the country's truly great cultural heritage sites. The legacy of this formidable icon of the church has continued, although he may well be turning in his tomb, if he is aware the town is now being promoted as one of 'Monks, Music and Mystery'.

In order for the town to survive the ancient doors that were locked to the public for over a century have recently been thrown open and tourism accepted as a means of survival.

Visitors can stay the night, break bread, converse and share mass with the monks. A tour guide gave us detailed and fascinating background on the Convent, Monastery, Chapel and various schools. The wonderful old school buildings which are now only used occasionally for weekend camps conjured images of the days when ten strokes of the cane was all part of the daily routine. Some of the interiors of the religious buildings had magnificently painted altars, priceless artifacts and quite wonderful woodcarvings. The Art Gallery, which houses many truly wonderful life-size oil paintings, vestments, antique books, furniture and machinery is world class and a half-day appreciating the works and history of the town would hardly suffice. There are 27 buildings which are heritage listed. This alone is quite a distinction, while the whole town is registered on the National Estate, whatever that may be.

A 100-year-old wood-fired oven which is never extinguished, bakes 10 different breads daily while nutcakes, jams and honeys are diligently produced from time honoured recipes. Their internationally acclaimed cold pressed olive oil, is sold in exclusive outlets such as Harrods in London which would indicate that the dear old monks have hit the pinnacle with their processing procedures.

It is amazing how many Sandgropers are not even aware of the treasures of this little gem, especially as it is only a two-hour drive from the capital.

We were heading back towards the coast and as usual, after every excursion into the inland areas, were looking forward to returning to the closeness of the ocean. The fishing township of Cervantes was our destination, mainly because it is ideally situated next to one of Australia's most unusual phenomenon, The Pinnacles.

It was one of those crystal clear moonlit nights and we watched the stars twinkling over a flat motionless ocean. We were feasting on a dinner of local cray, when a plumptuous lady who obviously wanted a bit of a chat, interrupted us. She was walking one of those most unusual looking dogs whose skin is totally surplus to its body size. They look as though they were previously twice as big as they are now, but have been on a Jenny Craig crash diet, with amazing consequences. After a good slobbering session with this most affectionate creature, who did his utmost to lick me to death, we gleaned a bit of local info from his owner. She had been in a state of marital bliss for some years with one of the local fish processors, who it appeared, was having a few serious business problems. "My old man's cray catches are so bad this year that he's thinking of sending me out for a job" she confided, hoping that I was some sort of saviour who could help resolve this terrible predicament that had befallen her family. She rabbited on about how many tonnes he was holding this year compared to last and how Mother Nature could be so cruel. I thought to myself 'do I really want to know about all this cray crap', and concentrated on finishing my dinner with great relish. The excessively wrinkled dog was totally oblivious to his owner's problems and proved to be by far the most interesting member of the family. However this observation about the fishing fraternity having one of is worst years on record was repeatedly heard all along the West Australian Coast.

The Pinnacles are located in the nearby Nambung National Park. This is undoubtedly one of Australia's most fascinating sights, featuring thousands of unusually shaped limestone outcrops, which emerge out of the shifting golden sands.

Most visitors were being lazy on the day we were there, and driving through the laid out winding course, snapping away with their cameras from back seat windows. What a disgraceful way to treat one of our national treasures. Although an unexpected downpour drenched us, the three-kilometre desert circuit should be walked, providing everyone with the opportunity to enjoy close encounters with these amazing pillars. Some formations were over four metres tall, rising in the most unusual shapes, out of the stark landscape of mustard coloured sands. It was like walking the surface of an undiscovered planet where no man had trod before.

Colin was a young Ranger who was proud of his position and he fascinated us with the history of the area. Who would have guessed that the raw material of the limestone in the Pinnacles came from seashells in an earlier epoch which was rich in marine life? Consistent high winds and sand drifts caused the formation of these quite intriguing structures which are visited by hundreds of thousands of people a year. He pointed out the problems that the protectors of the Pinnacles were experiencing with idiots trying to climb up these slippery, penis shaped edifices and the irreversible harm these morons caused. But Colin was ever ready to evict such offenders.

The Indian Ocean Drive heading north along the coast, has been a costly but worthwhile initiative by the WA government which has bitumened a whole new tourist route across the coastal plains. Pleasant but mainly forgettable little fishing townships quickly pass by, while the low lying bush and heathland was the only vegetation which stretched out to the distant eastern ranges.

The black storm clouds, which we hoped had been left in Perth, continued to follow behind us and whenever a rest was called for, they caught up, preparing to dump another heavy shower on Morrison. Roadside tourist signs encouraged us to 'visit the sea lions in their colonies' or 'take a fishing trip to catch a big one', neither of which offered the slightest interest under the circumstances. Even the enticing 'explore the local caves' didn't stir Fay's normally adventuristic feelings, particularly as she has this peculiar love of checking out the world underground, whenever the opportunity arises.

The big bustling port town of Geraldton did not appear to have anything to offer us but it did open the door to an oceanfront camping spot just north of town. The weather was no better than an average English summer day, and as we set up camp overlooking endless kilometres of knee-high dried seaweed, lashed by dark frothy surf, the consensus that every night can not be a perfect one, had to be accepted.

One of Morrison's many treasures is a television set, which also includes a video recorder that is rarely used. As the evening weather promised to be miserable, I decided to cycle the few kilometres to the local video outlet with a view to obtaining some light in-house entertainment. There was a mountain-bike similar to mine outside the store, and I found that the only other customer was its owner, browsing the 'new release' racks. Tom was a bear of a man with salt and pepper hair, a much larger sprinkling of the former, and a warm Irish brogue. From out of County Cork he was, now living in a bit of a shack on the edge of town with his 'missus'. He cycled everywhere as motorised transport appeared out of the question, and was obviously a regular customer as he bantered away with the owner. Tom obviously had a 'dickey' right knee by the way he limped around the shop and when I asked him if the cycling helped or hindered, he mischievously replied with a half smile " I only pedal with me left leg, the other just follows around"

As we were about to depart to our respective homes, we doffed our helmets and I asked him which was his favourite movie of all time. "My wedding video" he stoically replied.

" I watch it regularly and always play it backwards, as it ends up with me walking out of church a single man".

It transpired that 'er indoors', rarely leaves the house and that the marriage was one of mutual sufferance, although Tom's acuity of wit at our brief meeting shone through like a beacon in a pea-souper

It would need a warming meal and a good bottle of red to accompany the video. The black clouds on the horizon indicated foul weather was ahead, our spirits and temperatures needed raising and the chicken in the fridge was about to find a new home on our gas barbecue.

Drunken Chicken in a Bag

This is a recipe that proved to be very popular when we served it at our Possum Creek Lodge B & B.
The concept is to poach chicken breasts in a mixture of juices and flavourings and this can be easily achieved on a hot plate or barbecue in about half an hour
Put a couple of chicken breasts, some sliced sweet potatoes, slivers of green capsicum on one side.
Then make a well-sealed oblong boat of double strength foil providing plenty of space for the food and accompanying juices. Place the chicken on a bed of sweet potatoes and surround with capsicum and pour over a cup of orange juice, dash of white wine, a good sprinkling of oregano, seasoning and top with a couple of strips of bacon.
If you really want to treat yourself, a nip of vodka, grande marnier or whatever is wonderful.
Seal top of boat tightly with extra foil and place on barbecue. Make sure it is not overcooked, so check it out after 20 minutes and on a medium heat and it should be nicely done and really juicy.

As we locked Morrison up before retiring, the black ominous sky threatened to disturb our night's sleep. At two o'clock in the morning, a great sweeping storm converged on us, violently shaking the van. The mighty heavens opened, the sea roared and intensive gusts of high-pitched wind-bullets screamed at us for what felt like an eternity. I normally love a good storm and being right on the ocean's edge when its full fury is unleashed can be frighteningly awesome. But on this occasion, Morrison shook as though he was having a minor epileptic fit and it wasn't till some hours later that sleep was even an option. We clung to each other, apprehensively peering through the curtains until peace was restored.

The small, almost undistinguishable sign on the roadside fence stated we were entering the Municipality of the Hut River Province. Years ago I had the pleasure of meeting the Minister of Main Roads, the Foreign Minister and various other dignitaries of this seceded municipality at an official inauguration ceremony on the Gold Coast. It was all very serious with participants wearing peculiar hats and costumes and being knighted by a ceremonial sword. Paying a few thousand dollars to have an official position in a new Sovereign State was no laughing matter, although there were many bemused observers who thought the whole episode a hugh joke.

So the opportunity to visit the Hut River Province intrigued me, and I was interested to see if Australia's first and only royal family had survived those early turbulent years. The entrance gates weren't exactly impressive, no guards on duty and not even a royal flag in sight. A small elderly gentleman scurried across the dusty forecourt towards us, gesticulating where we should park our vehicle. Wearing a well-worn green cardigan and brown faded working trousers and boots, this sprightly farming type with a mischievous twinkle in his eye offered us a warm handshake. We were in the presence of His Royal Highness, Prince Leonard, or as he was known for much of his life, Leonard George Casley.

Readers with good memories and interested in this sort of thing, may well remember back in the early 70s when the West Australian Government put restrictions on how much wheat their farmers were allowed to grow. The Casley holding covered 18,500 acres and Leonard, quite rightly took umbrage to this ridiculous restraint, proclaiming there were immeasurable amounts of land in the state, so why have restrictions. Being hocked up to the eyeballs with leasing commitments, which that Government had previously encouraged, he had a choice of losing his land and all his wordly goods, or finding another way. He decided to secede from Australia.

Prince Leonard if nothing else has a brilliant mind, particularly in the areas of law, mathematics and physics and through hours of burning the midnight oil, found numerous anomalies in this country's constitution. After years of wrangling with the taxation office, postmaster generals, various Governor-Generals, ministers and frustrating beaurocrats, the secession was a 'fait accompli'.

He proudly showed us around his offices, cluttered with glass-topped cabinets housing letters, gifts, medals and souvenirs from governments, dignitaries and royalty around the world. We were privileged to see the cabinet room where decisions are regularly made by the cabinet of his municipality, which just happens to consist of his sons who are all Princes. He has consuls and representation in dozens of countries, and is generally treated in a true right regal manner by his subjects.

There is a souvenir shop with Hut River printed on everything from hats, fridge magnets to teaspoons. His Royal Highness personally stamped our passports, proving our entry and departure and informed us that a drivers license could be available for a couple of hundred dollars. We didn't have the pleasure of curtseying in front of Princess Shirley, his wife of 50 years, as she was ensconced in the royal kitchen making Lamingtons, but did doff our hats to Prince Ian, next in line to the throne, who drove by on his tractor.

There is no question that Prince Leonard is an eccentric genius, a loveable sort of rogue that most Australians admire for upstaging various governments. He enjoyed talking and was highly knowledgeable on a wide range of international and political issues. We admired him tremendously for his tenacity in believing in and executing his constitutional rights and ensuring the continuation of his family's future. He still harasses the powers that be in Canberra, on matters which affect the municipality, and his comments provided a breath of fresh air on numerous mundane political issues.

Unfortunately the place had a ramshackle, run down, definitely unroyal feel about it and was in urgent need of a bit of a tidy up. The plans that were envisaged for developing the property back in the 70s including an airport, duty free shops, hotel, casino and caravan park never eventuated.

The good Prince could have chatted on with us all day, particularly as we were the only visitors but we had reached information overload. As we departed he reminded us, with a smile on his face, that we were leaving the second largest country on the Australian continent. Thought provoking stuff indeed from this little Aussie battler who has our total admiration.

Early on in our trip we had thought it an amusing project to make a list of motorhome and caravan names that were innovative, interesting or at least humourous. The list never eventuated because 'out of the ordinary' names were difficult to find. One exception though did adorn an aging Bedford bus, which we came across on a couple of occasions. The faded, scratched paintwork was original and hadn't been touched in 30 years, while a panel beater could have been busy for days bringing the old girl into some sort of shape. Frayed, tatty curtains hid what was undoubtedly a ramshackle interior, and the whole rig looked like it urgently needed some TLC. 'Hi, I'm your new next-door neighbour', was proudly displayed across the front. Very funny, I thought, but we were pleased that our mobile lifestyle allowed us to easily alter that scenario by simply starting up Morrison's engine.

We were approaching the township of Kalbarri via the southern coastline. And what an entry it was, along 13 kilometres of breathtaking cliff formations. We were exhilarated by the views of Eagle Gorge, Island Rock and Pot Alley and the precipitous drops to the crashing waves below. A couple of sea eagles hovered just above us waiting for their next hapless prey.

It's too late in our lives to think about resettling a long way from home, far from relatives and loved ones, but if we were much younger, Kalbarri might well be high on the list of possible new places of abode. It has all the chill-out atmosphere of a small resort town but with a progressive 'going places' feel to it at the same time. Combined with natural beauty and friendly people, it is an infectious sort of place that brings a smile to your face just walking down the street. Nestled along the banks of an estuary, right on a broad bend where the spectacular meeting of river and ocean creates a dramatic entrance. Our arrival coincided with particularly big seas and the sight of fishing boats breaching the huge swells and crashing waves was quite scary.

Since Alfred Hitchcock's memorable film 'The Birds', I have always been a little cautious when a flock of feathered creatures head directly towards me. The reason I mention this is that just outside town there is an attraction called Rainbow Jungle, which is Australia's largest parrot breeding aviary. From a desolate piece of land, over a period of 14 years, Lisa and Ian Bromley have amassed over 350 birds covering 50 different species. Ian was, and probably still is, a frustrated landscape gardener, and has built an amazing complex of walkways, ponds, and waterfalls that connect the various aviaries. He used over 300 tons of local rock to complete the challenge whilst Lisa has created signage in each aviary detailing the numerous bird species.

There is one particularly large, walk-through, free flight aviary that brought recollections of 'that' movie. Something or someone sparked a disturbance, and what seemed like hundreds of screeching parrots, whizzed by our heads, many missing us by centimetres. They repeatedly winged their way around the walkways, appearing for the world as if they were F1 cars competing in a race against the clock.

Alexandrines, Major Mitchells, Plum Headed Parrots, Purple Crowned Lorikeets, were but a few of this amazing collection with the kaleidoscope of colours being an ever moving rainbow. There was one particular species of parrot that had been consistently used by the early settlers when making their rather popular parrot pie. The nervous look on their faces indicated that their predecessors could well have been the catalyst for the old saying 'a bird in the pot is worth two in the bush'!

Once again ready for some exercise after the previous few days driving, the idea of early morning kayaking down the Murchison River had great appeal. Picked up at 'sparrows' with two other couples, who like us were half asleep, we bounced around in the back of a dilapidated old 4WD along deeply pitted dusty roads until we were 20 kilometres upstream.

There is something a little dreamlike about a totally isolated environment in the early morning, just as the sun is casting its first rays through the trees. The river was glasslike as our paddles gently sliced through the water, having no desire to disturb the abundant bird and animal life on the nearby banks. A mother emu and her young striped family of chicks gazed at us suspiciously, large white crane-type birds on long orange legs stood in shallow waters searching for breakfast, while dozens of black swans motionlessly glided by. A large brown osprey perched majestically next to its untidy nest of twigs atop a tall gum, while a sea eagle plummeted into the water, plucking out its unfortunate breakfast victim with effortless ease.

Fred was our host and ran his little business whenever the weather permitted. "Suitable for all ages" he proudly pronounced "In the last few months we have had the youngest fella ever in a kayak...only nine months old he was, and just lay in his mum's arms while dad did all the paddling". Fred was a hive of information about the outback, environmental issues and any of his clients that warranted a mention "Only last week, we had a 93 year old geezer 'ere who really showed the young ones what paddling was all about. Doubt if we'll see 'im back again though, as I thought he was going to have a heart attack, what with all 'is wheezing and coughing.".

Our genial host was cooking a particularly greasy breakfast over a large stone barbecue, which I am sure would have finished off the 'old geezer' even if the paddling didn't. Mind you, after our paddling efforts, we all tucked in with gusto to the bacon, egg, toast, grease and all without a thought about the health issues. Fred was a man of the bush and he certainly looked the part. He epitomized the word scruffy. Long unkempt straggly hair and beard, a face that has spent its life under the sun and generally giving the appearance of a finalist from an episode of the TV series 'Survivor'. But looks aside, he proved to be a fascinating true-blue character with a dry sense of humour and an infinite knowledge of his big back garden.

Like many West Coast towns, Kalbarri has marvellous sunsets and the ones we saw were a little more dramatic than most, as the cloud formation and backdrop of crashing surf provided the perfect canvas. An added dimension was the fishing boats in varying sizes returning from the deep, carefully negotiating their passage through seemingly treacherous waters, temporarily disappearing behind jagged rocks and pounding surf. On a far beach, a dozen or so horses were galloping, with flaying hooves kicking up sprays of sand, while riders firmly hung on. We felt privileged to be viewing this glorious display of nature's sensual delights.

In the busy tavern that night we shared a drink with a friendly Pom who confided that this evening was the last time he would be smoking and drinking for two months. Bill threw away a half-empty cigarette packet which I thought rather extravagant and downed his last schooner in a somewhat flamboyant manner. "Off to Madagascar tomorrow on a rowing boat" he proclaimed "trying to break a world record of 64 days". Statements like that normally indicate an intake of excessive amounts of alcohol, but it appeared this slightly overweight and seemingly unfit 30-year-old was in fact telling the truth. He certainly did not portray the style and image of somebody who would undertake such a challenge. He informed me that his partner Robin, who had the common sense to have an early night's kip, had in fact already achieved a solo Atlantic crossing, and weeks of training had seen both of them in world-beating shape.

I recalled that there had been an unusual- looking sort of futuristic craft tied to the jetty that day, painted out in Union Jack configurations, surrounded by a small gawking crowd. It was becoming apparently obvious that Bill wasn't just suffering from a few schooners too many, but had in fact got Madagascar in his sights.

True to his word, with his partner Robin, they were towed out of Kalbarri Harbour the next morning with television cameramen shooting away from helicopters, cheering onlookers waving them off and many believing that any one with a half a brain, would be mental to attempt such a challenge.

A couple of days later a TV report showed two men being rescued from an upturned boat in the middle of nowhere. The craft was supposed to be one of those that automatically righted itself in the event of a large wave or other object hitting it, but in this instance it remained in the upside down position. Bill looked as though he was searching for a packet of cigarettes and would be clearly happy when a schooner of beer was in the offing. Their attempt unfortunately failed and the journey from London must have seemed a long way to travel, to have some mystifying mishap curtail their challenge after only a couple of days at sea. Anyway, for a couple of Poms, Madagascar can be unpleasantly hot and sticky at that time of the year.

Prince Mukramm Jah, the eighth Nizam of Hydrabad, was once worth $2000 million and ruled some 16 million subjects. For some inexplicable reason, best known only to the Prince himself, he came to West Australia, settled in Perth and purchased an enormous property just outside Kalbarri where he spent many months each year. Stories in these parts still abound about the good Prince, and locals treat his past association with the area with a mixture of intrigue and pride. So when his old property Murchison River Station is mentioned, a little folk lore license still exists, even though there is a new family now running the place.

The current owner Steve Roscic, who at just under seven feet is a tall man by any standards, is the first to admit that he was the last one with his hand held high when the property was auctioned. He also admits to snapping up a bit of a bargain. The land area covers a massive 250 square kilometres, 60 of those have direct ocean frontage and about 30 are along the dramatic meandering banks and floodplains of the Murchison River. Steve and his charming wife Anne bought the place in 1987, with a view to their two sons Calum and James taking over the running of it. A fascinating morning was spent with them as they immersed us in the history of one of West Australia's largest and oldest pastoral properties.

Steve was happy to talk about his predecessor, Prince Jar, whose spending prowess has indelibly left its royal mark. The Prince had a penchant for very large pieces of farm equipment, and scattered around the paddocks lay dilapidated, unusable, rusting farm machinery including a massive immovable 100-ton dozer. "The Prince had enormous local media coverage when he married a Perth secretary, and made Helen his real life Princess" Steve recalled. "Unfortunately, ten years later she was the first Australian female to die of Aids, contracted after an association with a bisexual friend of one of the Prince's associates".

One of the old original settler's cottages is still standing. On the flaking mud-rendered walls, hung newspaper cuttings and memoirs of events and mishaps of this Sandhurst educated Prince. He was certainly worlds apart in every way from the self-styled Prince Leonard, who we had spent time with the previous week.

Back in the 1840s, the property's first owner, Count Charles Von Bibra was given the title to what was then nearly one million square kilometres. He trained horses here for the British Army, which were then transported to India. Today the main form of wildlife are feral goats of which 6000 are mustered annually and transported live to the abattoirs, where they are killed by a Muslin Priest for export.

There is a causeway across from the homestead, which leads to the ocean side of the property, and in times of flooding, it takes a long arduous 240-kilometre drive to reach a point only 100 metres away. That to me summed up the enormity of running an operation of this magnitude.

We were unfortunately a little early for the height of the wildflower season, which is prolific over thousands of square kilometres during the months of July to September. Even so, the roadside banksias were in full bloom and their combination of pale pink and orange turning to a light ochre were a show unto themselves. Day after day, mile after mile, the trees were heavy with blooms that cheered a sometimes monotonous countryside. A few weeks later, and with a few drops from above, it would be a veritable Garden of Eden. I read somewhere that there are over 800 distinguishable species of wildflower in this part of West Australia and I find it commendable that someone has been given this enormous task of differentiating and actually counting them all.

Kalbarri National Park is a delight. Stretching from ocean cliffs through a twisting river of crystal clear waters and dramatic gorges this 183,000-hectare treasure has to be seen to be appreciated. Photographs do little justice. Memories are stored in the mind and the vastness of this spectacular scenery leaves visitors in awe of its beauty and stature.

Around 400 million years ago, sedimentary rock formations created magnificent red and white-banded gorges for 80 kilometres to the ocean. Discoverers subsequently named the 'The Loop', 'Z Bend' and 'Natures Window' all of which are the gathering points for the lazy admirer or the adventurous hiker about to set out on one of the trails. The Murchison River zigzags her way through stark, arid landscape leaving 80-foot high cliff faces of dramatic proportions. Healthy feral goats with coats of many colours munch contentedly away at peace with the world, while eagles float effortlessly in the stillness of the day.

Birdos come here in increasing numbers to photograph, sketch or just spy on the extensive bird community. There are over 200 different species to check out, which should keep most Birdos pretty occupied for years to come, especially as the catchment area is larger than some Australian states.

Morrison had some work to do; the ocean was calling once again and we had to au revoir this memorable piece of Australia. It was just a hop skip and a jump to Monkey Mia and the people-friendly dolphins. The 'hop' was a few hours drive thru   . unloved land that offered little to anything or anybody except the eral goats that were often quite stupidly suicidal. Their awareness of speeding vehicles was non-existent as they potted around on the roadside. Paprika coloured soil glowed under the newly sprouted leaves of the recent rains while monotonous low bushland seemed to go on and on forever.

The 'Skip', from the main highway roadhouse to Denham was equally boring and inhospitable until a rather bizarre occurrence broke the monotony. As we slowed down to cross a cattle grid a howling, growling, yapping racket split the silence of the morning. This appeared somewhat extraordinary as we were right in the middle of absolutely nowhere. It could well have been a raving rabid rottweiler or some other such wildly agitated hound, but there was not a beast or human in sight. Cautiously peering out of her window, Fay noticed these agitated barkings appeared to be coming from amplified speakers set by the roadside and rather bravely decided to take a closer look. A high security fence stretched as far as the eye could see and indeed there were speakers built into supporting columns, which were motion-activated by vehicle, human or animal movement.

The Barking Dog Fence was built to keep feral animals on one side and protected species on the other.

This whole peninsular is called Cape Perron National Park and certain commendable visionaries have slowly introduced a restoration plan which will remove feral animals and reintroduce native mammals. The shape of the peninsular, with its narrow isthmus is perfect for controlling what lives and dies there. Project Eden intends to turn back the clock, see the extinction of goats, foxes, rabbits and feral cats, all introduced by the white people since they set foot here 150 years ago.

The quiet and quaint township of Denham was a pleasant surprise. We really didn't know what to expect, particularly after hours of driving through pretty average countryside, culminating in the howls of raucous 'dogs'. Overlooking a broad expanse of crystal clear water, the place had a character all of its own and is the obvious stopping off point if dolphins are on the traveler's menu. 'The Jump' to the resort of Monkey Mia was a doddle after the boring hop and monotonous skip and we were getting very close to those dolphins.

It had been 15 years since Fay was last here and she was more than interested in evaluating the numerous changes and in checking out the recently completed resort. She had vague memories of driving down a long, winding, dusty, pot-holed road and finding a handful of people, knee deep in water feeding the dolphins. In those days avid dolphin lovers paid $5 for a small bucket of fish and freely waded into the water to feed them.

These days everything is controlled by the very affable Rangers. As the bottlenose dolphins are wild, numbers and the exact time of their visits varies, however one or two dolphins usually visit the shore up to three times a day, more frequently in the morning. The rangers do most of the feeding but one or two lucky gawkers are selected out of the big crowd to pop a fish into a perpetually smiling mouth, however it's a harsh word from their minders, if you dare try to touch one. Fay had a 'pick me' look on her face and had the pleasure of feeding Nicky who is aged 24 whilst Puck looked on. They all have names and are recognizable by their fin markings or body scars and each one has a documented family history.

The ecologically aware resort hugs the pristine white sandy bay and visitors are clearly reminded how the management is continually protecting and sustaining the marine life and environment. What had to be done, with the advent of increasing hordes of uncontrolled visitors, has been done in a way that most people would understand and appreciate.

Monkey Mia apparently got its name from a 19th century trading boat called 'The Monkey', that used to ply these Indian Ocean waters, while Mia is thought to be an Aboriginal word meaning 'place of'. The indigenous connection has now come full circle with 50 percent of the operation, recently being handed over to the leaders of the local tribe, resulting in employment for one or two fortunate members.

Evenings on the beach are something quite special. Numerous boats having returned from their fishing activities create a flurry of activity around the filleting tables. Men wearing aprons stand brandishing razor sharp knives, while scurrying wives carry buckets of iced water ready for freezing the fillets from the wide range of recently caught reef fish. Keen fishermen have been coming here for years and many have their own special spots and holes. One rather grumpy Perth retiree told me this has been his home for a month every year since the 60s. He takes his half-cabin runabout out most mornings, seven to ten kilometres to his 'secret' destinations. Returning with a sizable catch, I questioned him on the restrictions, which he would have known were strictly five fish per person per day. He became even grumpier as I jokingly counted the invisible people still sitting in the stern, who would have made his catch of 20 barely legal. Depleted fishing stocks is a serious worry to authorities and there are heavy fines for abusing the law, but I suppose there will always be the odd greedy fisherman who pushes the boundaries, ultimately spoiling it for others.

As the orange coloured sun vanished into the sea, a church-like silence of awe and appreciation settled on the beach. Nobody talked much, there was a companionable silence and small groups of people gathered to soak in the ethereal atmosphere The quiet was only broken by the occasional awkwardly landing pelicans, creating quiet ripples on the darkening bay.

Small groups, tinnies in hand, gathered around the barbecue areas after sundown and the talk invariably was fishing. I found it intriguing that red meat for dinner was by far the preferred choice. I suppose when you've been pulling them in by the boatload for years and years, then the old taste buds can get a little over-saturated.

Steve and Harvey are a couple of comedians who have the most enviable job imaginable. They skipper a 60 foot ocean racing catamaran, fastest in the Southern Hemisphere, with the unusual name of Shotover, which sails from the jetty a couple of times a day, packed with enthusiasts, who want to see and know more about the local marine life. The day is filled with humorous banter interspersed with thrilling sightings and lots of fascinating facts.

As the voyage progressed, the captain and his mate were getting worried that it might be one of those rare days when no mammals are seen and everyone gets their money back. We were looking for dugongs. These alert, shy and curious creatures can live up to 70 years and are closely linked with the mermaid myth. After a few make-believe sightings, which were set up by the gesticulating antics of the crew, things improved. Of the supposed 10,000 dugongs in the bay, two of them sidled up to the boat for a breath of air sending us all into a frenzy of camera clicking. Further excitement erupted when a sponge dolphin emerged next to us with its colourful cleaning tool mounted around its snout. Tiger sharks, some up to four metres long, turtles, flying fish and manta rays made up some of the more interesting species that are prolific in this vast waterland. However, we were out of luck in trying to spot a longtom who very cleverly skips his way across the ocean on his tail.

Back on land, still smirking from the humour of a totally enjoyable afternoon, we found ourselves strolling into the resort's art gallery. We both appreciate the talents of budding artists, especially as Fay has recently taken up this challenging hobby. Hung on the walls were a myriad of the most unusual shaped frames imaginable. Michelle Wardley is a petite fresh faced talent who sits in her work area within the gallery and attacks the next project with a totally different concept to painting. No canvas or brushes here. She uses a palette knife with oils onto hard board, surfboard, or driftwood and creates stunning ocean related scenes. Frames are collected from beach, tips or forests and each exhibit has a beautifully worded message underneath, describing the reasons and background for the work.

Our conversation was interrupted when who should walk in, but Steve, our skipper cum comedian from Shotover. Apparently these two well-suited lovers were finalising their plans to leave Monkey Mia that month, had bought their own catamaran in Queensland and were about to start a new adventure. Fortunately Michelle's gallery will remain, managed by the resort, and her new works painted on the East Coast waters will be freighted over for sale.

We departed this very special place as a procession of tinnies and runaboats were jostling at the ramp to start another day, guaranteeing more fillets for the freezer, more smiles from the dolphins and more happy laughter from guests on the Shotover.

For decades now, pies have been generally accepted as an icon of Australian tucker and although I have no idea on the quantities annually consumed, they must add up to many millions. Some pie makers get away with murder, filling their soggy crusts with crappy tasteless mince, while others have built a reputation of providing innovative combinations and first class ingredients. Fay, who tends to be a bit of a health fanatic and likes to watch the calories, would normally not go near one. However, we had the good fortune to stumble upon a roadhouse at Wooramel, about 100 kilometres short of Carnarvon, where the pies and pastries are the best we have tasted in years. They are all freshly made on the premises and taste like they have just come out of Grandma's kitchen. We left there feeling a bit like the cat that ate the cream as we dusted the crumbs from our T-shirts.

Carnarvon surprised us in a lot of ways. The immediate impression was the dramatic transformation from the harsh scrubby bush land that is all about, to an extensive area of verdant, well tended plantations. Located on the Gascoyne River, the busy township is the West's most important produce growing area. Back in the 1920s, local farmers were finding the variable weather conditions impossible to cope with, and it became increasingly difficult to earn a living from the dry land. Some bright spark worked out there could well be fresh water streams underneath the main flow of the Gascoyne. Today, irrigation water is drawn from acquifiers, which are replenished during river flows, with each grower receiving 72000 kilos per annum.

Initially it was just bananas but in the last few decades virtually every kind of fruit and vegetables are now successfully grown in this near perfect climate. South River Road is well known as the fresh produce shopping lane of Carnarvon. It has a dozen or more produce growers offering remarkably cheap and mainly unsprayed products from their roadside sheds.

The farm owners were all flat-strap, but had time to say g'day and have a chat. George had the face of a man who had spent a lifetime toiling in the heat, but his back was straight as a rod, an unusual feat after years of backbreaking work in the fields. His huge gnarled hands sorted out our purchases as he passed on some finer points on his special tomatoes or favourite avocado. He told us that there were nearly 160 different commercial growers in the area, and their properties which average ten hectares stretch over 16 kilometres along the banks or within close vicinity of the Gascoyne. Virtually isolated from other growing regions, bugs and diseases are unknown and the necessity of spraying is not an issue. About 96% of the produce is exported to Perth with the industry now worth $30million a year.

We emerged from each shed laden down with supplies for the next few weeks. A supply of unripened produce for later on was stored away in Morrison's now tightly packed storage bin.

The one mile jetty at Carnarvon is, strangely enough, one mile long and is famous as a top fishing site. A little train takes the elderly and lazy types to the end, but as we didn't feel we were in either category, we walked, rods in hand and with high expectations.

At the end of the jetty, there was an interesting mix of fisherfolk with quite distinctive attitudes towards this intriging pastime. A small group of well dressed, jovial, middle-aged European gentlemen sat on the decks with legs wide apart, dangling their lines through gaps in the timbers. Small bream proved easy to catch, the challenge was extricating the fish through the spaces in the decking. Each man had a bottle of beer in one hand, which did somewhat inhibit their retrieval process, but when they caught the last train back, each one carried a large plastic bag full of the rewards of their patience.

Then there were the energetic ones who had the smell of bigger fish in their nostrils. By sundown, a small group of us working individually and together pulled in ten huge Mulloway (also know as Dhufish), in just over an hour. Each one of them exceeded a metre in length. One young Japanese guy seemed to relish his suicidal jumps over the railing to a lower level and proved that he was a master at gaffing. The turbulent waters deep below held no fear for him as he balanced on his precarious perch, while his 100% spiking record ensured the safe landing of each fish. Watching these silvery beauties thrashing around on the deck, seemingly hoping for a second life at every last gasp, made me realise why Fay never really had her heart in fishing. However, she was sporting enough to walk the one mile back to Morrison to collect the camera and record our epic catch. One fish was enough for us, which I cleaned and filleted at the specially provided bench on the jetty. It provided us with 14 good-sized portions, 12 of which were frozen, for future enjoyment. It was cold as we all trouped back down the jetty in the pitch dark, laden down with fish and tackle. But the cold was quickly forgotten. With a warming bundy in one hand, I threw a couple of fillets, seasoned with Cajun spices, into the sizzling pan.

An easy morning drive lead us through mundane, arid country that makes up a large portion of the West Australian land mass. Suddenly, like an oasis in the desert, we were face to face with crystal blue waters and bleached white beaches, luminous in the radiant sunshine. Coral Bay lies at the southern tip of the fabulous Ningaloo Marine Park and is the only settlement bordering the park. It used to be an isolated little hamlet, uncommercialised and off the beaten track. But its beauty and easy access to the Ningaloo Reef could not be hidden forever and things have certainly changed. Ningaloo is not only the largest fringing coral reef in Australia, but also one of the largest reefs worldwide found so close to a continental landmass. It is about 200 metres off shore at its nearest point and less than seven kilometres at its furthest.

With the influx of tourists to Coral Bay, the shortage of drinking water had become a problem. In 1980 they seriously started to search for this precious commodity and lo and behold, 3000 feet down there was a plentiful supply. It came gushing out like oil, the only problem was that it had twice the normal salt content of potable water and was also a nice warm 68 degrees. Desalination reversed the first problem, while visitors quickly learned about the other. Still, within a short period of time, an oasis was created.

Today Coral Beach is a hive of activity providing all sorts of opportunities for visitors who like to be close to marine life. Spotter planes search for the whale sharks, which are the big attraction here during the months of March-June. The whale shark is the gypsy of the sea; showing up to feed when the coral spawns, then disappearing as mysteriously as it came. To swim with these gargantuan creatures as they move effortlessly and serenely through the water is the thrill of a lifetime. The whale shark can reach a length of 12 metres and are the world's biggest fish and also are one of its most gentle.

Meanwhile turtles, manta rays, dolphins and dugongs can be viewed from boat or plane. Fishing and snorkeling trips can be arranged, diving courses and ultraflights for the adventurous or you can just mooch around the beach and café scene. With its busy bars, backpacker outlets and internet cafes, Coral Bay seemed to appeal to the younger set that were there in droves.

The jet black storm clouds that had been behind us all the way, abruptly appeared on the horizon and foul weather blew in dropping bucket loads of the wet stuff. We timed it to perfection and headed north once again appreciating the ability to run, at a moment's notice, to where the sun shines.

Thousands of termite mounds, dotted across the scrubby fields, highlighted our trip as we diverted from the main drag north and headed along the North West Cape to Exmouth. They seemed to be not of this planet, but somehow specially positioned there for an extra terrestrial event. Some were over two metres tall, all reddish brown in colour and like people, all had their own uniqueness. A few were in tight little groups as though having a meeting, while many were standing in solitude in their own spacious blocks of arid land. We were to see termite mounds of varing shapes, sizes and colours as we journeyed on and they never ceased to fascinate us.

We passed the RAAF Base at Learmouth, which looked deserted, devoid of people, planes or any activity, although the high security fencing and gates around the place suggested plenty to conceal from prying eyes. Instead of hanging around waiting for some "Top Gun" to take off, we continued on to Exmouth. It was lunchtime and hot, so we wandered down to the beach with a swim in mind.

Collecting shells and beach pebbles has never been high on my list of priorities, and I always thought it to be the domain of children and little old ladies with plenty of time on their hands. Encouraged by Fay's continual fosicking, I must say that I've slowly become sucked in to this passive pastime. The colours, textures and shapes can be quite extraordinary. The subtlest shades of pinks, mauves, mushroom, greys and brilliant whites are truly a marvel of nature. As the collection grows, gets sorted and packed away in little boxes, I wonder what will eventually become of them, but Fay assures me that there is a master plan in place.

Exmouth will never forget the day Vance came to town. It has experienced a few cyclones this century, but the category 5 terror which hit them on the 22nd of March 1999 with wind gusts of more than 280 kilometres per hour, was the mother of all cyclones. Tropical Cyclone Vance, bore down on the North West Cape and within a few short hours had wreaked havoc on the township. The resilient residents wasted no time in recovering. Just five weeks after the cyclone, the roof was back on the pub, the bar renamed Vance's Bar and Exmouth was back in business. We felt that this sort of pub deserved our patronage, so we had a cooling ale as we planned our trip out to the Cape Range National Park.

Tragedy can often bring humour and while many pubs we visited had various slogans on their walls, Vance's Bar gave some amusing antidotes on the effect that drinking has on the excessive imbiber. 'Alcohol may make you think you are whispering when you are not.' ' Alcohol makes you think you can logically converse with members of the opposite sex without spitting' 'Alcohol may cause a disturbance in the time space continuum, whereby small and sometimes large gaps may seem to disappear'. And so the list went on.

The well stocked shops in town supplied us with all necessary provisions and we looked forward to playing castaways for our few days away from civilisation, on the northern and less commercial end of the Ningaloo Reef

Driving around the northernmost headland on our way to the National Park, numerous tall out-of-place looking satellite receivers appeared which apparently served the very useful purpose of keeping the USA in touch with her own navy. The Harold Holt Naval Communication Centre also passes those very secret messages from

Canberra to the US Command Centres, and we were continually reminded with large signs to 'Keep Out' .As if we would want to go in anyway?

At the gate of the National Park we found information about the numerous oceanfront camping spots, that are dotted along this extensive strip of sand dunes and pristine beaches. These picturesque sanctuaries for travellers who appreciate their closeness to the sea were in most cases, virtually sitting right on the beach. The placid waters of the lagoon lapped gently within metres of Morrison's wheels, while the surf crashed and sprayed high on the surrounding reef only 200 metres away. Black footed rock wallabies, red kangaroos and emus were our neighbours, while recent rainfalls gave a verdant look to the heathland.

With snorkels in hand we were off to adjoining Turquoise Bay which is aptly named and symbolic of all that is special in the Ningaloo Marine Park. The waters here are indescribably picture postcard blue and framed by a gently curving, white sand beach. The slow moving current carried us effortlessly from one end of the beach to the other, a distance of less than a kilometre. With the assistance of our snorkel and flippers we watched with fascination, as an underworld of marine life drifted by. Reef fish of every conceivable colour, size and shape passed within centimetres of us, unconcerned at our presence. Some darted in and out of remarkably formed coral shapes, feeding on plankton and other minute delicacies, their remarkable colour configurations looked as though they could well have been hand-painted by artists of extraordinary vision. These perpetually warm waters are home to 500 different species of fish that breed and play amongst the 250 different types of coral.

At the completion of the snorkel drift there is a sandbar and the secret is to get out of the water here, otherwise the suddenly fast moving current will have you quickly out with the sharks near the reef. One very noisy American tourist apparently missed the sandbank and made quite a spectacle of herself as she straddled a submerged coral outcrop and screamed for help. The beach crowd thought she was just another American shooting her mouth off and did not take her seriously at first. But as the screams became more frantic she was eventually rescued.

Around these parts, fishing always seems to be brought up in conversation. A couple who haled from some obscure country town in the middle of New South Wales have travelled here every year for the last decade, and spend a month or so camping on the beach. They bring with them an inflatable two-man kayak, which was pulled high and dry and loaded with rods and tackle. "Mate, if you get out there towards the reef and hook a big one, there's nothing like being pulled through the water in this 'ere little kayak" said the amiable tousled haired fellow, who was stocking up for his morning session. "In the last few days, me and the missus have caught a few large spangled mackerel, made friends with a couple of inquisitive turtles, and got real close up to the odd dolphin" he enthused. The missus didn't seem half as enthusiastic as her old man, hardly saying a word. Country girls are often that way, but before he pushed off for another few hours in his little piece of heaven, he did mutter something like "bit quiet this year though; when there's a drought on the land, there's normally one at sea".

The reef goes as far as the eye can see in both directions and is omnipresent with its booming surf and constant spray. The crystal clear water contrasts with the rich red limestone cliff faces, behind which ancient gorges apparently exude quite powerful auras. We had one amazing sunset behind these cliffs where the vanishing heavenly body created golden outlines around architecturally shaped mysterious clouds. We were transfixed by the beauty of it all.

Back in our camping spot, the evenings often draw nearby campers together, sometimes with the most unusual mix of people. A large rotund man, with a few days stubble on a face that could well have been straight from the movie 'Deliverance', introduced himself as Ron, all the way from Rapid City, Dakota. He was in the 'appraisal business' he informed us, brandishing a bottle of Rum, and if anyone wanted appraisals done when they were next in Dakota, he was the man. It was an offer we all thanked him profusely for, particularly as he had a fondness for regularly filling our glasses from the bottle of BlackLabel Bundaberg which seemed to be permanently affixed to his armpit. I kept his card, just on the million to one chance that I might need to take him up on his offer, but give me a break. Ningaloo

Reef, Dakota appraisals, these yanks never give up do they?

Young Jane was quite the opposite. She was an eight-year-old sweetie who had taken a sabbatical off school for six months to tour West Australia with her two older sisters and Mum. The girls completed three hours study every morning and for the rest of the day soaked up the environment, nature, people and the big world that we like to call ' The University of Life'. Jane did the rounds of the campers who quickly fell in love with her infectious spirit and inquiring mind. She wanted to know everything about life and will return to school a wiser and a lot worldlier young lady than her fellow classmates.

Life in this National Park can be traced back over 7000 years from the Aboriginal middens found here. At the right times of the year, the flora is quite outstanding. Pure white Manilya lily's, bright red Sturts desert peas, yellow Kangi wattles mix with mustard coloured Ashby banksias, morning glory and other wonderful wildflowers.

Sitting outside Morrison, with the sun's rays just appearing and with a few hours before our departure, we reminisced on the memories of our stay here. We only came here for a couple of days yet were finding it difficult to tear ourselves away after 10, which says a lot for this magical piece of the country.

Within a short time of us leaving, the whole area was front-page news. An unprecedented half a metre of water fell within a few hours, disconnecting communications and leaving many homeless.

Our timing was perfect and we were on our way north, once again just before the bad weather arrived.

CHAPTER SEVEN

ENCOUNTERS OF CONTRADICTIONS

The Pilbara region covers an immensely varied area that reaches from the north-facing Indian Ocean coastline, across to the imposing Hamersley and Chichester Ranges. The long drive through the stark beauty of land as flat as a billiard tabletop, with fascinating rocky outcrops and a backcloth of majestic mountain ranges was absorbing. Rocks of all shapes, colours and sizes litter the roadside and surrounding heathlands. The reflection of the sun extracted warm shades of reds and browns from the roadside gravel that extended through to the broad vista of the distant ranges. Innumerable riverbeds, broad, sandy and forgotten, that had not seen a drop of water in years, waited patiently for the next big descent from the skies. Lonely isolated gums, huge and gnarled stood proud, somehow surviving in these arid conditions. Emus gave us a curious look and quickly disappeared into low scrubby land, while wedge-tailed eagles soared majestically above; their sheer grandeur leaving no doubt that they were king of all they surveyed.

The roads were long and straight, the bitumen ribbon a shimmering image, Fay had given up on the scenery and was dozing in the passenger seat, and there was minimal traffic to interrupt my thoughts. Driving in these conditions gave me time to think, to plan, and to appreciate a rare moment of solitude. I recalled an old saying, 'Man cannot discover new oceans until he has the courage to lose sight of the shore' It seemed quite pertinent in these surrounds.

In the middle of absolutely nowhere, a lone cyclist passed us, coming from the opposite direction of course, slowly, methodically pedaling away in the heat of the midday sun. It was in the mid 30s with not a breath of wind and the broad smile etched on his face, could well have been a serious grimace. Garishly dressed in bright reds and purples, hidden behind huge wrap-a-round sunnies, he raised a finger in acknowledgment of our presence.

I thought, 'Must be mad', 'Probably a Pom', 'Mad dogs and Englishmen, out in the midday sun'. Maybe he had lost a bet, like the Irish guy who ended up dragging a fridge around Ireland. Or maybe I am getting too old and not fully appreciating the challenges that some people set themselves. This guy was certainly finding his new oceans, even though he was in the wilds of the Australian outback.

We have a large coloured map inside Morrison, which is affixed to the top of the cab, permanently looking down on us. On long drives, particularly when Fay is at the wheel, I gaze up and appreciate the enormity of this country. West Australia alone, which covers an estimated 40 percent, would take a lifetime to explore fully. I was happy in the knowledge that in the few months that we had travelled through this most beautiful state, we would probably have seen more than many Sandgropers do in their lifetime.

Karratha is a town with a few pertinent characteristics, one of which is the oppressive, sweltering heat during its summer months when the temperature regularly exceeds 40 degrees. But we found some early indications that this frontier town could well be hot in more ways than one. Scanning the local rag in the various towns that we visit can often be an eyebrow raiser, with the editorials and classifieds giving us a clue as to the feelings and attitudes of the residents.

In the Karratha Classies, which is the local weekly giveaway, we noted that there were only a few tickets left for the stage production of ' The Vagina Monologues' which was appearing that week at the local theatre. Sales had been brisk as nothing quite as risqué as this had been previously presented.

On the opposite page there was a large advert welcoming everyone to a 'Pap Smear' lunch, with guest speakers who would talk about the lighter side of this unpleasant medical procedure. It didn't mention what was on the menu or if the speakers were, in fact, talking on this delicate subject as guests were actually eating. My furtive mind was already imagining what succulent delectables could have been prepared for this auspicious event. It was a fund-raising lunch and all in a good cause, but time and other reasons prevented us from attending and allowing us to give readers a more in-depth report.

Only a few kilometres away from these interesting happenings, we camped at a look-out surveying The Intercourse Islands that were spread out below us. There are three of them, all with slightly different names and are part of the extensive Dampier Archipelago. Why they were named the Intercourse Islands no one seemed to know, but I am sure there would be some intriguing stories to tell, related to these christenings.

Back in town, one of the big Friday night attractions apparently is 'Jelly Wrestling'. The highly excitable crowd scream and shout for their favourite performers, who are normally wrestling with their own sex or occasionally end up in an extremely messy foursome. Males and females all having a go at each other, with bodies smeared all over in sticky jelly can be a big turn-on for many. Some participants are so titillated with these proceedings that occasional after-fight dalliances are not unheard of.

Was it just my mind concocting sexual leanings in this part of the world, or was it the smile on everyone's face that gave me the impression they are a pretty contented lot? The excessive temperatures would encourage folk to stay indoors in air-conditioned comfort and no doubt have more time to make their own fun.

Karratha was not high on our list of places to visit, but due to the miserable state of banking arrangements in this country, we had little choice. Since leaving Perth, our so-called and quite ineptly named National Bank was conspicuous by its absence in all but one town that we had visited. Shareholders are obviously happy with the billions the company is making, but it seems customers have become a distinct second when it comes to service.

Out of necessity, face to face encounters with my bank are unavoidable, which brings to mind the following quip. What is the difference between a banker and a wanker? The latter knows exactly what he is doing!

As it turned out, we were glad we called there, as it is a pleasant, well laid out town. There are attractive shopping centres, all the banks you could wish for, and a people-attitude that is second to none. Locals were so warm and outgoing, it would take a devious minded city type to think that something else was afoot.

Just a short drive away and about a kilometre out from Dampier is Tide Pole Island.

It is home to a modern day Robinson Crusoe who paddled out there on a 44-gallon drum back in the early 60s. Sam Ostojich's eyes looked as though they had seen a million sunsets from his deserted outcrop. His deeply tanned weather-beaten face has stood the rigours of time well. "I just fell in love with the place" he quietly recalled with his strong Yugoslavian accent. "In 1965 I started building my home out of rocks, driftwood and anything washed up on beach, and still have not finished. I'm 82 years old now and don't have as much energy as when I was younger, but I will keep working at it."

He told me he's got running water but no electricity and uses a gas-powered fridge and cooking stove. In a moment of generosity Hamersley Mining Company, who own the 300sq metre island offered him a 99 year old lease. I thought that pretty superfluous as he had been squatting there for 40 years. He is so well known around the area that the island is known as Sams Island. "My family all think I'm, how you say, 'mad' he joked, "but I feel very safe out there and happy with my own company. I come to town in my dinghy for shopping and like to go back real quick"

We wished him well. He's found his bit of contentment, away from all the dramas and traumas of a troubled world and will certainly be remembered by the locals as a likeable hermit who did it his way.

A few kilometres north is a little fishing town called Point Sampson. Taking time out, we relaxed there for a few days, finding a sunny and sheltered possie right at the end of the all but deserted small fishing harbour, overlooking a turbulent ocean. Some shabby looking commercial fishing boats were tightly secured, waiting for the merciless winds to abate. During a temporary respite in conditions, there was a flurry of activity and the gallant crew of one boat took to the high seas, fighting their way through the enormous swells. As Fay watched this battle with the elements, she struck up a conversation with the only other person dockside. She was a charming and seemingly knowledgeable lady but was showing signs of worry on her face. She had every reason, as her young son was skippering the boat in question. He had been playing around with boats since he was knee high to a grasshopper, and his father had given him the helm of this fairly sizable craft for the first time. Fresh faced, he looked right out of school, but with the confidence of a seasoned professional, he steered the boat out through the breakers for what promised to be an uncomfortable week. They breed them tough out here and the kid couldn't have had a more challenging debut. "If he's going to learn, he might as well throw himself in at the deep end" mum murmured.

There is a bugger of a fish in these waters that really tested my patience. Fishing from the rocky tops at the end of the long jetty wall, I battled an aggressive little creature who had a nasty habit of regularly grabbing my hook and vanishing into a hole or behind a rock. The big tugs on my line told me something substantial was on the other end but it was like pulling in a brick wall. A seasoned local passed by with a grin on his weather beaten face, and informed me that it was a blowfish, which has teeth like a razor, blows up to the size of a football and is totally inedible. I had lost half a dozen tackle so an alternative amusement had to be found.

My trusty crab net was dropped in near the mangroves and quickly got the results for which it was intended. Within the space of half an hour a crab was netted the size of which would not normally be seen in a fish market. No weighing scales around here, but from the open claw tips across, it would have measured nearly half a metre.

This monster did not want to believe that this was his last day in the mangroves and his aggressiveness saw him emerge from the confines of our eskie and march down the slipway towards the water. As I happened to be back on the other side of the harbour dropping more pots when the jailbreak occurred, it was left to my brave little wife to deal with it. 'Her outdoors' hastily grabbed a broom which was the only piece of suitable equipment available, in an endevour to prevent the quickly disappearing crab from departing the scene. Screams rent the air, and they weren't from the crab, which was now in full attack mode against this formidable weapon. The sight of this amazing 'woman against crab' scenario could well have been another entrant in TV's Funniest Home Video show.

The only cookbook we carry on Morrison is Stephanie Alexander's 'Cooks Companion', the bible of the kitchen, which informed us that crabs should be drowned in cold fresh water. This muddie had perfected the art of underwater breathing as he was still ready to attack anyone that went near him eight hours later. Eventually he gave in and was devoured the following evening in a humungous meal that left us 'up to pussy's bow' by the time we had finished him.

Mangrove Muddie... with Coconut Curry

Crabs are plentiful around much of Australia's coastline, depending on the time of the year, especially where there are mangroves.

Live crabs can be quickly killed with a long sharp knife through the brain, but there is an argument that if death is through natural causes, ie drowning in fresh water, then the meat will be more tender. Either way, when it's left this world, clean out the brains, separate body from shell, cut into 6 pieces, crack claws and it is ready for cooking.

Stir-fry in heated oil for a few minutes and set aside. This helps seal the flesh.

Keeping a little of the oil in the wok, stir in a tablespoon of green curry paste, a little garlic and ginger and a cup of stock. (Preferably fish or chicken). Add 2 tablespoons each of brown sugar and fish sauce, mix well and finally add a cup of coconut milk. Cook for a few minutes, then return the crab pieces to the wok and simmer for a further five.
Garnish with some coriander and serve with rice.
The heat can be increased or decreased with the amount of curry paste which can be varied according to taste...Enjoy, particularly if you are wearing a bib

Point Sampson has a few good things going for it, besides the fact that it is very quiet, ruggedly picturesque and has memorable crabs. One of them is the tavern, a typical small town watering hole packed with locals, mostly involved in the fishing industry. There are certainly no fashion statements being made here, and nor does there have to be, with the drinkers at the bar looking as though they have just arrived off the high seas, or are ready to depart. Dave looked like the place was his second home. He hadn't worked, shaved or had a haircut in 15 years and the tats all over him were a work of art. He reckoned he showered daily, which was an unusual way to strike up a conversation, but made me a little more comfortable having this knowledge. I bought him a couple of Swans, which is what everyone seemed to be drinking and found out all I wanted to know about the social life of Port Sampson, which wasn't very much.

It was Friday night, and like most pubs everyone gets a chance to win a raffle, which Fay gets much delight in getting involved with. Copious quantities of complimentary food appeared on the bar which was such a good quality and variety that it had the desired effect of keeping us there for many more drinks but made going out to dinner a very low priority. They are also famous in these parts for their fish and chips and hungry patrons drive for miles just to appreciate this superbly cooked fare. When we informed the waitress that our journey from Byron Bay had taken several months, she seriously thought that we had driven all that distance for a taste of their prized fare.

Laurie and Suzie live on a magnificent 42-foot catamaran, with the unusual name of Coal Miners Dream, which was temporarily moored in the harbour. Strong winds had brought them in while on their way from Bunbury to Darwin and they were getting a bit anxious as to how many more days they would have to spend there, even though they enjoyed their nightly visits to the Tavern. Their schedule was totally controlled by the weather and although the sea-going travellers would not agree, it made me appreciate the convenience of our land-bound mode of getting around. Laurie loved making his own home brew on board, and had gallons of the stuff to last their long voyage. He generously invited us on board to sample a few glasses of his potent nectar, and such was its strength, I had a departure I would rather forget, fractionally missing the bloody dingy in the dark and falling in the water. Fortunately the sea was warm and the swim back to Morrison cleared the head. Home brews will be treated with more caution next time.

Suzie had never previously sailed the open seas and showed a little trepidation on their forthcoming trip, which would eventually see them in Bali. But Laurie had spent years, building the boat himself as he worked out his final years at the Coal Mine, and was quietly confident of his and the boat's abilities.

Loos are something normally not worth mentioning but in this instance the 'Exec Loo' warrants a couple of lines. We had occasion to visit these super duper depositaries along the coast, and were intrigued with the streamlined, motion activated soap dispenser, taps, and hand dryer, together with the computerised flushing system and other futuristic features. Fully tiled and about three metres square, they have automatic doors, and warnings that after 10 minutes these doors may open, leaving passers-by with some interesting sights. A flashing green light advises if the cubicle is occupied and an automatic sliding door invites those inside who are in urgent need. Seeing one installed in a shopping centre or busy tourist area would be quite normal but having one at the end of our harbour, overlooking the ocean, seemed a bit like 'a shag on a rock'. However, we made full use of this modern-age facility during our stay even though it did appear to be an amusing addition to the surrounding scenery.

There were few if any people around here that didn't give us the time of day. Everyone was super friendly and even the odd mongrel dog smiled at us, for whatever reason, I cannot imagine. The wind was still raging its guts out, strong enough to blow a dog off its chain, so we packed up and headed towards the minute Heritage Hamlet of Cossack, which is a sort of a ghost town. Besides the one or two magnificently constructed buildings of last century, oodles of history about the past, and various depressing reasons as to why it is now quite ghost-like there did not appear much reason to linger longer.

About an hour or so on the road to Port Headland there is a place called Whim Creek, which in actual fact is not much more than just a pub. The building is all that remains of what used to be a copper and gold miningtown in the late 19th century. It was lunchtime, a thirsty time of the day in these parts, and it didn't seem unreasonable to call in and check the place out. Whim Creek is famous for two things. Firstly, it has experienced and survived more than one horrific cyclone and secondly it makes great Bara Burgers. It's a lovely outback pub, photos and newspaper cuttings adorn the walls highlighting its encounters with the elements. Disused old mining equipment litters the surrounding gardens of what was once known as 'The Pink Pub of the Pilbarra'. There is a large inviting sign at the entrance which promotes their wild life zoo. A quick walk around proved that the zoo was no more than a huge aviary containing dozens of gaily plumed parrots. Apparently the animals all decided to go on holiday during one of the cyclones and haven't been seen since. After ordering the recommended culinary delight, we sat for an eternity in the beer garden surrounded by these caged birds waiting for lunch to arrive. Maybe Barramundi were not too plentiful in the waters around here and were proving hard to obtain, or God forbid, the microwave may have broken down. The thought came to me that we and the other diners could well be the inmates of the zoo and were there for the amusement of the dozens of birds, all lining up on their perches, gazing at us. We observed the varying conditions of our fellow diners, hoofing into their mountain-high burgers, which obviously intrigued our feathered friends.

A voice with the pitch of a Doberman boomed out from a doorway, competing for attention amongst the babble and shouted 'Number 33'. It was the number on our docket for our long overdue 'Bara Burgers', and my arm immediately shot in the air as though I hadn't seen food in days. I caught the attention of the face behind the voice and those edible edifices, some eight inches high, somehow remained erect on the plate, as our waitress, blue thongs clenched between toes, dangerously swayed between the tables towards us.

The members of the menagerie were obviously impressed, particularly the larrikin cockatoos, as they harmoniously squawked their approval.

The hot afternoon sun was beginning its downward descent and it appeared the right moment to say goodbye to Whim Creek and head up to the distant mountain range.

There are many unique parts of Australia and the Hamersley Range can certainly be placed in that category. Its length alone, which is in excess of 400 kilometres is pretty impressive, but it's the visual impact that hit us as the dramatic outline slowly drew closer. As we approached, reflections of reds from the vast and intriguingly shaped mountain ranges become clearly apparent.

It was dusk as we drove along the floor of our first gorge, the highway surrounded on each side by shearing dark red sculptured cliff faces. Our first night was spent high up in the range, overlooking a deep chocolate tinted gorge with millions of stars seemingly within our grasp. The only movement that broke the indescribable tranquility was the falling of a leaf, the blink of a wallaby, or the restless rustle of a bird. Sitting out under our heavenly ceiling of twinkling lights it was a time to contemplate and appreciate nature. Conversation seemed quite secondary in these surrounds and a new appreciation of nature enveloped us.

By morning, heaven had turned to a comparative hell with lashing rain and howling winds surrounding us. The bad weather that we had successfully strived to outrun for the last couple of weeks had eventually caught up with a vengeance. Loath to get out of bed as we gazed through Morrison's fogged up windows, we wondered how our friends in Point Sampson were faring, captured in their small harbour, trapped aboard their catamaran, travelling options minimal.

Heading through the ranges, blackened trees passed us by in their thousands, ravaged by fire, with branches like fingers pleading to the heavens. The recent rains had given the fertile red soil a new lease of life and bright green new growth was emerging. Fresh verdant lines of scrub appeared to be newly painted on each side of the highway. Football size clumps of spinifex covered the plains and hills and from a tired grey, were changing back to their traditional greens. This sunburnt country savours every drop the Almighty delivers and the almost instant change is dramatic.

The Hamersley reach a height of around 1200 metres and ground temperatures in certain parts have been known to reach an oppressive 75 degrees celsius in summer. Granite greenstones form much of the landscape while red and white layers of silica provide amazing reflective shades from the sun's rays. Mountains and hilltops appear like islands in a sea of unmolested flora.

Golden Kangaroo grass resembling vast oat crops in full bloom provide a balance of colour as if from the palette of an artist. Mulla Mulla bushes with their fresh white flowers blend with the pinks of the Desert Rose.

Violent volcanic activity shaped this region many millions of years ago. The awesome landscapes might look tough and as resilient as the iron in them, but they are clothed with a fragile mantle.

The visitor centre in Karijini National Park is probably the best presented of any that we have visited so far. The information and historical background presented in various painted and photographic ways, provided an excellent insight into this wonderful part of Australia.

Unfortunately, the gravel roads to various gorges and waterfalls were in such a bad state that we were advised to stick to the bitumen. After travelling such a long distance, it was upsetting that CALM, who manage West Australia's parks cannot get their priorities right in this particular area, by not only endeavouring to improve reasonable access to these most picturesque sites, but by also offering better advice of the problem to intending visitors.

The inclement weather vanished as quickly as it had arrived, only 24 hours were lost, before the inspiring mountain shapes took their colour again. Finding the challenge irresistible, we climbed up two of the States highest mountains, 'Bruce' and 'Nameless' on consecutive days.

Why the white man had to rename these magnificent plateaus with forgettable titles when the local Aboriginal tribes have known them by their traditional names for a thousand years is difficult to understand. I mean, Mount Jarndrunmunhna sounds pretty good to me, instead of ' Nameless'. My god, which genius got the renaming rights to that one? It imperiously looks down over the township of Tom Price which prides itself on being West Australia's 'top town' or at least the 'highest', whichever way you look at it.

The walk up Mt Bruce, the second highest peak in the State, with a wind that was as cold as it was strong was quite a test of our capabilities. A young couple who we perceived to be from the good old USA by their accents, which pierced these chilly heights, were descending from the top. Looking somewhat blustered and windblown after experiencing the howling gale, the petite young lady was laden down with what was obviously an overpacked backpack. She proudly told us it was loaded with rocks, which her boyfriend told her would prevent her from being blown right off the mountain. I know the Americans have been credited with some wonderful innovative ideas over time but this concept seemed to totally defeat its object as she stumbled and gasped over the descending trail. On our return to base we saw no evidence of anything untoward, so presumed she made it to the car park. The small pyramid-shaped pile of stones, next to where their car had been parked, appeared to be testimony to their safe return.

Aboriginal history runs deep here and it is easy to see the spiritual attraction that has drawn them to these mountainous parts over the centuries. The ranges have remarkable shapes and distinctive features. Some with table top flatness as though some massive electronic saw has sliced off the top half. By the side, but joined by saddles, are curious sculptured shapes that a landscape artist would drool over. There are soaring peaks with many having unusual rings of colours

116

around them, in the reds and whites that have made this area world famous.

Mining is the lifeblood of the Hamersley. The townships, roads, employment, and tourism structures are all beneficiaries of Australia's leading export. Without the ore this would be an inhospitable, barren land with visitors few and far between. The train system is something else. Watching a two-kilometre length train pull 226 wagons carrying 20,000 tonnes of ore on its 260-kilometre journey to Dampier, we marveled at this amazing piece of engineering. There are over 600 kilometres of track, privately owned by the mining companies and seeing one these monsters passing by highlights the enormity of the operation.

'Her outdoors' was really keen to see the mines, and so we trundled aboard a conducted bus tour, hard hat and goggles in hand, to inspect the Hamersley open cut mine. It was a freezing cold morning up in this high country, however we soon became mesmerised with the sheer size of this venture. As we looked down on the monstrous trucks and machinery, carving deep into the earth's crust, we could easily comprehend the importance of this project to the nation's economy. Sculptured roads cut layer by layer into the cliff face created an enormous canyon-like effect. Our knowledgeable guide knew the answer to every question that was thrown at him, and there were plenty from our group of inquisitive onlookers. "We've been mining here for 25 years" he enthused "and its hard to estimate, but there are at least another 30 years work left in this particular mine." This was one of only six Hamersley mines in the Pilbarra and trains are transporting the valuable commodity 24 hours a day to the port, for shipping around the world.

The town and mine of Tom Price were named after one of the early instigators of ore exploration in the area. He was American and died shortly after returning home and being advised that the West Australian Government had approved his years of efforts in the mining industry. The other high profile identity who we enquired about, Lang Hancock, apparently wasn't responsible for such discoveries at all. He was astute or lucky enough to have purchased land that had to be traversed by the mining companies, and negotiated a royalty of $1 a ton, which his family holdings still receive to this day.

The myth of his endeavours will remain forever, even though it was a nice lucrative deal, getting such a big earn from the mining industry without getting his hands dirty.

The town's shopping centre was busy with people and bird life. The copious number of friendly parrots strolling the pathways and gardens amused us, and their crisp whiteness contrasted with the dark skins of many of the shoppers.

Round the campfire that night we met some interesting travellers and one intriguing character had a knack of telling a good yarn and reading some wonderful bush poetry.

Sam had been an achiever, in a myriad of variable challenges throughout his lifetime. He looked back on happy times in radio broadcasting with the ABC, running large pastoral operations, filming environmentally sensitive issues and for many years marketing the Great Barrier Reef. With his new partner, Frauline Bern, he was free to roam, explore, and had a special affinity to the land and its history. So his story-telling had a certain poignancy and a wonderful feel as though he had personally experienced every word.

After a couple of amusing Bob Magor bush tales, Sam enthralled the small intimate gathering with a tale about an old mate of his that really suited the setting.

Forest Hamersley, was a member of the Hamersley family, whose illustrious name was given to this mountain range. Back in the 60s he was an airline pilot and ferried people about the State for MMA, affectionately known in the airline industry as Mickey Mouse Airlines. Forest, whose nickname was Bush (say no more) was a wild boy with rules of his own. He also owned a large sheep farm somewhere to the east of Geraldton that was his pride and joy. One day he informed his few passengers, a group of Japanese businessmen, doing goodness knows what up in these parts, that there would be a slight diversion to the preordained flight path so that he could take a look at his property from 5000 feet.

To his astonishment, the rams and ewes, which should have been separated at this particular time of year, had broken down a dividing fence and were enthusiastically doing things they weren't supposed to. With the gleeful approval from his passengers, he landed the plane on the bare flat land, and with their assistance separated the joyfully copulating animals into their allotted fields.

They were all having a lot of fun and the Japanese contingent had their cameras clicking. Bush did not give a thought to the fact that he had been out of radio contact for two hours and pandemonium reigned back in Perth as search and rescue plans were being put into place. Although much loved by the airline management for his charismatic attitude to the job, this little episode put him distinctly out of favour, and he was dismissed the next day. The GM with a sheepish look told him that his behaviour did not come within the guidelines of the airline's policies.

The airline seemed to have a track record for employing interesting characters and stories abound of in-flight incidents that gave credence to the nickname Mickey Mouse Airlines. A young blonde hostie, we'll call her Angela, was making her first flight from Port Headland to Perth and was obviously a little nervous. The passengers included some keen fishermen who were taking their frozen catch of fish and various crustaceans back home with them. A good looking chap handed Angela his package asking her to take good care of it, and if she would like to join him for dinner in Perth that night. On landing in the capital, she used the intercom for the first time and wanting to locate this particular traveller was clearly heard to call

"Can the gentleman who gave me the crabs in Port Headland please stand up". Guffaws erupted throughout the small aircraft, no one stood up through sheer embarrassment, while Angela hid behind a rather red face.

MMA ceased trading some years later

The only reason we had to call in to Port Hedland was to collect our regularly diverted bundle of mail from our home Post Office. Since leaving home, we called our faithful Postmaster on a weekly basis, informing him of our next intended destination. He methodically writes down the name of the town along with the postcode and says, "Right". No further conversation is encouraged. Given that it is a small two person operation, it strikes me as peculiar that even though we are paying for the call, not once has he enquired as to our journey, our health or if we will ever be back. On one occasion he did, in a matter of fact sort of way comment "Some more money would be nice". I presumed my account was getting low and sent him another $100. Obviously a man totally devoted to the job on hand.

Port Hedland isn't really a town that impressed us and I suppose it's not a destination that is near the top of travellers 'must see' places to visit. Besides its associations with iron ore and salt, it really isn't worth a mention, although the town does hold claim to some sort of record, which I read was a Guinness Book entry. The world's longest train was coupled together here in June 2001 by BHP to a length of over seven kilometres and weighing in at 100.000 tonnes.

There were a couple of incidences that tickled my fancy in Port Headland. One was some advice from a young jogger who was profusely sweating in the afternoon sun. He welcomed a reprieve from his daily exercise and was ready for a chat as we strolled leisurely along the beach. He warned "Don't forget to wear your thongs while you are swimming. You just don't know where those deadly stonefish might be lying in wait for you"

Good advice indeed and with that thought in mind, we gave the water a complete miss. Fay looked somewhat perplexed. The actual concept of swimming with thongs, tightly gripped on by her toes was a worrying one, as she already has enough to worry about coordinating her arms and legs, without additional rubbery burdens.

The other item of intrigue was a request in the form of a notice. A handwritten sign on a scabby piece of cardboard affixed to the window of the bottle shop requested patrons to be properly attired prior to their purchase. Thongs, singlet and shorts were the minimum level of dress code in downtown Port Hedland, which I thought quite reasonable. The main thrust of this important message though was the maximum amount of alcohol that could be purchased by one person; a four litre can whatever that might be.

On the banks of the De Grey River, 100 kilometres north of Port Headland, the dreaded 'croc' word was mentioned for the first of what I suspected would be many occasions. We were now on the outer perimetre of crocodile country, and at this point Fay declared that she would not be putting so much as her shadow in the water.

How things were to change as we became more attuned to the ways of this wild land. It must be said that few have been sighted here, and then only in 'The Wet'.

Our neighbours along the riverbank appeared to know the area well and always call in for a week or so each year. Ron was a highly intelligent sort of retired gentleman who had worked out a system for 'safe swimming'. He sat outside his caravan, with wife Joyce by his side, and watched for a day or more for any croc movements before he immersed himself in the slow moving current. We passed by their caravan numerous times, and noticed eyes transfixed towards the far broad sandy banks. Unflinchingly gazing, as though some memories of a distant past caught up with him, while Joyce had perfected the art of knitting and gazing at the same time.

What also drew us to this lovely couple was their magnificently marked Burman Ragdoll cat called Max. This playful pussy had saucer-like china blue eyes, thought he was a dog, and preferred blondes. He took an instant liking to Fay and on hearing her voice bounded out and requested the obligatory pats and strokes that his canine counterparts do. His proud owners are fourth generation Edgars and have a family history in West Australia that goes back to the turn of the last century. Their campfire tales of their ancestor's early pioneering days held us all, including Max, quite spellbound.

Our neighbour on the other side was the 'matchstick man', duly named not because of his beanlike appearance, but because of a creative ability to build outback scenes from thousands of glued matches. Talented old timer Kevin travels around West Australia for many months a year leaving his wife at home for reasons he wasn't prepared to divulge. Out of the depths of the storage space in his aging caravan he produced dozens of these cleverly constructed works of art, which he sells at any local markets he may be passing.

The banks of the river where we camped for a few days provided us with an adventure into fairyland. Bleached river gums with gnarled trunks of the smoothest texture, mix with steeply arched paper barks, their branches pointing to the water in some exclamation of life. Coloured birds flit and call from tree to tree in the sheer delight at being alive. Fay found one particular paper bark that stood out from the rest. Tiny faces appeared etched in its living being, topped by a dominating pair of bulbous eyes over a huge gaping mouth, and with branches like the waving arms of some Pagan God, it set her imagination running riot. A kingfisher poked his head out of what appeared to be an ear, intently watching us before disappearing inside. My little wife is occasionally prone to superstitious beliefs and this breathing monument of timber gave her the distinct feeling that it was in fact a haunted tree.

The number of paperbark trees inspired us into cooking dinner in a way that has been used by the aboriginal for thousands of years.

'Babe in the Wood'

This is our recipe for pork wrapped in paperbark.

Choose your tree well and select a quantity of paperbark from the trunk that has few holes and minimal insect life. It should be lightly washed and brushed clean and large enough to wrap around a pork fillet twice. The secret to this dish is the marination of the pork fillet, which ensures the moisture of the meat is retained, but does not prevent the flavours of the bark eminating through. Smear the bark with oil/butter and roll the marinated meat. Secure with rushes, vines, or even twine will suffice, lightly dampen the outside and place on to a hot plate. Turn over after 10-15 minutes and the fillet should be cooked through within half an hour.

Slice cooked meat and serve on bed of spinach with boiled baby potatoes tossed in extra virgin olive oil and your favourite herbs.

Marinade

¼ cup each of soy sauce, vinegar (pref red wine), mirin. 1 tablespoon of honey, olive oil, hoisin sauce and sprinkling of chopped or bottled garlic and ginger. Mix well and let the fillet sit for at least an hour before cooking

Sitting around our riverbank campfire each evening, with the sun's final rays filtering though the tapestry of leaves and branches, we felt like we were in heaven. The perfumed smoke from the multi coloured embers drifted from one direction to the other as if guided by some magical force in the stillness of the evening. Catfish occasionally broke the silence with gentle flops in the black mirror like waters. A blue winged Kookaburra, common to these parts with a Pavarotti inspired vociferation, bade us goodnight.

As we packed and prepared for departure to our next destination, we envisaged what conditions would be like in the wet. While the river was peacefully meandering down through its wide sandbanks, it is difficult to appreciate the force and depth of the raging torrents that sometimes makes these areas inaccessible. The underside of a rail bridge near our campsite, was over eight metres high. Used twice a day for transporting BHP iron ore to Dampier, its uppermost supports were clogged with flood debris of all sizes.

I had never had the opportunity to stay on a working station and was looking forward to the experience. Our arrival at PardooStation coincided with what looked like the filming of an episode of Roadrunner. Two hyperactive cattle dogs were chasing an emu round and round the gardens, disappearing behind huge cattle trucks and racing past us, as though the entertainment was orchestrated for our arrival. Beep was a three-year-old emu who had been raised on the property, and as the homestead pet, was enjoying its afternoon frolics with the blue healer and the red cloud kelpie.

Pam and John Leeds and their two sons are the current owners of this nice little spread of just over 500,000 acres. In the ten years since moving here, they have experienced all the problems of living off the land in a climate that is prone to drought, heat and cyclones. A fleet of modern cattle trucks and their tourism facilities have been added to cattle grazing with their stock currently running at thousands of head of Bos Indicus and Santa Gertrudis. Their additional activities have become necessary to keep the property financially viable.

The open-plan park with its plentiful shade trees was a casual, relaxed place where we eventually stayed five days. It was full of colorful characters; many were regulars spending the winter months here before returning south. As we had quite often heard it before, the comment "Oh we're from Bunbury" lead us to believe that this southern city must be pretty quiet at this time of the year.

Pardoo Station has miles of magnificent coastal frontage and as usual along this entire coastline, fishing was a popular topic at evening gatherings around campfires or sunset cocktail soirees. Whether it be baits, lures, tackle, secret holes, how many and what type caught, and the monster that got away; there was no end to the tales.

While Fay could take or leave the fishing, she has special memories of these totally unspoiled beaches which are famous for their extensive shell accumulation . She had developed the idea of returning home with sufficient shells to make a large mirror, but after a few days of scouring and collecting, I imagine she would have adequate supplies to open her own shell shop. Walking kilometres each day and filling her beach bag with a grand assortment of larger types she could then be seen, sitting with legs apart searching the sands for a selection of the miniscule variety to add to her magnificent bounty. While assuring me that she was being careful, I had the feeling that she was oblivious to the dangers of the dreaded cone shell.

Death within six hours, preceded by paralysis and breathing difficulties if you touch one of these spiteful little devils. Warnings are given that they may be found along these beaches at certain times of the year. This venomous, but quite beautiful gastropod with harpoon-like barbs should not be touched at any cost.

Ron and Jackie have made this place their home every winter for the last few years and are part of the scenery. Acknowledged as the most successful with the rod out of the part-time residents, they invited us to tag along with them, and we got a few tips as we jogged along in their 4WD to the chosen beach of the day. Threadfin salmon were biting that week and as the tides can peak at over 6 metres, the keen fisherman has less than three hours to maximise his efforts. The warm waters quickly crept in covering the broad sandbanks in no time at all. There were sufficient numbers caught to top up everyone's freezers, so we were all feeling very pleased with ourselves by the end of each day.

Further down the beach, Val and Barry, floppy hats pulled well down, strutted down the dunes well before the arrival of the tide. He was struggling with rods, tackle and a large white bucket and the few expansive inches around his waist would not have made the task easier for him. Val had an ironing board securely tucked under one arm, which was so old and rusted, it looked like it had been ironing shirts since World War Two. It was an unusual piece of equipment to carry along the beach and she set it up overlooking the incoming water with no visible signs of an iron or basket of clothes, let alone a power outlet for the iron even if she did have one. It didn't take too long to work out that its singular purpose was for the filleting of fish. It was well utilised at the completion of the day's fishing. The original owner would probably find it most amusing to see it being put to such an interesting purpose.

The most colourful character around the place was Des, a lovely old guy, who looked and was in his 90s. Affectionately called the Pink Panther due to the bright pink diver's boots he wore, which always bought a smile to our faces as he waddled by. He had as much success as his fellow fisherfriends with the rod, proving there's nothing quite like a few years experience.

It was hard to imagine that only a month or so ago, a cyclone hit Pardoo and over 400 cattle were lost, many on this serene picturesque beach. Carcass's rot in the now parched heathland, bleached bones scatter the dunes and high tide marks indicate how quickly ocean front pastoral properties are subject to the vagaries of the weather. Ron & Jackie picked up a bleached scull to take home to decorate their bar, but my little wife declined one of these beach treasures thinking it all a bit gauche and preferred to stick with her shells.

Back at camp we were soon cooling off in the full size stone-built swimming pool, which is a real bonus out here in the middle of nowhere. Particularly in this climate. Unlimited clear, fresh, cool water, from an artesian bore 90 metres deep, constantly flows from an old piece of suspended piping.

"Numerous pastoral properties have looked at becoming involved in the tourism industry, but only a few have gone down that road" said owner Pam. "It's really a question of whether they have the ability, and the enthusiasm to provide the sort of service that is expected these days." Pam, apart from managing a large household of workers and family, spent a large percentage of her day in the all purpose shop cum office. She was warm and obliging and appeared to revel in looking after us all. With distractions such as her energetic emu racing round the joint, there was never a dull moment and we could see why people came back here year after year.

Our five days at Pardoo should have been five weeks, but the road was calling, Morrison was rested and it was time to move on.

Something akin to a baby emu suddenly arose from the nearby roadside growth and made great bounding steps alongside Morrison seemingly in an effort to fly. It's cumbersome body and longish neck made the task look impossible, but eventually it was airborne with its slow- flapping wings taking it towards the faraway hills. We were mesmerised, particularly as we were absolutely certain that emus couldn't fly. It was a point that we debated to a stage where we wondered if the heat was getting to us and we had imagined it all. Some days later, a ranger informed us that it was indeed our first sighting of an Australian bustard and we were lucky, as they are lazy bustards and are rarely seen flying.

Cape Keraudren was only a short flight away by any bustards standards, and the ten kilometres of badly corrugated roads which led in from the highway, shook Morrison's nuts and bolts to their foundations. It did though prove to be well worth the effort.

The area is a recreational reserve of some 5000 hectares and is a haven for marine, terrestrial and oceanic life. The inquisitive white-bibbed kangaroos, pretending to hide in knee high grasses and then bounding away like large brown rubber balls, were like some sort of welcoming party.

Of all the places we have visited along this magnificent coastline, Cape Keraudren is in a league of it's own. Perched on elevated land with a 360-degree view of the ocean, river estuary, cliff faces, rocky outcrops and a mountain backcloth it is a landscape to take the breath away. Groups of caravans, tents and motorhomes have settled into the many dramatic locations overlooking the continually changing oceanscape. They mostly come north for the winter and at rates of $25 a week to be living on multi million dollar real estate, why wouldn't they?

As dusk approached on the first night, we traced the footsteps of two faceless characters across the rocks on a quickly receding tide.

Coat hanger type hooks in one hand, bucket in the other, they stopped, stooped and prodded into darkened holes with great concentration. Disgorging the unsuspecting octopus from their hideaways proved fruitful and their buckets were soon filled with slimy groping tentacles.

With chairs facing west, most campers were outside to watch the disappearing sun and the whole perimetre of the earth changed from orange to deep red to a purplish hue.

Then something quite unbelievable happened, and it is something that we may well never experience again. Within a short period of the sun diving into the vast darkening ocean, the new moon, a sliver in comparison, accomplished the same feat in the same spot. Venus, vividly changing from reds and greens thought this a commendable idea and quickly followed suit. We thought that something was terribly wrong in the solar system, but a couple who passed us on an evening walk informed us that this was quite a rare and unique happening and we need not worry that the world was coming to an end. We thanked them for the information and invited them to join us in a celebratory drink. A brave little Margaret River Sauvignon Blanc did the trick. We just sat there, stars twinkling over us and could not imagine a better setting and a more fitting end to another perfect day.

Motorhomes have not yet become as fashionable over here as on the East Coast, with caravans and tents being the customary form of mobile holiday travel. Morrison stood proud as fellow campers ooohed and aahed and wondered when the new cult would take on in this slower-to-change part of the world. We farewelled our newfound friends and left early the next morning for what was to be our longest single leg. It was a mere 450 kilometres to Broome.

Some things are a little slow to change away from the cities and simple things like trying to obtain brown bread at roadhouses brings stares of amazement at most of these otherwise well run places. The service station at Pardoo was just another in a long line of 'white bread only' vendors. "Any chance of some wholemeal, multigrain or even soy and linseed" I meekly asked the owner who just stared at me without a smile.

He was obviously recovering from a recent personality by-pass operation, so I took pity on him. Although his look inferred that I was accusing him of being colour prejudiced.

When will these service operations realise that these are changing times and traveller's tastes should be addressed? His suggestion of frozen white-sliced was declined and we decided to stay on cracker biscuits until we reached civilisation.

A good hour on the road, and in the middle of absolutely nowhere, an extremely wacky sight came into our vision. On the opposite side of the road was a large dilapidated truck with numerous indigenous characters gathered around it. They were dressed in colourful clothing, bright shirts, carnival type trousers and wide brimmed hats, and on seeing us approach started waving their hands and dancing some sort of ritual dance across the road. It was eight o'clock in the morning so it was difficult to comprehend whether they were celebrating the birth of a new day, required some mechanical assistance or were already well inebriated. We suspected the later. Given that I'm not much of a mechanic and with a nervous co-driver next to me, I decided to do the only cowardly thing that came to mind and gave them a friendly wave as I pressed my foot firmly to the floor. A following truck would no doubt assist them and it was too early anyway to join them for celebratory indulgences.

The straight highway to Broome was devoid of interest and as we were on a mission to get there that day, we reluctantly passed up some of the enticing byways to the coast that we passed on the way. As Fay always says "Good to leave a little bit for next time". We passed an abnormally high number of recent roadkills, suggesting the roos along this section of highway must be particularly suicidal or stupid. One particular ravenous crow stood his ground and was unmoved by Morrisons three and a half tonne hurtling down on him. Missed by only a metre, I saw his glinting eye concentrating on the bloodied intestine hanging from his beak. Nothing was going to disturb his breakfast.

I noticed more and more as we headed north, the cursory wave of the hand that drivers of caravans and motorhomes give each other as they pass. The further away from the city, the higher number of acknowledgements are given. I feel as if I'm a member of a club of well wishers offering some sort of comradeship in these distant parts. After an hour or so of this, my right hand became firmly ensconced at the top of the steering wheel, so I just had to raise my fingers with a minimum of effort. After a busy day, the process is reduced to one index finger. When someone doesn't return my signal I feel a little sorry for them as the driver is obviously unaware of this secret fellowship.

Looking up at our large ceiling map, I noticed we were on the western perimetre of the Great Sandy Desert, a huge inhospitable tract of land that for some unusual reason is compared to the size of Germany. Nice little bit of trivia. It is largely inaccessible with only the fabled Canning Stock Route opening up the area to keen four-wheel drivers. The parched road ahead seemed a lot more attractive at this point of time. A handful of soaring eagles had perfected the art of hovering right over the white line in front of Morrison, ostensibly pointing in the direction we were travelling.

'Welcome all to Broome' they seemed to indicate with their wings, as we left the highway behind and trundled into this wonderful isolated oasis of the North.

CHAPTER EIGHT

PEARLS BIGGER THAN A CAMEL'S TEARS

'**B**roome in June' has a certain ring to it, and we were looking forward to our visit to this highly acclaimed winter retreat and enjoying time with friends who were flying in that week from chilly southern climates.

Setting up camp in a caravan park, after residing in national parks, on cliff tops and by isolated river banks and beaches for the last few weeks, was initially a bit of a culture shock, but with our friends arriving we had little choice. Driving around Cable Beach Caravan Park was like revisiting suburbia. There were over 500 sites, many separated by hedges and lush trees, which at least provided a little privacy. The majority of these preferred sites where we were lucky enough to snag a spot, were in the old section, and are occupied year after year by the same retired couples who renew acquaintances over the winter months. With the exception of a few 'new kids on the block' such as us, the same plots are reserved annually giving it a home away from home feeling. Friendships are renewed, groups gather around evening dinner tables and there is even the odd birthday party. Our geriatric next-door neighbour proudly watered his tomatoes, runner beans and various other dubious looking vegetables each day, seemingly taking hours to achieve what could be done in a few minutes. Guess he has to fill his day in somehow! His annual agenda was to plant on arrival either in pots or into the ground, with his runner beans disappearing up the ropes of the lean-to. By the end of his stay, there was plenty of fresh produce to feast on and even more to take home to the family. The whole place looked like an oasis surrounded by his massive collection of potted palms that were left behind each year for the park owners to water.

Occupants tended their own green lawns and colourful flower beds with a morning watering ritual, which did give the place a nice lived-in appeal. Ladies gathered to play cards or knit outside their vans while men tinkered with boats, played with their fishing tackle and amiably pottered about

People go to bed early here, no vans were a-rocking, and evenings were pretty quiet after 9 p.m. We gained the distinct impression that our presence would liven the place up a bit and hoped they would take it all in good spirit.

I must say I got my fair share of morning entertainment as I sipped my first cup of tea and observed the parade of ladies heading off to the amenities block. Toothbrushes in hand, shuffling in their gaily-coloured slippers, they paraded a grand selection of quilted dressing gowns, with the occasional pastel nightie peeping through. However, there was not one single set of rollers evident, which I thought remarkable. The blue rinse set apparently does not worry about such formalities on holiday.

There was one big difference here. Unlike a normal community, this lot can move in a flash. In the event of a cyclone warning or any other impending disaster, the whole park could be packed up within hours. Getting out of the joint might be slightly different though. Imagine 1000 people, queuing to settle their accounts, endeavouring to keep in an orderly line, and causing chaos in an already congested town. It would seem like a scene from the movie Independence Day.

The town itself is a multinational society with distinct cultural influences flowing through everyday life, and it has an architectural touch that is casual, relaxed, and distinctly 'Broome Style'. Everywhere there is colour as the rich, red sand of the Great Sandy Desert meets the slash of white beach with the powder blue sea beyond; the whole scene puntuated by the fresh green of the ever swaying palm trees. These brilliant primary colours are reflected in the paintings to be found in the many art galleries and provide a photographic dream for both the amateur and the professional.

Today Broome relies on tourists and the resurrected pearling industry for its existence.

Prior to the 1980s it was a rough and tumble town, with no decent access, plenty of places for a brawl, and in need of a visionary to encapsulate its potential. It took an Englishman, a knighted one with lots of money, to visualise Broome as an international tourist destination. Lord Alister McAlpine, a likeable eccentric, fell in love with the place, spent $500 million on Cable Beach Resort and the rest is history.

The Resort, where our friends chose to stay, has a special feel about it, with its manicured gardens, ponds, and latticed bridges in reds and greens. Meticulously presented colonial style bungalows and suites evoked a sense of peace, style and contentment. Large stone statues of horses and exotic animals imported from Asia stand as a memory to 'The Lord', who had a great eye for antiques and artifacts.

Cable Beach, which fronts both the Resort and our Caravan Park, was voted in some international magazine as one of the five top beaches in the world. Who are these lucky people who get the envious job of going around the world comparing one beach with another? Be that as it may, it is a magnificent, broad, classic white sandy beach, backed by graceful sloping sand dunes and has a good rolling surf that is far preferable on the full tide. The warm waters are always inviting but the ten metre fluctuations make the swim a long walk if the tide is out.

Around the turn of the century, Broome was without a doubt, the pearling capital of the world. At its peak, 400 luggers were based here and sailed off in search of the underwater treasure. The finest single specimen was the 'Southern Cross' found by a young boy on the beach in 1883. It was a cluster of nine individual pearls in the shape of a crucifix and was originally traded in a bar, at nearby Cossack, for a few pounds. It was eventually sold to the Vatican for 24,000 pounds. I wonder where it is today and what it would be worth. War and depression brought about a decline in the demand for pearls and the introduction of plastic buttons in the 1950s was almost the death knoll for the industry. However, pearling was revived in the 1960s with the development of cultural pearls, and is now a multi-million dollar industry.

The girls thought that 'pearling' meant trolling up and down Dampier Terrace swanning in and out of the various retail outlets, drooling over the showcases and trying on innumerable pieces with astronomical price tags. To get a complete understanding of the industry, its history and impact on the area, we thought that a trip to a working Pearl Farm called Willie Creek, might be a bit more informative. So we all bundled into the tour bus and headed off.

It's always nice to have a bus driver with a great sense of humour and hosts that provide interesting information without waffling on too much about technical rubbish that goes over everyone's heads. The addition of a boat tour over the working pearl farms all made for an amusing junket. Of course, at the end of the day, they were keen to offload a few pearls, at which they excelled themselves.

Bill Reed is a man who knows his pearls. He has been closely involved in Broome's dramatic change over the decades. Over early morning coffee in his grand old Kimberley-type home, he enthralled us with his knowledge of the town and its romantic and often flamboyant history. As the owner of Linney's Pearls, one of the foremost pearl retailing outlets, he has seen many a success story over the years. Let's be honest though, you don't hear too many sob stories when you run an exclusive pearl shop.

"Over the next few years there will be an explosion in cattle, horticulture and agriculture" he confided in his deep throaty voice, thickened with a lifetime of chain smoking. "This place is on the move and its not, as most people think, just tourism and pearls".

He informed us that the pearling industry in Broome earns around $100 million a year with 95% of all pearls exported equally to the USA, Europe and Asia. We could have chatted for hours, but Bill was off to open his shop for what would no doubt be another successful day's trading, while we decided that the beach was a great option.

I decided to cycle by road to a far off point at the end of Cable Beach where small boats and 4WD drive vehicles could just be seen, and then return along the sand. The 30 minutes ride into a headwind along bitumen was nothing compared with what I anticipated would an easy return journey along glorious wide stretches of flat beach. How wrong could I have been, it was a bloody nightmare. For much of the way, my tyres sank into centimetres of soft sand and it all became so exhausting, I felt like I was like pedaling with concrete boots on my feet. Cable Beach may well be one of the world's top beaches, but certainly not for cycling.

However, the sunsets are legendary. As that lucky old sun drops into the Indian Ocean in a kaleidoscope of colour, visitors from around the world line up along the boardwalk with cameras and videos at the ready.

Sunset camel rides along the beach are a 'must do' thing here with a couple of different operators competing for the tourist dollar. Abdul the Camel man, sounded the part, particularly as he was a cousin of our recent acquaintance, HRH Prince Leonard, who highly recommended him. We had a royal, unprintable message for Abdul but unfortunately the very night we booked his services, he had a memory lapse and didn't show up. Apologies are unheard of when you are a far-flung relative of a 'royal person', and as we didn't even get any sort of an excuse from this ill-manered operator, we ended up booking with his far more professional opposition, the 'Red Camels'.

Sitting astride these passive creatures with their large expressive eyes, extraordinary long lashes, and haughty yet serene faces we were transported back into an era of sheiks, Arabic tales and nomadic lifestyles. Cable Beach seemed the perfect place to indulge our fantasies and as we padded along the evening sands, Broome showed off one of her perfect sunsets in this most romantic setting.

Our train was by far the longest with 20 camels all strung together, head to tail, sporting deep red hump cloths and black shiny leather saddles. Their proud owners, John & Janet, bought the business a couple of years ago, coming from city jobs in cold southern climes to live in a whole new world of camels and sunshine. They have taken to it, like ducks to water, calling each beast by name and treating them all as members of the family. A very fit John ran alongside all the way, answering all manner of silly questions shouted by the various riders, as the train slowly padded along the darkening sands. As the sun slowly vanished into the ocean, the camels appeared content that their day's interaction with humans was nearly over. But as with humans, there is always one in a crowd that is different. This one particular fella was not so happy with his lot, and his continual guttural, heart-rending braying not only brought copious amounts of white foam to his contemptuous leering mouth, but amusement to the entire entourage.

Fay and I were lucky enough to be riding a beautiful passive fella with brown curly hair called Kabul who was specially picked for us by John. Back in 1998, a chap named David Mason had the strange desire to walk all the way across Australia from our hometown of Byron Bay to Carnarvon, mostly with three camels and Kabul was the lead camel. We had a real good one-sided chat with Kabul about his extraordinary journey and why this David character had not ridden him but just walked by his side, covering the 5500 kilometres in seven and a half months.

Our little expedition around the continent seems quite a breeze compared with this extraordinary feat.

The ride had been enjoyed with friends from Sydney, Sandi and Jiff who are an adventurous sort of couple. It wasn't just the way they appreciated their first-time camel ride, but the keen interest Jiff took in one particular camel that intrigued us. I must admit that Sasha, with her long eyelashes and 'come and get me smile' was by far the best looking dromedary in the train. She only had eyes for our pal, who was totally captivated by her.

Over the ensuing days, with a flair that Houdini would have been proud of, he disappeared and suddenly reappeared with a permanently engraved smile on his angelic face, ignoring suggestive innuendoes on his whereabouts. I'd be a liar if the camel farm was not foremost on everyone's minds.

There is an old Arab saying; 'when the beasts of the earth were formed, the camel was made up of the leftovers. The head of a sheep tacked onto the neck of a giraffe, grafted on to the body of a cow. The neck bent itself in shame at being put to such use. The tail of an ass was pinned over the legs of a horse, which tapered into the pads of a dog with the claws of an ostrich. The monstrosity was banished to the desert, where its miserable existence gave it the hump. But of all living things, only the camel knows the hundredth name of Allah, hence its supercilious expression when it looks at mere man'.

Graham was a friend of a friend, who kindly offered to take our Perth pal Barry and I out for a mornings ocean fishing in his little runabout. It was hit and miss stuff with a flurry of activity for ten minutes then nothing for half an hour. Barry was 'man of the day' and pulled in a couple of big ones, so dinner that night was looking good. Prawns were the preferred bait so let me tell you about a little idea I was given back down on the WA coast by a real keen couple who hated to see wasted bait. Take a kilo of prawns, peel but leave the tail on and soak in a mixture 1/2-cup of salt, 1/2 cup of sugar and 1/2 a teaspoon of boracic acid. They last for months in the fridge and the fish love them. Does away with all those nasty smells and throw outs.

It was the last night in Broome for Sandi, Jiff, Suzanne and Barry so an 'under the stars' dinner party was planned to be held in Morrison's back yard. Fay busied herself with finding flowers for the table, and in an attempt to create a bit of atmosphere set out dozens of candles which eventually lit the place like it was some religious gathering. I opened another green can and gave much thought to what we were about to eat.

It was a special night, so we had stocked up with goodies at the supermarket, and I was exchanging stares with the large Coral Cod that Barry had caught that morning. He was a good four or five kilos, with warm red looking skin and startlingly bright blue speckled spots. And he didn't need scaling.

Pearl Luggers Coral Cod

Coral Cod have a wonderful texture and taste that generally do not need a lot of flavouring. I wanted to prepare something a little different to serve to our dear friends who had joined us. I mixed some garlic, lemongrass paste, lime juice, chopped coriander, sugar and ginger into a paste and coated the sides and inside of the fish. Cuts into the flesh allowed the flavours to seep through. Sealed in well buttered foil and cooked in the covered barbecue, it only took about 40 minutes to cook through. The flesh just fell off the bone and was delicious, but ensuring it is not overcooked is important.

Accompanying this tasty culinary delight, we decided to have another little gastronomic offering, which takes a little time but is well worth the effort.

Green Paw Paw Salad with a Balltearing Dressing

This is a wonderfully refreshingThai inspired salad for those hot days and if green paw paw is difficult to get hold of, try replacing them with carrots which are plentiful everywhere. Shred 1 cup of green paw paw or carrots, 4 shallots or small golden onions cut finely, half a dozen cherry tomatoes, quartered, handfuls of chopped coriander and mint, and some crushed peanuts. Mix the following dressing:

2 red chillies, 4 cloves of garlic pounded together to make a paste, small chopped onion, 3-4 tablespoons of fish sauce, 6 tablespoons of lime juice, and 3 tablespoons of brown sugar. You can adjust flavours so that the sauce is equally salty and sour with a touch of sweetness. Mix well, let sit to allow flavours to emerge, and then pour over salad.

The evening was highlighted by some wonderful wines brought along by our guests. Jiff excelled himself, as he always does, by concluding the evening's drinking activities with the opening of a brave little 1997 Muscat de Rivaltes-Chapoutier, which he had brought all the way from his cellar in Sydney. Regardless of the contents, which were really too good to swallow, the bottle was unique in that it had Braille printed on the label. This old French company is the only producer in the world to feature this useful addition for unfortunate people who can't see what they are drinking. The name of the guest will not be revealed who was smart enough to comment on how certain inebriates might benefit if and when they became blind drunk.

Broome's central shopping and browsing area is called Chinatown and my initial feelings were quite mixed. It is unlike any other Chinatown and in many aspects was a bit disappointing. Whenever I have to visit a city and when time permits, I love walking around these quarters observing the life of the Chinese, gazing at the barbecued ducks hanging in windows, admiring those lovely orange and red lanterns and soaking up the Oriental atmosphere. We ambled around Broome's Chinatown a number of times and saw little to indicate that the Chinese were in town. They were the original shopkeepers here, back in the early pearling days, and apart from Fong Sans Bakery, Yeun Wings General Stores, Johnny Chi Lane and something called the Shekki Shed there was a distinct absence of all those things I love about most Chinatowns. There were of course one or two Chinese eateries like Son Ming, Chins, Wings and some place called Tokyo Joes, but these were all on the perimetre of town, as if the Chinese weren't allowed into this recently refurbished centre.

Fay kept telling me that it was all to do with the history of the place and I fully appreciate the part the Chinese played in originally putting the town on the map. The fact that back in the early pearling days when brothels, opium dens, gambling saloons and soup kitchens were part and parcel of the seedy streetscape, was not lost on me, however there is litle evidence of those early times remaining.

Today there is a lovely collection of 'wriggly tin' buildings, all quite similar in silvers and greys mixed with dark timbers that give the tarted up Chinatown a clean fresh organised look. Unfortunately though, not one single building has an inkling of the real image of the Orient, which I truly think a shame. Strolling through Johnny Chi Lane, we absorbed ourselves in the historical information, which was framed on the walls highlighting the changing times of the town. Looking back on the eclectic mix of Malays, Chinese, Japanese and other assorted nationalities, it was easy to see why Broome proclaims itself as Australia's first truly multicultural town.

'Staircase to the Moon' is a rather special phenomenon which only occurs up in these parts. It takes place three days after the full moon between April and October. We decided to extend our visit a few extra days, specifically to view this natural 'happening', which brings people out in their thousands. The golden stairway effect is created when a full moon rises in an already darkened sky over the shoreline at low tide. As the moon starts its ascent, rays of light hit pools of water that are left behind on the rippling mud flats by the receding tide and the total effect is mesmerising.

The Mangrove Bay Hotel is reputed to be one of the best viewing areas, so we lobbed in an hour or so before the event, and found most of the best seats already taken. About 500 avid moongazers, mostly with cameras and videos perched on tripods, were already settled to record this auspicious occasion. As the advertised time of rising approached, a hushed, expectant silence fell over the crowd, broken only by a lone didgeridoo, which signaled the arrival of the moon. Through a red glow, the golden ball gracefully emerged changing from red to orange to yellow, creating the illusion of a stairway leading up to the moon. There was much oohing and aahing until finally it moved high in the sky and its bright white light shone down on the exhilarated gathering that seemed set to party on in celebration. Local musicians performed on an impromptu stage and the bars were humming, leaving hundreds of empty seats around the outer railings. It was an evening certainly not to be missed, if only to witness the preceding dramatic performance by Mother Nature.

At the end of the peninsular, about six kilometres out of town, there is a place called Port, which has a long jetty and attracts loads of visitors, and many a local who is unfortunate enough not to own his own boat. It is indeed a veritable little fishing spot and attracts a diversified mob of individuals, all hoping for a free feed. There were so many people jostling for position, it was busier than Central Station on a Monday morning. Toby was a plump young eight-year-old who was on holiday from the back of Burke and had never even seen a fishing line before in his life. He was an absolute novice compared with the other few hundred hopeful souls who were happily passing the time of day. Within minutes of this cuddly little farmer's boy throwing in his line, which his father had expertly baited with a frozen mullie, he was hauling in a large, thrashing Trevally, which would handsomely feed the whole family that night. As everyone stared at him with a mixture of jealousy and admiration, I thought such are the vagaries of this often-frustrating pastime.

I got the clear impression that many of the regular oldies came here for a chat, a bit of socialising and if they were lucky enough to actually catch something; well what a surprise that would be. The odd Whoopee might even be heard.

There is a flat piece of land right behind the museum, which sits on some high cliffs overlooking the turquoise ocean. The views are something to die for and it made a nice change from the Caravan Park, which we checked out of after our friends left. There wasn't a soul around as we set up camp for the night, except for the occasional Aboriginal straggler who was making his way home after a hard day at the office. One of those 'Britz' motorhomes pulled up right beside us and out jumped a hyperactive loud-voiced Yank and his little lady. I find it sometimes interesting to try to work out a person's nationality before they open their mouth, but on this occasion it was instantaneously obvious. For a horrible moment I thought they were going to disturb our peace for the whole evening and not just a few minutes.

"Ya really think its safe to camp here buddy" he drawled. I was just going to comment that snappy crocs would emerge through the night, mosquitoes would crucify him or failing that the black fellas might consider them to be a good bit of tucker, when he interjected "Delilah here and me, we always try to stay in a Coles or Woollies car park. Feel really safe there". I was too gobsmacked to reply, thinking how much this guy must be missing of our great country by heading for all the shopping trolley infested bits of concrete in suburbia. Yanks never fail to amaze me.

The old quarter of town has many elegant colonial homes, mostly set back from the tree-lined streets and hidden behind their own expansive gardens. One of these important historical buildings is McAlpine House which is now operated as an upmarket Bed and Breakfast, and where the good Lord spent much of his time. Guests can sleep in his huge four poster bed, lie around the lovely pool and reminisce about the times when a pearl master originally built this beautiful property, back in the boom times. As the bubbly resident manager escorted us around the property, a feeling of nostalgia swept over us, bringing back memories of our 100-year-old homestead in the verdant Byron Hills, which we ran as a B&B for many years.

As we wandered around town chatting with long time locals about their memories and associations with Broome, it was wonderful to note that there was not a single bad word to be said about Lord Alister McAlpine. Apparently he was a warm, worldly raconteur, considered to be a bit of an eccentric who came north from some commendable building endeavors in Perth, and certainly left his mark on this town. He was a great collector and Broome was the pearl in his collection. At one time he owned 80 properties including the Sun Garden Cinema and the Cable Beach Resort plus operating a large pastoral holding. Indeed, a man who had an eye for beauty, a man of vision, with tremendous energy and passion and above all, he didn't tread on toes. How some of our locally born entrepreneurs could learn from this leader of men, albeit he had unlimited wealth to help him on his way.

The world's oldest open-air cinema took us back to a bygone era. Sitting under the Kimberley stars on a frangipani-perfumed evening with palms swaying above, it was not hard to mentally revisit the pre World-War-One days when the Sun Garden Cinema first opened with silent movies. The packed houses of varying nationalities required announcements to be made in four different languages. They had a resident pianist called 'Fairy', so named because of her frizzy peroxided hair and short frilly skirts. She happily played away throughout the films, perched at the side of the screen, with her appropriate but rather limited range of popular tunes.

Quite novel in the world of enterainment was the situation when, on the odd occasion, a king tide would lap around the feet of the absorbed patrons.

When the talkies arrived in 1933, there was much concern that moviegoers should not arrive with their dogs, whose barking continually drowned the crackly soundtracks. A few canine fights on the lawns, followed by boisterous interjections from an unamused audience, resulted in signage affixed to the entrance stating 'Please leave your dog at home'.

Up to 1976 all the seats were segregated, with cushioned cane chairs at the front going to the local business community. The back stalls were kept for the different nationalities of boat people, who were only allowed in through a special side entrance.

Around us, staring downs from the walls were black and white photographs of those early stars. Mary Pickford, Douglas Fairbanks, Mae West, and Charlie Chaplin framed in immortality. We watched that evening's showing of Gosford Park, which took us back to earlier days in England, when the world of servants was as interesting as that of their masters.

Behind the large screen are the toilets, ladies on the left and gents on the right. It was quite easy to lose our concentration on the actual movie, when inconsiderate patrons emerged, finalising what should have been finished business with their apparel.

As we walked out it was difficult to comprehend that out here in what must have been an Australian outpost, a cinema was packing them in before Hollywood was established. Original 35mm projectors from 1926 and 1950 pointed us towards the exit, and it would have been nice to extract a cool drink from the massive soda fountain that used to be the main feature of the foyer.

Next morning we had coffee at Henri's. Sipping our 'caps' on a street-side table on busy Carnarvon St, we watched what appeared to be an affluent, orderly society going about their pleasure and business. No riff raff here; the town didn't seem to attract that element.

The Aboriginal community have called this place home for aeons, and on the surface appear to have accepted the dramatic changes that have affected their lives. A small group of them live in a shantytown area on the sand dunes right on the doorstep to town. We had previously watched them crouched around their fires at twilight, shadowy figures in the dimming light, their chatter drifting through the still night. I had suggested popping over for a bit of a chat with them, but Fay quickly dissuaded me, remembering a local businessman's advice, 'white man not welcome there'.

We had extended our stay from seven to 14 days and still hadn't had our fill. Our memory banks still see the ever-changing seascapes that the massive ten-metre tides continually made, and the wizened black fella walking home with a line in one hand and a huge trevally in the other. Pearls in shop windows by the ton, camels and sunsets and a radiant sky that didn't proffer a single cloud during our stay. A friendly, warm multicultural society, romantic balmy nights, and a wonderful matrix of gourmet cuisine.

We departed, knowing that one day we would definitely return.

CHAPTER NINE

NEVER SMILE AT A CROCODILE

The road from Broome to Derby can only be described as boring. The one singular item of interest were more termite hills; hundreds of thousands of camel-coloured ones which stretched like suburbia into the parched distance. Cities of termite strongholds, created by these prodigious white ant builders, were fashioned in fantastic images. Getting closer to Derby they change in colour to browns and greys, alter their sizes and become more contorted in appearance.

I read somewhere that there are over 60 species of termites in Western Australia alone. Another absorbing job for somebody compiling a list of different termite species and I'm grateful it is someone else and not me. Who the hell would want to sit in some laboratory spending their life comparing different types of termites?

For those few readers who may have a fascination in termites, and I am sure there must be a handful out there, the following information should prove riveting. Each mound or hill, some of which are up to three metres high, are controlled by a King and Queen who live to around 50 or 60 years. Fortunately for them, they are the only fertile ones, but have millions of non-fertile little workers who run around all day, priding themselves on being the earth's best organic recycler.

Over the centuries these busy little things have provided another most unusual facility. In bygone days, certain aboriginal tribes used these mounds as a sort of mortuary for interring the remains of their deceased. The termites quickly sealed up the entrance that had been created and got on with their termite business. We did not see one termite hill with a cross, mark or dried out bunch of flowers on the top, and wondered how grieving relatives could work out where their loved ones had actually been placed.

That night we camped on the banks of the Fitzroy River, not far from a sign indicating that crocodiles may be present and that their favourite food was human beings along with any of their canine companions. We lit a fire which Fay reckoned would help deter our snappy friends, sat back under the stars and absorbed ourselves in what was a truly Australiana scenario.

One of the most extraordinary sights in this part of the world is the bottle shaped boab tree, the true giants of the plains. They are everywhere in all sorts of shapes and sizes, each with a formidable bulbous trunk looking exactly like what they are; large water storage containers. They apparently originated from Madagascar thousands of years ago and are quite unique to this part of the world and only one other faraway island country. The strange shape of the big boab beside our campsite, silhouetted against the night sky by the flickering flames of our campfire, was even more architecturally spectacular than the termite mounds.

Derby, or as the locals call it, Durby, did not hold much appeal for me, but we were lucky enough to be in the vicinity at the time of the Durby Derby, which is a significant event in the Kimberley, so we decided to call in. The ladies were all dressed up in their finery, which probably only gets dusted down once a year, and paraded a few garishly outrageous floral hats that were specially created for the occasion. The men were a real assorted lot. Young jackaroos were there in long black jacket-suits, sweating it out under the Kimberley sun while others characterised the occasion more amusingly with freshly pressed white shirts, black bow ties, akubra hats, bush shorts and muddied boots. The betting ring was a frenzy of action even if the half dozen bookies weren't exactly being generous with their odds.

We had hoped The Toe Sucking Cowgirls were one of the performing acts that night, but were out of luck. They had performed in town the previous two evenings to rapturous applause, and with a name like that are certain to be a drawcard. I made a mental note to check their appearance in future towns we visited, while my little wife showed a distinct lack of interest. I couldn't imagine why.

Derby has the highest fluctuating tides in Australia. They were ten metres that week and the fishing was abysmal, with not even a nibble, so we camped inland during our short stay.

The Boab Prison Tree is exceptionally expansive, so large in fact, that it was used to regularly house captive teams of Aborigines back in the 1880s. At 14 -metres around its girth, it makes one hell of tree and it offered us a sense of security as Morrison lay in its shadow each night. Life must have been hell for those poor unfortunates who were chained and crammed into its oppressive pitch-black interior.

The local Aboriginal community maintains that the tree is imbued with special mystical forces and holds potent powers. In the darkening twilight with a cool drink in one hand it certainly looked foreboding and mysterious.

Lined up next to this massive offering of nature was a manmade monument to cattle. Myalls Bore, a concrete cattle trough 120 metres long, is the largest in the Southern Hemisphere, and was built in 1916 offering water to 1000 bullocks at a time. As they arrived from their arduous overland trip which normally took many weeks, enduring parched and inhospitable terrain, the stampede over the final hurdle towards the welcoming water would have been a sight to behold.

Derby's Annual Bush Poets Breakfast started at seven in the morning and was a real hoot. It was advertised as the fourth such event but regular poets who could count on all digits argued that it was the fifth. Be that as it may, the venue adjacent to the town swimming pool, was packed that Sunday morning, which would have made attendance at the various churches so disappointing, it would hardly warrant the vicars opening their bibles. The audience sat around on camp chairs, surrounded by boabs and swaying palms in a wonderful garden setting and absorbed every spoken word.Some of the characters that ambled their way on to the hastily built stage to deliver their recitations truly epitomised the outback spirit.

The star of the proceedings, a heavily bewhiskered character called Keith Lethbridge, barefoot and dressed in coloured patchwork overalls, had the attentive audience eating out of his hand. He was world class and proudly signed his books to a line of patiently waiting admirers after the show. It was a wonderful morning with offerings, many humorous, from 20 talented performers who were proud to proclaim that Bush Poetry is alive and well. We certainly had to agree.

By midday it was approaching 32 degrees, the sun was beating down and a few refreshing laps in the town's inviting Olympic size swimming pool seemed to be an excellent way of unwinding after the adrenaline pumping morning of poetry reading. Imagine our total surprise at the absence of any other person in the complex, except the kindly manager who explained that the locals wouldn't dream of swimming in waters that were only 21 degrees. " Much too cold for them" he explained, his bulbous frame indicating he was in need of a few laps himself. I found it hard to imagine all these wusses staying at home with their air conditioners blasting away, waiting for the really hot steamy weather to arrive before they took the plunge.

"If you want some real fun" our friendly manager called out. "Come back next weekend for the mud football match". Unique to this part of the world, and why wouldn't it be with the extensive mud flats left by the receding tide, the game is a very loose interpretation of the AFL code. Apparently it is a rough and tumble affair and the players are hardly identifiable after a couple of hours on the 'field'. A photographer's dream, another deserted day guaranteed at the swimming pool, and lots of empty pews in the churches.

The infamous Gibb River Road opens the door to the real Kimberley; a vast, mostly deserted wilderness area that claims to have fewer residents per square kilometre than almost any other place on earth. Mighty river systems produce thundering waterfalls, rugged ranges and deep spectacular gorges. Mother Nature certainly has fun with the landscape here and it is appealing only to those who choose to explore with a sense of true adventure.

Reputed to be one of the most challenging roads in Australia, the Gibb River Road had been slightly improved by a recent visit of a grader on certain sections, which offered our Morrison some respite from the bolt shuddering corrugations and rock filled floodways. The old saying 'The road to the future is always under construction' seemed to have a double meaning as we carefully drove along endless kilometres of this treacherous byway.

There are two distinct seasons here. The 'Wet' and the 'Dry'. The vast majority of visitors like us, come between April and October, lured by perpetual blue skies, pleasantly warm days and cool evenings, low humidity and roads that are normally open. The 'Wet' is somewhat different, offering dramatic raging rivers and waterfalls; intense thunderstorms followed by dramatic sunsets and a tropical climate that is indicative of the close proximity to the equator. More humidity, more mossies, lots of closed roads but for the true adventurer, a real challenge. We made ourselves a promise that one-day we would return to see 'The Wet'.

A few hours drive from Derby, we headed off the Gibb River Road, leaving the fabled rough central section to those more daring and better equipped. The diversion brought us to what can best be described as a true Oasis in the middle of very average scrub country.

When I was quite young, I recall my dear mother narrating extracts from the bible, probably with the main intention of getting me to sleep more than offering me any religious teachings.There was one particular story that always caught my attention. Adam and Eve in the Garden of Eden was a winner and it was guaranteed to activate my dream senses in an emotional sort of way.

When we walked through a fissure in the massive rock face that opens the door to the Windjama Gorge, I immediately felt that this was the closest place on earth that anyone could associate with that fabled Garden from biblical times.

Imagine being on an ancient ocean floor bed; sheer rock cliffs of massive dimensions and proportions rising 100 metres or more on either side of a meandering mirror-like stream. Prolific bird life abounded, twittering, chatting and squawking in a delirious fashion. Butterflies of amazing colours flitted from ghost gum to weeping paperback to river fig. Flood water levels were marked by huge branches and trunks, picked up like matchsticks, and suspended high above. Sleeping fresh water crocodiles lazily watched schools of small fish swim by in translucent waters, too lazy to fill their already fat bellies. Is this paradise or what?

We relaxed on a sandy bank, under the shade of a huge gum, scrubbed clean with time, and had lunch only metres away from a substantial croc basking in the shallows. He opened one eye and showed total disdain at the morsel of food thrown towards him, effortlessly pushing himself into deeper waters to pursue more productive pleasures.

On each side of us rose a winding range of majestic razor-toothed peaks, heralding an era that goes back 350 million years, when this hidden valley was permanently under water. The Leonard River has carved out a three and a half kilometre passage through the sheer faced gorge walls creating a geologist's dream. Prehistoric marine fossils are to be found on these vertical structures while spinifex and small rock figs breathlessly hang on to small creviced ledges, 40 metres high. Wild passionfruit vines tenaciously hugged the lower gorge walls and in the slow moving crystal clear waters, archerfish prey on insects by ejecting fine streams of water at them.

This was one occasion when walking was absolutely effortless, due to the constant sights and sounds that absorbed our seven kilometre return journey through the gorge. The hundreds of pink and white parrots treat dusk as playtime, and flying en masse from tree to sandbank and back again, bade us a screeching 'au revoir' that filled the evening air.

As we sat down to dinner that night under another starlit sky, it was difficult to take our eyes off the imposing outline of the jagged range. Far into the distance, rows of sharp tooth-like pinnacles, resembling the lines of a crocodile's jaw, provided a dramatic backdrop. If an artist put brush to canvas, it would be difficult to believe the richness and dramatic colour this part of Australia has to offer.

This stimulating moment created a celebratory desire to toast nature with a glass of bubbles, and try a recipe that seemed perfect for the occasion

Walkabout Emu with Never Never Sauce

This large flightless bird does not produce a lot of meat for its size, but it is high in protein and quite low in fat and cholesterol. Not every butcher stocks it, in fact it is not easy to come by, and as ours had been in the deep freeze for some time this was a good opportunity to try it.

Emu should be marinated well, and never never overcooked. Trim the skin from 250-300 gms of fillet and cut into 2cm slices. Marinate in ½ cup of red wine, garlic, and 2 tablespoons of olive oil for about 3 hours.

The accompanying sauce should be made prior to cooking with the meat being drained from the marinade and grilled or barbecued for 5 minutes on each side.

Never Never Sauce: Heat 1 tablespoon of oil in deep pan and add chopped bacon rasher, 1 finely chopped onion, and when par cooked add a finely chopped carrot and celery stick. When cooked, stir in 2 tablespoons each of tomato paste and plain flour and slowly add 1 cup of water with a dissolved beef stock cube. Stir until thick, season if required and add a little red wine to adjust consistency.

Serve with potatoes and green vegetables

The Aborigines call them firebirds, as it is their habit to hover over bush fires, patiently waiting for their prey to escape the heat. As the morning campers pack up and wend their way to their next destination, innumerable numbers of these large black kites mysteriously appear, and with minimal motion, cruise majestically overhead and survey all beneath them. We watched them with a sense of awe and an uneasy feeling that perhaps we were intruding in their domain.

A few kilometres down the track we stopped to view some ruins and were suddenly confronted with one of these large black aggro birds whose claws were ready for attack. It hovered, head high and only metres in front of us and my dear little wife was quite taken aback, in fact petrified she was. We must have sprung the bird's nest, so brandishing large sticks we slowly retreated, while Mum scrutinised us with a look that could kill.

The ruins in question used to be a police station where one night an Aboriginal tracker called Pigeon, shot the white sergeant dead and released his chained fellow countrymen. He was a bit like a black Ned Kelly as he started a mini uprising against the white man, hiding out in these ranges for a number of years before being killed.

Fellow travellers thought that Tunnel Creek, which was the next place of interest on the way to Fitzroy Crossing, was quite an experience and should not be missed. Morrison handled the gravel roads with aplomb, although his nuts and bolts received a good testing on some stretches that had not been graded for years. He glided through the half metre deep floodways with the greatest of ease and by now was well used to the choking bulldust that puffed up from every passing vehicle.

An amazing 750-metre tunnel has been carved, by nature's amazing processes, through the Oscar Range. The trick is to wade through the chilly, often knee deep water in the pitch black, trying to avoid the really deep bits. A good torch proved essential as we cautiously wended our way through. It was invigorating stuff in the darkness, beaming our torch up to the amazing rock formations, and trying to find some of the thousands of bats that apparently wake up when the tourists have all gone home.

Golden straw-like fields stretched far into the distance to meet the dropping sun as we headed for Fitzroy Crossing, while friendly bottle-shaped boab trees waved us by, highlighting mysterious intergalactic rock formations.

Numerous highway wanderers who had passed through the Kimberley area had offered advice on how little, not how much time should be spent in Fitzroy Crossing. Word quickly gets around when there are more appealing places to visit, but we had plans to spend time at the annual rodeo and decided to take each day as it came.

We had heard about the Crossing Inn, which advertises itself as an historical watering hole, but which is really just a posh tin shed. It's a bit of a walk from town and as it's the only drinking spot around, is obviously well patronised by the local community. My co-driver thought a cooling lunchtime drink here would be well warranted, and even at midday there were a hundred or more serious drinkers gathered in small groups under the shade of the nearby trees. Regular trips over the road for another carton of green cans for each group, indicated these guys would not be driving home, even if they did own a car.

At the bar, we stood out like white balls on a black bull and suddenly found ourselves confronted by an amiable young lady called Beryl, who proceeded to introduce us to her Aunt Vera, Sister Alice, Mum and a few other friends. Now Beryl was a real darling who could have been a contender for a 'Miss Indigenous Australia' title back in the 70s, except that her left eye had unfortunately been gouged out in some kind of marital brawl.. Everyone was real friendly and the conversation flowed in a limited fashion although it couldn't be called typical of your average drinking spot. There was a big sign on the bar wall. NO SPITTING. NO SWEARING. NO FIGHTING. AND NO HUMBUGGING.

While getting an Emu Mid Strength for Beryl, from the young lady behind the bar, who was the only other person who wasn't as black as the ace of spades, I enquired into the terminology of humbugging."Its what that group are doing to you and your wife right now" she smiled. What the hell, the cost of a beer for a good chat, was but a small price to pay.

They've got a great sense of humour too. A tall crinkly haired fella with striking black features and a single huge white tooth started talking a bit of business.

"Turns over $7 million a year this 'ere pub" he informed us, as though it was a bit of inside information and then smiled and inferred that most of it was treated as black money by the management. Big laughs all round at that one, but the 1000 cartons sold the previous day at $42 each indicated that the place was not exactly going backwards, and it was enlightening to hear from such a voice of authority.

I have always believed that every day should be a learning process. This day was no exception, and I gleaned the absorbing reason why VB is by far the best selling drink in these parts. One of the establishment's most prodigious imbibers informed me that besides Carlton providing the first lightweight aluminum can up here, VB unlike some other competing brands, can handle the dramatic changes in climatic conditions. We had to hand it to them, these new drinking friends of ours certainly knew their poison.

Small town supermarkets are much the same everywhere, with the one at Fitzroy only being remembered for its few peculiarities. That particular day's discount-special of frozen kangaroo tails at the bargain price of only $5.00 each, did not include accompanying recipes, but had my taste buds salivating, until the generator packed up and the shop went in to complete darkness.

"It happens most days about this time" advised a voice from somewhere, "don't worry folks, should only be about half an hour". With hand grasped firmly on my wallet, the thought of kangaroo tails for dinner became quite secondary. Shadowy figures were moving around the aisles, bumping into racks of foodstuffs, while muffled moans of anguish made me think that certain people could have alternative motives to doing their daily shop.

I decided to return later for my kangaroo tail and was most happy at not being body-searched as I left the darkened premises.

There are Post Offices and then there are Post Offices, but my visit to the one at Fitzroy Crossing was memorable. I was the only white person in a queue of maybe 30 customers who patiently waited and waited, while the exceptionally tolerant lady behind the counter slowly unraveled everyone's problems. There are interesting people to be met in Post Office queues, and in some ways I thought I could have been anywhere but in Australia. The language which was flying all over the place in shouts and emotive pleadings was pretty hard to distinguish. In fact I couldn't understand a bloody word of it. My efforts at conversing were well received and understood, particularly with a tall proud looking elder who had a grand grey beard down to his navel. Wearing a smart three-piece, charcoal-grey suit and an unusual sort of stockman's hat that had seen a long hard life, he repeatedly asked me if I was going to the rodeo.

After 45 minutes I eventually placed my order for stamps and an express envelope and quietly enquired as to the reason for the young lady's overload of duties that day.

"No one else turned up" she smiled. " It's like that sometimes as my fellow workers often decide to go walkabout at the last minute". I waved goodbye to the grey bearded elder and told him I would see him at the rodeo later that day.

Everyone in town goes to the rodeo including Beryl. She was already there having another Mid Strength and a friendly chat with the local sergeant. He asked her if she was going to behave herself.

"Don't want to go back to prison" she exclaimed, with a dark cloud on her face "Spent three months there for beating up my husband" she whispered in my ear. She couldn't remember what she hit him with, but I got the impression it was something quite sharp. Apparently this area has the highest incident in the world for women receiving steel implants in the left forearm, due to continually using it as a shield in confrontations with the 'old man'.

Here in the outback, the rodeos are the real thing. They epitomise everything that is wholesome and traditional about Australia. Old fashioned values, unheralded heroes of the saddle and the wonderful livestock this country produces. The interaction between the smartly attired, akubra headed riders and their handsomely groomed horses, who seem to be able to turn on a sixpence, is an exhilarating sight.

Russell Greene is one of Australia's most recognised rodeo announcers and travels the length and breadth of the continent introducing the entrants, amusing the crowd with his acuity interwoven into his lifetime of outback experiences. He's the man with the mobile microphone and covering 75 rodeos each year, just loves his job.

"Knowing the contestants, the stock and the people involved is a big help" he explains, but interacting with the crowd, displaying an affable sense of humour is a special art, which he has perfected well. His true blue eyes are the colour of these northern skies. His huge paw like hands previously held him on to the backs of the country's most challenging bulls and broncos for eight years. These days he's a butcher back in Wangaratta, when he's not calling out the next contestant, and this weekend in Fitzroy Crossing he's doing what he loves most.

Some people may think a man has got to have rocks in his head to sit astride 1000 kilograms of infuriated bull whose only desire is to ditch it's rider as soon as possible. I tend to agree. These brave souls are cowboys for a day and they make the most of those few precious seconds of glory. We are told that the kicking strap, pulled around the animals nether region is like wearing a jockstrap four sizes too small, so its understandable the beast gets a little agro.

Exploding into the ring with relentless energy and determination, these massive Brahman and Santa Gertrudis have the sole intention of dislodging their rider as quickly as possible. The chosen beasts for this weekend's fun and games have been given some very unusual names. We saw gut-wrenching performances from the likes of The Undertaker, Road Train, Cocaine, Anaconda and Pulp Fiction. Rated riders came from far and wide and many of the fancied didn't even last the required distance. In this, one of the world's most dangerous sports, competitors must stay on -board for eight seconds, hold one hand high in the air and never touch the ground. A dozen or more hopefuls, in flared embroidered chaps and tall stock hats, were sitting around the fences, overlooking what some called 'the arena of life'. The daredevil heroics had started, and the crowd groaned as the first rider was tossed in to the air and crunched into the dirt in only four seconds.

There was a few dollars on the favourite, Mark Lambeth, but he bit the dust in even less time and decided a good drink would be a better way to spend the rest of the evening.

"Everyone's first ride is the worst" he recalled, 'You just black out and its all over so quickly. Its becomes a real addiction, a buzz, I wouldn't miss it for the world". We were looking at a couple of other battle weary warriors but swollen wounds and damaged pride would not deter them from future encounters.

The bucking broncos have always had a fascination for me. Can't imagine why. Russell was telling us that they could be classified as a special breed due to them not being much good for anything else. "Couple of contractors supply them and although they are fine tuned and primed for the day they only spend about eight minutes of each year actually working". Now where have I heard that before; they sure would not have a problem getting a job in some government department.

One of these broncos got a bit carried away with his bucking at a recent rodeo and badly twisted his bowel. He was on the verge of saying goodnight to the world when some smart arse suggested he be taken to the Horsepital. Russell took the matter in his own hands and grabbing a water hose inserted it right up the agonised animal's anal area turned the tap on, and in a short while had saved the it from being another pet meat statistic.

Night-time arrived and the big social event of the year in Fitzroy Crossing was about to start. Country and Bluegrass hits of yesteryear blasted out from huge speakers, while camp fires blazed in the cooling night air; a gathering place for the intermingling groups of blacks and whites. The guys and girls from the stations work hard and long, and on these rare occasions play equally hard. Standing amongst these clean cut, well behaved young people, I was very proud to be Australian. The cream coloured akubras stood tall on these guys and the Jillaroo's in their skin tight jeans and fresh country faces gave me a renewed confidence in Australia's future.

I gazed into one of the campfires and thought 'you can't get more Aussie than this'. Everything Australian seemed to come flooding through my mind; Vegemite Sandwiches, True Blue Mates, Diggers on Anzac Day, Dame Edna Everidge, The Flying Kangaroo, Kylie Minogue, Cuddly Koalas, Bronzed Bodies on Bondi, Greg Norman's Akubra, Home and Away, Rain on the Rock, Pie Floaters, Pavlovas and Lamingtons.

What a bloody marvelous country this is. It damn well brought a tear to me eye.

After a long stint at the rodeo party that night, we did not get to leave the grounds and parked Morrison next to where the bulls were munching away. They lined up and inquisitively stared at us. Perhaps they were thinking that Morrison was one hell of a big white bull.

Kids as young as eight were up and about at daylight next morning, and it was cold. Hard to believe that the temperature would soar to 35 degrees by lunchtime, and this is the middle of winter. There was much activity as horses were watered and the morning's events got under way. It was wonderful to see these youngsters getting so much enjoyment out of what is a lot more than just a sport. It's a lifestyle they will be involved in until their latter years, although the look on one tiny tot's face as Mum put him on his first bareback poddy calf ride, was one of absolute terror.

We farewelled Russell as he saddled up his pretty young wife Jodie who travels the circuit with him. She's one of the country's most successful riders when it comes to roping and barrel racing and they looked like a couple who personify what the rodeo is all about. Leaving with bulldust well cemented between our toes, we got a farewell wave from a tiny young aboriginal boy, wearing an enormous ten-gallon hat, bright red shirt and colourful patterned chaps.

The rodeo is alive and well and is the heart and soul of these outback towns.

It can be frustrating, but it is also enlightening to turn the radio on and find that the only available station is 'National Indigenous Radio'. If a choice had been available then maybe we wouldn't have taken the opportunity to listen in to the local community's involvement in broadcasting and promoting their own indigenous issues. The music may have been a little dated and the conversations somewhat stilted, but it was real old fashioned entertainment which followers of John Laws and the like, may well have forgotten about.

No one likes to work weekends though, so its 48 hours of preselected music and to hell with mundane things like the news and weather. If World War Three should break out over the weekend, we will all have to wait till Monday to hear about it up here. Still, we enjoyed the local radio stations wherever we travelled, which often provided us with a greater understanding of the area's issues.

One of the good things that Fitzroy Crossing has going for it is Geiki Gorge, just 18 kilometres out of town and another piece of Mother Nature Magic. We walked the riverbank in the twilight of the day and next morning took a boat trip down the mighty Fitzroy.

We were awed by the amazing configuration of the soft limestone cliffs, on which millions of years of constant erosion from massive river floods have created fascinating shapes and images. One of the rangers reminded us that the floods of February 2002 were the worst in living memory and pointed to a height above the information rotunda where wild rushing waters proved to be in excess of 25 metres above normal levels. We found it hard to imagine the work involved in getting the place shipshape for the influx of tourists in the dry season, in such a short period of time. But it is second nature to the people who live here.

There are circular timber posts along the walkways that have information messages affixed to the top, providing details of associated flora, rock formations and so forth. I initially thought they had been provided for the benefits of small people, young children or maybe the odd pygmy on holiday. The signs in most cases were jutting out of the sand by only a few centimetres and to read this important piece of information I had to kneel on the ground. Fay was as usual, as bright as a spark, and pointed out that the paths in fact had risen by a metre or so because of the floods, indicating the magnitude of the sand deposits.

Barramundi or Barra as they are affectionately known are a big prize here, but word from the locals, on such important matters, was that they just weren't biting: 'Waters too cold', 'Been a funny year weatherwise', ' Fished out'. I heard it all but reckoned that the community liked to keep the secret places to themselves, although not one person was spotted with a rod anywhere.

Fitzroy Crossing was the first place since leaving home that troublesome flies really became a nuisance. I have always maintained that the manufacturers of some insect repellants are a bunch of ratbags for producing potions that have not the slightest bit of beneficial use. Fay did a little experimentation and found that some particularly aggressive flies were actually attracted to one particular brand, which shall remain nameless for fear of litigation. They seem to be getting smarter, as they dive-bomb into crevices such as nostrils and the corner of eyes, knowing of course that such deterrent's won't be found in such places. Each time we emerged from Morrison, it was like being met by a welcoming committee that clearly said 'bugger off, this is our patch of land.'

Around about this same time we received an email from some Perth friends who were holidaying in Barcelona. "We've counted only five flies during our travels over here" quipped Bill smugly, knowing we would be swotting them by the dozen. Various 'Spanish Fly' jokes came to mind but I will exclude them in order to maintain the high moral values of this publication. It does appear somewhat unfair that these little bastards should taunt us in their millions, yet stay away from similar European climates.

Fortunately, flies seem to go to bed at dusk so we spent a night or two in perfect isolation in the fields stretching out beside the gorge, with no sounds or movements except the fluttering of birds and the odd rustling of an inquisitive wallaby. Metre-high golden pastures surrounded us and in the mornings the sky was rich with buttercoloured sunlight filtering through the newly budding trees. It was a crisp clean air after the nights drop of 20 degrees. In these conditions, it was easy to listen instead of talk, watch instead of think and appreciate nature as never before. Then as the day warmed up the bloody flies returned.

Halls Creek was around 300 kilometres away and about two thirds of the way there, we found a champion little camping spot right on the banks of the Mary River.

Shady gums, white cockatoos and happy campers around their campfires greeted us as we arrived just before dusk. Mary Pool was the name of the place and we were amused to find our next door neighbour was none other than Mary Pool. "How could I not stop here" she laughed "and my sister-in-law Caroline is down the road at a little spot called Caroline Pool for a few days".

This was indeed riveting stuff, and the only reason I mention it is the fact that there was nothing else of much interest happening that evening, except a rather original meal that I concocted on the spur of the moment.

The now defrosted kangaroo tail from Fitzroy Crossing was about to be trialed and it seemed as good a time as any to make use of the embers on the fire and try out a variation of an old and favourite recipe

Kangaroo Tail Osso Buco

Osso Buco is normally a great winter dish involving Veal Shin, so we thought an interesting variation with our recently purchased roo tail would provide an equally nourishing meal. Cut the tails at the joints, roll them in seasoned flour then fry them in butter and oil till they are brown. Place pieces in the bottom of the camp oven and cover with some red wine (not a good vintage drop), chopped tomatoes, lots of garlic, seasoning and topped up with beef stock. Cook slowly as possible and top up stock if meat becomes exposed.

In the meantime, imbibe a little more wine and pray that your Osso Buco will be edible. Eat when cooked which is a good suggestion for most foods. Serve it with boiled potatoes and green vegetables

Ours was delicious, but then we might have been lucky with a young Skippy.

The sun's new rays were filtering through the riverside gums and the next door neighbours on the other side, who we hadn't met the night before, were up and about and checking us out.

161

We had a feeling one would emerge sooner or later and it was here at Mary Pool that we encountered our first and hopefully last, 'Mr. Negativity'.

George invited himself over, mug of tea in hand, and in his unwashed and unshaven state, he wasn't the perfect early morning guest. Within minutes he was whinging like a proverbial Pom. "Been everywhere and I'm always disappointed" he confided. "Can't wait to get back to my fishing at Ballina". I enquired as to why he should be traversing the highways of this huge continent when he should really be where he wants to be, back at home in 'God's waiting room' on the New South Wales coast. It appeared his bossy wife, simply told him where to drive and under sufferance followed her directions hating every bit of it. His utterances about his daily problems are too numerous and boring to bother relating, but it did occur to me that when somebody retires before they are 40 as he did, there is still a big chunk of life to leisurely fill in. Not wanting our perfect day spoiled by this groaner, I got rid of him as quickly as possible, while Fay refused to emerge from Morrison until he was gone.

On the road to Halls Creek, a large black porker was on the edge of the highway, its pink snout foraging away at some package that an inconsiderate motorist may have thrown out of their window. He was oblivious to the huge road train, the length of a liner that roared by, causing far-reaching reverberations with its load of cattle. This was probably the only thing of the mildest interest that occurred on that monotonous morning drive into what was amazingly called the Oasis of the Kimberley.

Acquaintances, who have not had the pleasure of appreciating the undeniable delights of the outback, often ask a question that to them seems somehow important. "How do you occupy your mind on those long hauls between places of interest?"

Well readers I will let you into a little secret. While I am concentrating on the occasional oncoming vehicle, counting termite mounds or involving myself in other such mind therapy, my erstwhile navigator, with not much navigating to do has other distractions. At the same time as I can achieve a 100 kilometre leg, she has been known to treat and pamper two legs and two feet. If time allows, even a manicure. Whipping out her box of magical Sothy's beauty products, and with legs positioned on the dashboard, this self-taught therapist turns out the smoothest skin from thigh to toe, of any woman on the road. This weekly treatment is but a precursory for other parts of her anatomy, for which the dashboard is definately not the place.

Motorhomes and caravans were heading back to the west in large numbers. We seemed to be one of few pushing on towards the Top End. Early wild flower spotters were obviously amongst them, but many motorhomes would be congregating en mass at The Campervan and Motorhome Club's forthcoming Annual Convention in Northam, near Perth. One day we will make it to one of these gatherings, which we hear, are great fun but for now further exploration has our insatiable interest.

Halls Creek has lots of colorful shop frontages, all heavily barred, a lovely green sporting oval but the folk there have a really bad attitude or at least they did the day we were there. From the visitor centre, service station, supermarket, to the bottle shop, we were never welcomed, never saw a smile or heard a thank you, and got the impression that visitors just weren't welcome.

When will these drongos realise that without we pilgrims venturing into the outback, life could become even more uneventful and certainly less profitable.

There was a glimpse of humour from the local butcher who proclaimed by means of a large sign that they offered 'Tough, Tasteless, Fatty Meat at City Prices', and wait for it "Iffy Seafood". James and Lorraine were the only people who showed any warmth to a stranger and the food we purchased was exactly the opposite of their quirkily advertised products.

I called into a tawdry café for a sticky beak. Colourful plastic streamers guarded the entrance, only partially stopping the interminable flies. Some Aborigines fiddled with their food and mumbled in a mixture of pidgin and triabelese. The plastic tablecloths had seen a couple of wars and the greasy well-thumbed menus had not been changed in a long time. What happened to all the cafes and fish'n chip shops throughout this nation that were run so successfully for so long by Greeks and Italians? They all seem to have left for greener pastures in the cities and we now have a new generation of Asian shopkeepers who can not make good chips to save their lives.

The black people we chewed the fat with were a more friendly mob. They loved a bit of a chat, as they sat under the shade of the roadside trees, sipping a cool VB or three, which is the only lubrication you will see these people consuming. A lot of city people have a preconceived attitude about Aborigines, which unfortunately is often incorrectly paraded on talk-back shows and the media in general. The average indigenous person is mostly unaware of much of the political haranguing that covers this country like an umbrella, and just wants to get on with his accustomed way of life.

Just outside Halls Creek there is another of Mother Nature's little tricks in the form of The China Wall. Covering many kilometres of barren rocky landscape, this fascinating white quartz formation rises clean out of the earth up to heights of four to five metres. At first impression, the idea of some past master race building this massive dividing wall, would seem possible. But common sense prevailed as we realised that no one in their right mind would want to build anything out in this barren inhospitable land.

Once again we had missed the Toe Sucking Cowgirls by just a day. We heard that the townsfolk of Halls Creek just loved them. It is apparent that the locals much prefer their country music to the continuous line of grey nomads who continually interupt their day, demanding a bit of service. However, it was good to see that they still had some appreciation of what could be loosely called 'the performing arts'.

In the meantime, we're out of here.

CHAPTER TEN

KANGAROO TALES OF BUNGLE BUNGLES & BARRAMUNDI DREAMING

With Halls Creek behind us, we headed towards an area known as the East Kimberley, famous for its diversified and dramatic landscapes.

Turkey Creek emerged out of the heat-haze. First impressions proved correct, it was a 'one horse town', although it was the base for various adventurous escapades including helicopter flights over the Bungle Bungles. This experience has long been on 'her outdoors' list of 'must do' things, but being a fairly expensive excursion, we preferred to book a plane flight from Kununurra in a few days time. Much better value, considering the time spent in the air and so much more to ogle at.

Aboriginal art galleries aren't exactly my cup of tea but my art-loving wife couldn't say no when she heard that one of the most formidable indigenous galleries in Australia was only minutes away. The problem of actually getting into the joint proved challenging in itself, as special permission has to be obtained. These guys don't make it easy and if the phones aren't operative, or the 'curator', for want of a better word, is having an extended 'smoko', then hanging around in the heat can be somewhat frustrating.

The waiting proved to be well worthwhile, even for a sceptic like me.

The walls of the Warnum Art Centre are hung with the works of over two-dozen past and present Aboriginal artists, drawing on traditional events and contemporary experiences of their lives. Thousands of different coloured dots in abstract shapes and contortions can be quite hypnotising, and I found if I really concentrated, then a vague dreamtime story materialised. There was one particularly large well-hung piece, and I'm not referring to the strange lady next to me, that took my fancy. The dots seemed to fuse into one great multi-coloured blob, or was it just the humidity in the non air-conditioned room.

Ruth proved to be a fascinating fellow art admirer, but was really more interested in telling me about herself and why she was all by herself in a place like Turkey Creek.

It appeared that husband George pulled on his hiking boots that morning and headed out for a day's walking, appreciating the joys and mysteries of the Bungle Bungles. "This time last year he was on death's doorstep" she confided. "The 'Big C' had crept up and he was told to get his affairs in order. He had been fit, healthy but always a bit of a worrier was George". I asked her what had changed this dramatic order of events, giving him enough energy to climb mountains when he should have been knocking at the Pearly Gates. " Well, he had a friend who had read somewhere that laughter was a deterrent to illness as it released something called endorphins, which is a sort of self anethesis" she continued as if proud to tell the world of these amazing facts. "So he went out and hired every comedy video available. Faulty Towers, Billy Connolly, AbFab, and other

Pommy funnies and just sat in front of the tellie hour after hour, day after day laughing his head off. Every comedian that appeared at our local RSL saw us in front row seats, while friends bought George comic books by the dozen. At the end of the year he went back to the doctor, who informed him that he mysteriously had a clean bill of health. Which of course gave him further reason to laugh"

I had often noticed that people who are surrounded with happiness always appeared to be blooming, while the whingers of this world tend to cocoon themselves in self-pity and ill health. Ruth returned to her 4WD to patiently await the return of her hubby whose life had been given a second chance through nothing simpler than laughter.

Laughing heartly just for 'insurance', we set off through the mountainous terrain that encompassed the Purnululu National Park, home of those mysterious Bungle Bungles. Like turning pages in a picture book, the scenery changed dramatically in the space of a few kilometres, stirring our senses in wonderment. The far ranges were intensely blue and velvety in the dimming afternoon light. Smooth sculptured, rolling green slopes of the O'Donnell Range on the left and the flat topped Carr Boyd Range with their sheer cliffs on the right. The brilliant reds, glowing as if on fire from these rock-faces in the afternoon sun was quite awesome. This afternoon drive, winding through such remarkable ranges, with their ever-changing shadows creating wonderful colour changes, had a stimulating effect on both of us as we recorded the setting forever in our memory banks.

A small simple road sign read 'Argyle Project'. The long winding gravel road that disappeared over the range looked innocuous enough, considering this was the entrance to the world's largest diamond mine.

Huge pastoral holdings, all named after previous ladies of the household such as Alice Downs, Mabel Downs, and Lissadel, passed us by with road frontages and boundaries so expansive they defied imagination.

This was one afternoon's drive that needed no urgency with so much colour and shape to absorb and appreciate. In due course, Morrison hung a left and we diverted onto the eastern end of the infamous Gibb River Road.

Swirling red bull dust immediately swamped us from the oncoming 4WD's that had almost completed their journey across the full length of this last-frontier track. With the end in sight, they bounced along the corrugated gravel at alarmingly high speeds, like trail horses with the home paddock in sight. Fortunately, we were not going to experience the worst of this infamous road, which seriously depreciates a little further along with large potholes, boulders and other suspension-challenging obstacles.

Ever faithful Morrison was not happy in these conditions and was grateful when we found an overnight camping spot, just off the road and under the shadow of a huge silver-grey boab tree.

A rather well spoken English couple had staked their claim on the spot and were relaxing, G&T's in hand, precariously perched on small fold-up chairs.

Obviously pleased to see someone else to provide some companionship for the night, they sauntered over for a chat. Jeremy told us of their rather fwightful experience on this tweacherous overrated jolly goat twack.

"It was so bumpy, old chap, the fillings in my teeth became all loose" he said, showing me a mouth full of gold fillings. "Just like being on one of your bucking bwonkos", he confided in his very Cambridge accent. They looked a bit like fish out of water with their tweed- type outfits, while Camilla could have just walked out of a Bond St beauty salon. With not a hair out of place after such a courageous experience, her appearance seemed a little unusual. Well good luck to them I thought, giving our raw outback a 'bit of a go' and it must have been one hell of a challenge with their sort of aristocratic background..

It was a bit too much for Jeremy to stomach when I asked him if they would like to join us for dinner and that we would be finishing off the rest of a baby crocodile that I had shot a few days ago.

Our gullible wayfaring friends wandered back to their tent, and I was somewhat relieved at their 'no thanks, old sport' refusal as the cryovaced croc fillet that had been taken out of the deep freeze that morning, was really only sufficient for two.

Spicy Billabong Crocodile

Catching and skinning a croc for its meat is a bit outside the law in Australia, but a few years ago it was quite common in the outback to get a good feed by shooting one of these monsters. Steve Irwin has a few good tips on how to catch your own, but it is lot easier to find a retailer who can sell you a cryovac fillet, which has been taken off the bone and devoid of fat. It has a subtle taste, with a likeness to chicken and is quite unique. Cube about 250-300 gms and marinate for 3-4 hours with a mixture of the following.

Marinade; 3 tablespoons each of teriyaki and soy sauce, 2 tablespoons of white wine, 1 tablespoon each of fish sauce and sesame oil and a sprinkling of chopped ginger.

Cook the croc in a saucepan with the marinade for about five minutes. It should not be overcooked, else will become tough as a pair of crocodile shoes. Add a handful of chopped cashew or macadamia nuts in to the marinade before serving.

We enjoyed ours on a bed of ribbon pasta with accompanying snow peas, sliced carrots and peppers.

We were in the vicinity of El Questro, an immense one million-acre property that has become a resort of international renown, offering diverse opportunities to enjoy its 'off the beaten track' beauty. The vastness of the place is difficult to comprehend, but for those who have a quirk for comparisons, like me, just imagine this. It equates to a block of dirt that spreads from Sydney Heads, down the coast to Kiama, inland to Bowral up to Penrith and back to the Heads. Measuring 100 by 40 kilometres, it is a fair sized back yard in anyone's estimations. My pal Bill back in Perth came up with these figures, as he's very good at that sort of thing.

Looking after a working property and tourist operation of this magnitude is a frightening challenge and certainly not for the faint hearted. ELQ as it is known, has a wide range of activities for the adventurous, ranging from gorge walking, fishing for barramundi (from boat or helicopter), and anything you want to do on horseback or playing around in canoes. Natural hot springs are there to luxuriate in if you just want to be lazy. It is a getaway for all pockets. At $700 to $900 dollars per person per night, the exclusive homestead is a magnet for the wealthy, who appreciate that touch of luxury with their outback adventures. Cantilevered over the winding Chamberlain River it offers everything the well-heeled wanderer desires. If that's a bit 'exy', then there are bungalows straddled along the riverbanks or tented accommodation down the road at the lovely Emma Gorge. Tourers with tents, and a few motorhomes who had braved the floodways and pitted roads, set up camp around the Station Township or in secluded private spots along the banks of the overflowing Pentecost River.

There are a pot pourrie of characters around the place, which is expertly managed by a good-looking sort called Silk. Stylish black Akubra permanently perched on her head, skintight designer jeans and made up to perfection, she epitomised the style of ELQ. Looking rather young to control such a demanding operation, she nevertheless has her team of 50 employees under total control, and they think the sun shines out of her 'you know where'.

Evenings around the Township Bar present enough characters and sufficient material for a book on its own.

Will was a tall, rangy, youngish looking fellow with a mischievous smile, bright blue eyes and a complexion that screamed 'I'm English'. Chatting away to all and sundry he was just one of the boys but with a noticeable touch of panache. The ensuing conversation accompanied by a couple of beers found that he was, in actual fact, the creator and owner of this expansive property.

Born into a blueblood English family that isn't exactly short of a few quid, can certainly have a few benefits. The way in which Will utilised those benefits, particularly at the tender age of 22, in transforming this vast tract of land into an international destination would defy comprehension in most people's minds. A million acres at the princely sum of one dollar an acre is petty cash compared with another 11 or 12 million that he has thrown in to the place since. No airs or graces about this achiever, who fell in love with the big outdoors when he was a jackaroo in his teens. His dream was to own a cattle station and a friend mentioned this nice little spread in the Far North. He originally purchased his expansive outback holding to ride and fish in peace and his folk back in the UK thought he had gone 'bonkers'. Time has proved them quite wrong. His Australian wife Celia saw the tourism potential and ELQ became the renowned Station and Wilderness Park it is today. The elements have challenged many times, but he and his dedicated crew have survived the onslaughts of 'The Wet' and continue providing visitors with an opportunity to appreciate this magical piece of the Kimberley. Always after a thrill, he once water-skied behind a helicopter through one of his numerous gorges, much to the dismay of some of his more conservation-minded staff.

Big Buddy Tyson is the face of ELQ. This bear-like gentle soul who was born a bush baby, has been a bushman all his life and has been here since day one. He ambles around with a bow-legged John Wayne walk, sporting a white stockman's hat and has every reason to be proud of his life's achievements. Jet black smiling face, pearl white teeth, he laconically talks to anyone who wants to listen about his years of riding bulls, hanging on to bucking broncos, and mustering cattle back in the 40s. He has even painted-up and acted as a clown at the rodeos. He is the horse whisperer of the Kimberley and has a remarkable understanding of our four-legged friends.

He recalls "We had a horse, the managers own, whose stomach had swollen up something terrible and looked close to death. Vets in helicopters had been summoned, but couldn't land. I got back from the bush just in time and found he had a bad case of colic. All he needed was a couple of warm VB's poured down his throat plus a bit of space away from the crowd to let his guts go". Winking, he concluded, "After all, if a couple of VB's are good enough for me, then why shouldn't a sick horse have the best"

He is the only black fella I have drank with who could hold his beer and was still sober after closing time. Or at least it appeared that way.

There is nothing on the land that this lovable bushie can't do or hasn't tried, and his appearances on television shows and commercials, some with his mate Ernie Dingo have been the pinnacle of his life. He cracked a good whip and threw an occasional decent lasso as he enthralled his audience round the campfire at the weekly barbecue.

Buddy suggested we take a look at Chamberlain Gorge, which he reckoned was one of the more spectacular in the area.

The boat glided through the twisting gorge, past spectacular sandwich-like cliff faces towering up to 100 metres above us. Prehistoric rock-art from a bygone era was absorbing stuff, but the highlight for Fay was the tame barramundi, nearly a metre in length that repeatedly drifted under our moored boat. It motionlessly lazed among the dozens of small archerfish, waited till the right moment before pouncing with the speed of lightning, devouring the tasty morsels in a second.

Rock-art had never been close to my heart, but the ancient significance of the prehistoric Bradshaws and the wonderful Wandjani style drawings suddenly took on a new light, when our passionate tour guide Meg, gave an absorbing account of these primitive sketches.

Even in these winter months there was colour in the trees with the spectacular bright red Kimberley Rose blending with the buttercup-yellow Kapok flowers, whose faces perpetually turn to the ever-present winter sun, sendingout bursts of brilliant colour from the leafless branches.

Bob Griffin is a tour leader extraordinaire who meets some weird and wonderful characters in his job. He enjoys the luxury of flying around the country in a Cessna Titan, taking small groups mostly retirees and a smattering of singles that have lost their loved ones on 14-day Air Adventures. His party of nine well-heeled 'humans', as Bob affectionately refers to them, had been cooped up all afternoon and had just flown in to ElQ to 'do the town'.

" I just love showing off this wonderful country of ours, especially to folk who haven't had the opportunity to see places they have only dreamed about" he enthused. "The vast majority of our travellers have spent their life in the city, never getting off their backsides to visit the outback. Now they have a way of 'tasting' it in a safe and luxurious way, staying at a different location every night".

I suggested to Bob that there must have been many amusing incidents over the years, and he recalled a recent one that occurred at Mount Isa.

"Our normal motel was fully booked and we stayed at another establishment where the service in the dining room was abysmal. After ages of waiting, one elderly member of our group asked for his steak dinner to be sent to his room, and eventually tackled it in bed watching telly. It was like boot leather, the meal totally inedible, and he left it virtually untouched outside his door. He was first up next morning and to his amazement found the manager's doberman had just devoured everything on the plate except the steak.

It seemed that the normally avaricious mongrel also had his standards when it came to doggy dining, or could it be that he was a vegetarian"

His gregarious group took over the bar that night but there was one lonely looking guy who kept himself to himself.

Rodney always moves on his lonesome but prefers travelling with groups, partly because of the security and assistance of a tour guide like Bob. When I asked him about his love of Guinness, as I noticed he had downed four in quick sharp time, he was a initially a little reluctant to talk. The smooth dark liquid can do funny things, and after a couple more, he admitted quite shyly that it helped to put lead in his pencil. "Funny thing is though, I've no one to write to at the moment" he ruefully smiled, eyeing up a couple of old dears from his group who were also heavily imbibing. Perhaps this was to be his lucky night.

Sharing the confined spaces of a small warm spring with total strangers can be an interesting experience. Constantly moving 30 degree water, the sun filtering through tall Livistona and Pandanus Palms, smooth pebbles underneath, mossy banks and a gushing waterfall really was total heaven, until someone else slid in beside us.

We had just grabbed the only vacant one of half a dozen pools at Zebedee Springs, when our few idyllic minutes were shattered by four friendly Victorians who crammed in like sardines. They couldn't believe their luck at finding this paradise away from the freezing weather of their Big Smoke. Their over-worked Nikons and Cannons hardly stopped clicking, supplying enough pics to make their friends back home quite envious.

Having done a little reading back at the campsite, we passed on the fascinating information that these naturally warm pools are the only home in the entire world to a small white crab-like creature. This unique and very ancient aquatic isopod crustacean just loves these year round tropical conditions, is rarely sighted and very shy. We decided that one of these Melbournians, a matronly lady from Toorak, was one tinny short of a six pack when she enquired if they were edible and how many it would take to make a crab curry. While we were wondering if she was really as dumb as she appeared, her sister-in-law jumped out maintaining her private parts were being attacked by these inoffensive little critters. Oh well, thermal springs can do unusual things to city types, but their unexpected exit fortuitously made more room in the pool for ourselves and the crabs..

Fay's dear old mum is named Emma, and back home in Brisbane eagerly waits for regular reports of our trip. Spectacular Emma Gorge, which is part of the ELQ property, was therefore somewhere that simply could not be missed. It's an exhilarating gorge and the hour or so it took us to get to the upper reaches, clambering over rocks and boulders, crossing rock pools and flowing crystal clear streams was memorable stuff. Mind you, the temperature in the large turquoise pool at the top, with the huge waterfall cascading down the sheer red cliff walls surrounding us, was fucking freezing. As I plunged in I could not think of a more appropriate word to describe the icy waters.

Butterfly-filled trees and tropical vegetation are dwarfed against the towering heights of the gorge walls. Along the narrow winding track, fellow hikers offer smiles and words of greeting and it is then that we realised the extent of the varying nationalities that travel huge distances to these parts.

"Awesome buddy", "C'est Magnifique", "Jolly nice and all that", "Guten Morgen es war sehr sehon", "Questa e Bellisima".

It went on and on until I thought I was at some International Trade Fair. This really is a universal meeting spot and it was great to see the interaction and joy that the Kimberley scenery had created to this diversified global set.

The resort of Emma Gorge has a very classy feel to it and anyone's expectations of the ultimate outback retreat would be realised here. It is in complete harmony with nature and the surrounding landscape. It's also a top spot to relax over a leisurely meal after the rigours of the gorge.

At this point, we were gorged-out, it was time to hit the road again and get the dust of the Gibb River Road behind us. Heading towards a little bit of comparative civilisation at Kununurra, Morrison's radio suddenly came to life for the first time in 10 days. With no news reports or weather forecasts, a total lack of current newspapers, world disasters could have happened and we would not have known a thing about them. It made us realise how isolated this part of the world really is.

Since leaving Perth, we noticed small roadside signs, which regularly indicated how many kilometres from the capital we had travelled. It is gratifying to see that some government departments can occasionally come up with simple but informative data that benefits the driver. Kununurra is about 3000 kilometres from the capital and we were nearing the end of our West Australian escapade. My trusty little navigator worked out, that with all our various zig zaging from coast to mountains, we had covered exactly twice that distance.

Aboriginal stories abound in these parts but there was one we heard, apparently true, which deserves a place in these pages. Somewhere in the Kimberley last year, Telstra received a request for a telephone installation to be made at the home of an indigenous character, who actually lived in a large boab tree. On finding it wasn't exactly a residence, our esteemed telephone company refused to comply with the application. Our claimant threw a wobbly, legal threats took place through various government bodies such as ATSIC, and guess what? Today, in some far off field, the ringing of a telephone attached to the large bulbous trunk of a tree can be heard and everyone is happy. I never did find out where his accounts were addressed to, but that small point is probably totally irrelevant.

Kununurra is a refreshing little town, surrounded by vast irrigated areas of immaculate fields of greens and browns, supplying the nation with a wide variety of fruits and vegetables. Similar to Carnarvon, we found farms selling fresh produce; melons, paw paw and the like, straight from the land at ridiculously cheap prices. This once barren ground is one of the benefactors of the massive Ord River Irrigation System, which has turned Kununurra into a prosperous go-ahead township.

There are a few things of interest to look at around the town and some worthwhile walks in the nearby hills. The Zebra Rock Café just a short drive away is famous for its carvings, which are crafted out of a rock, unique to this area. This rock has quite vibrant zebra stripes that are dominant throughout each artistically cut creation. Noel and Aileen have been selling their wide range of souvenirs there for nearly 40 years and wouldn't trade their life for the world. Noel loves a bit of a chit-chat and when he's too busy to talk, suggests a conversation with the bird out the back is a reasonable option. The bird is not his wife but a large shiney black crow, with a sign outside his cage indicating that it actually talks. It apparently has a reputation for conversing with 'rolling stones' like us who have nothing better to do than hang outside his aviary, and endeavor to exchange a few pleasantries. Everyone has their 'off' days and this indignant feathered friend haughtily looked at us as a one sided conversation ensued. Not even a squawk was forthcoming as we decided to head back to town to finalise our plans for Fay's big day in the air.

We spent that night overlooking the airport runway, helicopters and small planes lined up outside our bedroom window. 'Her Outdoors' made it quite clear that she had no intention of being late for the six o'clock early morning flight over the Bungle Bungles. She had waited a lifetime for this opportunity and even the Second Coming would not have interfered with her long laid plans. First in the office, first in the queue, first on the plane, was she going to get the most out of this chance to see these unique monuments of nature. She was not disappointed, and nor was I, as our young pilot Jamie, who looked as though he had taken a day off school, gave us a trip we will never forget.

After all our kilometres of road travel it was a great change to take to the air. Everything looked so different from our low altitude flight and it was the perfect way to fully comprehend the geographical diversity of the area. The Carr Boyd Range was quite awesome in the early morning light, but the vastness and beauty of Lake Argyle really grabbed our attention. Calculations vary as to the amount of water this 1000 square kilometre inland-sea holds, but opinions fluctuate from eight to 18 times the size of Sydney Harbour. The 90 islands within the lake are home to 20,000 freshies (they're the friendly type of croc) along with exotic sounding birds like the Jabiru, Australia's only stork and the Dancing Brolga. The 'dancing' tag appears appropriate due to the bobbing and bowing, backwards and forwards movements, and much loud trumpeting during courtship. The couple apparently get very randy with all this action although any consumation of a new relationship waits till after dark.

The two-hour flight took us over vast pastoral holdings and we circled the Argyle Diamond Mine. Suddenly, Fay began wiggling in her seat with excitement and clutched my hand so hard, I thought she would break my fingers. As the lost world of the Bungle Bungles came into view, our fresh faced young Slingair pilot dropped to 500 feet and we were looking down on one of nature's true masterpieces. The vast maze of sandstone domes and narrow canyons, towering 200 metres above the surrounding lowlands is breathtaking. This has been home to the Aboriginal for well over 20,000 years yet the white population has only been aware of its existence since the early 80s, adding a touch of mystery to the lost world theory. The tiger-like stripes on the brilliantly coloured orange and black domes are unlike anything we have seen before. These domes are covered in a skin of silica and lichen, sealing otherwise fragile and crumbling sandstone. The area was much greater than we had imagined and continued to take our breath away as the plane completed one figure of eight after another. As we finally headed for base, we felt that we had experienced something rather special, which had transcended all our expectations.

Having been so impressed with Lake Argyle from the air, we decided to drive out to the lakeside and spend the night at the Lake Argyle Tourist Village. We crossed the 100 metre high and 325 metre long wall, which controls the release of water to the irrigated lands around Kununurra.

It was an interesting coincidence that the following morning as we were discussing the enormous amount of water stored in the dam, Alan Jones was presenting his segment on the Today show, and was also talking about this very subject. He was questioning, in his own inimitable way, why governments need to be continually handing out vast sums of money to drought stricken farmers, when four million litres of water a day from this Ord River Irrigation Scheme could be piped south to the benefit of thousands.

At the bottom of Lake Argyle lie many buildings, which were the heart of the famous Durack pastoral empire, established in the 1890s. Their combined holdings covered seven million acres, which is a pretty big acquisition for a determined family of Irish immigrants. The original homestead was being carefully dismantled stone by stone, courtesy of the West Australian Water Authority, when the waters of Lake Argyle rose more quickly than originally calculated. Many of the stones and and much of the timber had been moved to dryer reaches and with what was available a small version of the homestead was faithfully reconstructed near the Lake Argyle Tourist Village.

It took 20 builders and labourers over two years to complete this arduous task and it is now open to the public. It provides a realistic insight into the hardships, hopes and achievements of the early pioneering settlers. The ashes of the well know author Mary Durack lie in the grounds, along with other descendants of this great dynasty.

Reminders are everywhere that life certainly was not easy in those challenging years although family values were never higher.

The waters of the lake teem with a special breed of catfish and provide an interesting piece of trivia. State Government approval was recently given for a name change to improve their image and increase interstate sales. It appears to have been successful, the catfish is now known as silver cobbler and a substantial interstate demand has developed for their firm white flesh and pleasant taste.

People that state the obvious have always intrigued me and bring out either the best or worst in me depending on the situation. As we concluded the packing up of our camping spot, a genial old timer who had been watching our activities for some time shuffled over and said,

"On your way lad are you?" If he hadn't been such a kindly old soul I would have suggested that I spend 20 minutes each morning packing everything away just to practice my fire drill.

" Yes we are, in fact, actually, on our way, departing, leaving, taking off" I replied with tongue in cheek. Obviously satisfied with my reply, he did an about turn and returned to his rather dilapidated caravan.

The neighbours on the other side had kept to themselves and had been equally uncommunicative, but one of their decisions both amused and bewildered us. In this reasonably spacious park they had decided to park their large converted bus right outside the latrine block. Sitting under the awning of their commodious transport, books and drinks in hand, they appeared to be an attentive audience for the comings and goings of everyone completing their toiletries. The sign in the rear window of their bus, which went by the highly unimaginative name of 'Me and My Old Woman', said it all. It carried a familiar emblem, which indicated they were members of the Ulysses Club. 'Growing Old Disgracefully' is the clubs motto. They would certainly earn some brownie points for this exercise.

CHAPTER ELEVEN

CORROBOREES & COLD GREEN CANS
...A TASTE OF THE TERRITORY

Fay's finger pointed, and she proclaimed her findings like a mariner shouting 'land ahoy' from atop a 19th century schooner mast, distracting my concentration at the wheel. It was purely coincidental, that as we crossed the state line into The Northern Territory, she spotted a small white cloud, like a puff of cigar smoke in the distance. To readers from places like Melbourne and Sydney, this may not seem a particularly unusual occurrence but this was the first time in almost two months that a cloud had appeared in the clear blue sky. However, the excitement was brief, as the rogue cloud dissipated and the normality of cloudless skies was resumed.

A large roadside sign said 'Welcome to Nature Territory'; 'Clocks to be put forward one and a half hours'. Departing motorists were queuing on the other side of the highway, waiting their turn for boring quarantine inspections. Restrictions prevented certain fresh produce being taken into West Australia. No such hold ups for us.

Certain changes and differences were always felt as we passed from one state into another and we were now looking forward in great anticipation to the fabled 'Territory'. There are two distinct geographical areas in the Northern Territory and we were about to explore the northern half, known universally as the Top End. Great wild rivers, cascading waterfalls, rock pools, thermal springs, gulf country, wetlands and lily filled billabongs were just some of the delights ahead of us.

We passed along the broad Victoria River and into the inauspicious little town of Timber Creek. Given that this is the last and only town on the long road from the border to Katherine, we decided to pull in for the night. There is a country store cum tourist office run by Max Sharam, a local identity and raconteur, who operates boat tours on the river. He has lots of signs outside offering barramundi tours, croc viewing, sunset boat trips and the like. A brave proclamation at the bottom of these signs states, 'No Mossies…No Flies'. In this tropical climate, it was quite a courageous claim. Sitting behind his large table-like desk, piles of brochures, booking forms and papers scattered untidily everywhere, phone constantly ringing, affable Max seemed a remarkable busy guy for a 'one-horse' town such as this. "No guarantee's, but mossies and flies are definitely in short supply in this part of the world" he declared with absolute sincerity.

He directed us off to the Big Horse Creek camping area and was true to his word. We camped on the riverbank and not one itch or pesky irritation. Croc observers from the boat trips and various fishermen confirmed that Max was true to his word.

Barramundi is on everyone's lips in this part of the world so it's a good time to set the record straight on a few points. Yes, these elusive, hard-fighting and fine-eating fish do have a sex change. They are all born male and for some unexplainable reason most of them change sex when they reach six to eight years. I wonder what percentage of human males would make a similar decision in our ever-changing world if they had the choice? These much sought after creatures live up to 20 years of age, grow to a length of one and a half metres and can weigh in at a cool 40 kilograms. They also add millions of dollars to the Top End tourism industry.

I don't like making excuses but I had no luck at all at trying to pull one in. July is probably the worst month of the year, the waters are a tad cold for them and hanging around another few weeks was not on our agenda. So we just gazed at the photos on the walls in Max's office, and at the Roadhouse and just about any other wall that can accommodate a pic of these monsters being proudly shown off for the camera. Reconciling ourselves to the fact that the only Barramundi we would be likely to eat on this particular leg of the journey would be served in a restaurant, we put a tick against Timber Creek in the barra season on the 'must do next time' list.

We headed for Katherine, ascending up from the river through escarpment country and then into the grasslands that extended forever into the distance. With my co driver at the wheel there was little to occupy me at this stage, except observing more termite mounds. It seemed that a different family of termites lived here. Compared with their WA counterparts who had big bulbous habitats, these Territorian types were living in small, finely honed citadel style dwellings spread out in some suburban-like environment. Ho hum! Time for a nap.

We had not previously slept by the side of a Billabong, so the evenings at the Springvale Homestead just outside Katherine were intoxicating. Permanently full of fresh water, the billabong attracted tame wallabies in the evenings and scores of dive bombing rainbow bee eaters at sun up. We were well pleased at this outstanding find so close to a big town. The well loved nearby Homestead goes back a 100 years or more having survived numerous severe floods. Information on its establishment and the traumas and hard lives of the early day pioneers proved to be fascinating reading.

There is a little café nearby and in front of me in the queue was a cute little French Mademoiselle. She was from some obscure region where English was obviously not widely spoken and was having some difficulty getting her tongue round some of the words on the menu. The bemused lady behind the counter didn't blink an eyelid when in a strong French accent she requested "I will ave wun barramoondi an chip, an wun feesh an chip". The cook cum-dish washer cum waitress scribbled down the order and obviously decided that it would be too difficult to explain that barramundi and fish were the same thing. The French are the least travelled of all European nations but it was nice to see that this little lady was making a special effort in trying to interact when away from home.

It was a new day, and one that was to bring great excitement and much happiness. My first grandson was born. The mobile rang and I knew it was my son Scotty before we connected. His girlfriend Yvie had just gone through 20 hours of purgatory in delivering their son, and he was so excited that I thought he had experienced the ordeal himself. Zakk was a perfect bouncing baby, and Scotty wanted to tell the world. " Dad, you'll never guess what happened when I rang the Gold Coast Bulletin to place an ad in Saturday's classified column" he exultantly cried. " The girl asked how many insertions and I told her five times a week for three months". The emotion of the moment was more important than the accounting at that stage, but Scotty was most surprised to find the bill totalled $364. Such is the excitement of new parenthood.

Taking a pet emu for a morning walk does raise the odd eyebrow, even in Katherine at the Annual Show. Doc was a fully-grown three-year-old who followed his master around like a well-trained dog. Lead and collar not required here, as this passive bird with the largest attentive eyes imaginable, accepts a pat or touch of affection from all who pass him. His owner, Stewart, travels around the country with Doc, selling and promoting the benefits of emu oil. He goes to shows, rodeos, all manner of places and what a wonderful marketing tool Doc has become.

"Has he ever done a runner" I asked Stewart ?

"Occasionally when I take him into an oval, he like to give his legs a bit of a stretch" he smiled " but he always comes back".

Apparently he has never tried to peck anyone, which is pretty important when you've got a large feathered friend being stroked by kids of all ages.

Back at his rig, Stewart was flicking through large numbers of testimonials from satisfied users of his specially manufactured oils and capsules.

"It has wonderful recuperative powers in the treatment of diabetes, heart problems, arthritis and many other modern day problems" he proudly enthused. It appeared he had spent a year or two getting the bums rush by bureaucratic bodies in Canberra, wanting to stifle his remarkable products. After nearly pulling his hair out in frustration, he had just received his certificates from the Therapeutic Goods Authority, confirming that his range of oils were 'approved as an active ingredient'.

Meanwhile, Doc was eyeing up an attractive white poodle 50 metres away. "That's his only vice" Stewart whispered, "he loves to chase the odd dog or two….especially poodles"

Katherine is just a big country town with lots of colourful activity on the streets and police cars that seemed to be zipping everywhere. Roaming the streets and parks are mobs of characters from the local communities, preferring town life to their isolated outback villages, where there are alcohol limitations and minimal services. A few dozen of them seemed to make the main thoroughfare look really busy with their energetic pidgin banterings and heated discussions. There is much waving and shaking of arms while their gaudy attire could be considered decidedly eccentric.

I remembered a conversation back on the coast of Western Australia with some staid old caravaning couples. Based on their experiences, they were giving advice about dealing with Aborigines in the Territory. "Just keep your head down and don't look 'em in the eye" whispered one blue rinse type, as though a few black fellas were hiding in the bushes behind us. What a load of horse shit. Most of the blacks around town love exchanging a few words and always return a 'G'day' or 'How are you mate'. It is wise not to indulge in a deep and meaningful about current stock market movements, real estate values, or the United Nation's various peace policies, as these subjects will just bring a vacant stare or a nervous giggle. But they are more than happy to chat on about what's important in their world and some have wonderful philosophies on life and all its meaning.

We stocked up at one of the best Woollies on our travels and headed out to Katherine's premier attraction, Nitmiluk National Park. Home to the renowned Katherine Gorge, it is owned by the Jawoyn

Aborigines and managed by the Parks and Wild Life Commission in close harmony and cooperation with the indigenous communities.

The wonderfully presented visitor centre provides graphic details of the history and traditions of the land and its owners. After a century or more of mistreatment and abuse by the white man, the Jawoyn are back on their lands, maintaining their cultural practices and protecting the environment. They may wear white mans clothes, drive cars and hunt with guns but they continue to live according to their tribal law in the tradition of their ancestors.

After absorbing much of this, we decided to spend a day canoeing through some of the spectacular gorges that are a feature of the park. The deep waters snake their way through steep-sided rock walls of intriguing colours and shapes. The serenity was only broken by the commentary from an occasional tourist boat and the splashing of our paddles. The 15-kilometre return trip was smooth paddling, broken by the occasional need to haul the canoe over rocks and rapids. This tested the shoulder muscles but there were regular cooling dips with little concerns that a friendly freshie may be sharing the river with us.

Gratefully clutching our first thirst-quenching Rum and Coke of the day, we relaxed under Morrison's awning in the late afternoon sun and lazily watched as a serious 4WD pulled up a few metres away. The three male occupants hopped out and two of them busily scurried about putting up their three-man tent, setting up cooking facilities and getting a fire going. The big fella stood by and watched these proceedings, offering a bit of encouragement here and there, but looking very much a virgin camper. He slowly shuffled off across the park to the latrine block, obviously suffering some sort of discomfort. It could well have been gout, but it later turned out to be irreparable damage to his knees from playing too much rugby.

"Peter FitzSimons" he said, proffering a paw that would have done a grisly proud. After years of scrummaging and rucking for the Wallabies and other teams, this man-mountain is now on the public speaking circuit as well as writing for the Sydney Morning Herald and occasionally showing his bearded face on the Today Show. We all shared a glass or two from our dwindling supply of Margaret River reds, and chatted on about 'the game played in heaven'. Peter had been enthralling some corporate types in Darwin and was taking a quick camping holiday across country, with a couple of mates en route to his next job in Noosa.

They would have to be white line wizards to cover that distance in a few days, losing a great opportunity to appreciate some fine country they would be passing through. Next day, Peter once again watched as his mates disassembled camp, and they sped off with little knowledge of the pleasures of Katherine Gorge. We watched him on the Today show the following week, expounding his theories on wage caps for sports people always managing his art of being amusing, while riling fellow guests at the same time.

Edith Falls just a short drive away, seemed the perfect spot for a few days camping, so we headed north for a touch of peace and serenity. Friends from Byron Bay had raved about this place and recommended that we should stay at least a few days and truly veg out. The layout of the National Parks campsite, with its manicured little gardens beside each space, were well thought out, and along with the walks, rock pools and abundant bird life, was indeed another bit of Australian paradise.

Just a few minutes down the path waterfalls cascade into what is termed a plunge pool, which in fact is a fair sized lake. Further up the track more waterfalls, gurgling streams and ponds with a profusion of flowering bank-side lilies. The higher we went the more invigorating these crystal clear pools became, as we gazed into them from a perch right on top of the tumbling waters of a gushing waterfall.

In the total solitude, away from prying eyes, Fay thought it a marvelous place to indulge in the joys of gay abandon and discard her gear for a frolic under the waterfall in the starkers. Displaying her charms for my camera, she instantly disappeared under the water when a Liverpudlian voice from the trees shouted, "any room left in your waterfall missus". She has never been known to submerge for more than a few seconds, but this was a moment to really excel herself. Our Pommy visitor knew when he wasn't welcome and thoughtfully moved on; obviously upset he couldn't join the fun.

There is a brightly coloured bird in these parts called a Gouldian

Finch that has the most remarkably vivid markings, and 'Birdos' come from miles to spot this cute little feathered creature. They must have been on holiday during our stay; quiet as mice we were in our bankside hide, but didn't spot a single one. We did though have the pleasure of close encounters with a blue winged kookaburra, which was beating the shit out of a piece of steak he had nicked from some unfortunate camper's plate. He was having the time of his life, ignoring my camera lens, which was only a metre or two from his perpetually grinning face. It reminded me of an incident earlier in the trip when a fellow camper held a piece of meat in his hand as an offering to one of these delightful creatures. Ignoring the gesture, the bird swooped and nicked the full steak off his plate, leaving the not so happy camper looking pretty stupid .

Sitting next to the barbie was something we hadn't seen in a while. A full-blown idiot. He was American, big, loud mouthed and he was hard pressed to understand any basic English. He stood out like a shag on a rock with his garishly coloured Hawaiian printed shirt and matching knee-length baggy shorts. Do they realise what they really look like? Feeding the wild life here is definitely a big no-no, as indicated by the numerous signs around the place, yet this oaf irresponsibly ignored pleas from fireside campers not to provide dinner for the tame wallabies. A whole loaf of white bread is not exactly a nutritious diet for these guys and processed food can in fact cause serious illness. But this 'septic,' was totally deaf to any good advice, and was intent on supplying slice after slice to our now over-indulged marsupial friends.

On the southern approach to Darwin there is a little rural community called Howard Springs, which is starting to feel the effects of the quickly expanding capital's slow spread into their peaceful and idyllic setting. There is an expansive spring system here providing city dwellers with a great cooling off spot. It was the centre of much activity during the war years when enlisted men filled their leisure days creating waterways and swimming areas, which are still much-appreciated 50 years later. Fishing is definitely not the done thing here, although there are numerous swimming companions in the main lake. Protected barramundi, many around the metre mark, lazily drifted through the warm waters oblivious to the thrashing antics of first time visitors who think they are about to be attacked. It's a bit of a giggle watching a grey nomad reaching out for the safety of the steps, after someone like me has warned him there's a three footer right behind him. Mind you these big fish are not adverse to nibbling at the toes of swimmers, which can be a bit disconcerting.

We fell under the magic spell of Darwin and loved its tropical, laid-back feel. Tall majestic palms and lush verdant growth are everywhere, and as much of the city has been rebuilt in the 20 years since 'Tracey', a fresh cosmopolitan atmosphere pervades. Surrounded by aqua blue water, the nation's youngest city opens its arms to visitors offering lots to see and do in typical relaxed Territorian style.

. In the early stages of our journey, we had some preconceived ideas when it came to including cities, towns and commercialised suburbia. Darwin dispelled that notion. Australia's northern capital is invigorating; a mix of cultural character, mystery and beauty with a lively, vibrant, easy-going lifestyle.

The city is a melting pot of races with around 45 to 60 ethnic groups represented, but there is still a high degree of racial tolerance. With Australia looking increasingly to Asia for trade, Darwin is well placed to become the main link with the region. Everything flows smoothly from the traffic to the cooling drinks in the dozens of widely varied drinking and eating spots. Personalised plates seem to be featured on every other vehicle and at only $50 a year provide identification and a lesser chance of theft. A recent poll on changing from a Territory to a fully-fledged State was narrowly defeated.

Territorians are noticeable by their easygoing Australian drawl and short fragmented sentences. Talkspeak up here is slow and deliberate, and they dress in the casual way of the north. It's a young people's town although the lifestyles vary dramatically. Over at Cullen Bay, those who have made a few dollars live in a Sanctuary Cove type development, air conditioned power boats moored on their jetties, exotic cars in the driveways and houses you might be lucky enough to win in an Art Union raffle. The fortunate ones move south in the summer, away from the taxing humidity.

Cullen Bay Marina is really just a line of restaurants offering indoor/ outdoor dining overlooking lines of visiting yachts from around the world. With all these wonderful eating establishments to choose from, why would I pick out just one? Toilets, is the answer.

Most restaurant reviewers praise or criticise the food, service or ambience, and whilst all these are first class in Buzz Café, it's the little features like the toilets that cause the buzz. The 'Mens' has a large floor to ceiling two-way mirror facing numerous tables and chairs. Lunch was being served as I unzipped my fly, aquainted myself with the necessary equipment, and prepared to direct my relief at some old folk at a nearby table who would normally have choked on their prawn cocktails. This urinal with a difference suddenly flushed, with a waterfall cascading down the glass and the thought of being 'perved on' while doing what comes naturally, was temporarily shelved. On exiting, the oldies ignored me and I checked the mirror and was relieved to see the vision was only one way.

John Bonnin conceived, designed and operates Buzz Café and just loves crazy ideas. He has always dreamed of owning a top eatery in beautiful surroundings that provided something a little unusual. He spent two years completing his dream and has incorporated some wonderfully creative features. The huge semi circular bar and anteroom sinks are hand made from lava, which was flowing from a volcano in Java only eight years ago. Each sink weighs over a ton and the freight arrangements and cost must have been a nightmare.

Besides the features in the Mens toilets, which apparently have been viewed by just as many curious women, the Ladies room has its fair share of surprises. Toilet seats containing barbed wire and red back spiders ensure that the moment of relief is speeded up. Posthumously placed insects of the largest types imaginable are clearly incarcerated in the ceiling. Thousands of pieces of smoothly ground cola bottles surround the mirrors as the ladies recompose themselves before returning to their table with an exaggerated tale to tell. Teak and mahogany furniture of the most unusual designs, and artistic paintwork complete the picture of a restaurant that offers a lot more than fine food and a superb harbour setting.

John came to the Territory in the early 90s and after servicing remote outback places with his air charter company decided to return to his love of food and hospitality. It was a pleasure to see someone putting the fun back into eating.

Markets are a big deal up here and they all have a special infectious hustle and bustle about them. A mix of South East Asian and European cultures has created unique settings, exotic foods, collections of arts and crafts and the usual market characters. Thousands pack Mindil Beach for the famous Sunset Markets with dozens of Asian food stalls doing the biggest trade. Fire-eaters, live music, Indian street entertainers, balancing and contorting acts all combine to create an eclectic atmosphere.

We set up our picnic table right on the beach watching mini crowds rush to every vantage point at sunset, to see the fiery red sphere drop into the glass-like ocean. With the deed done, most onlookers soon scrambled back over the sand dunes and pathways to the activities and entertainment of the markets, and we were left to finish our wine and food on the relatively peaceful beach. A lone para flyer, who had spent an interminable time silhouetted against the setting sun, had enjoyed his moment of glory and decided it was time to go home.

Saturday morning at Parap Markets was quite different as we jostled past an intriguing variety of stalls offering fresh produce, seafood, creatively cooked Asian delights and locally made crafts and arts. Exotic smells emanated from Thai, Vietnamese, Chinese and Cambodian outlets, pungent coffee aromas filtered the early morning air and Oriental chatter was all about. We bought barramundi from an Indo Chinese lady who had difficulty conversing in English, fresh herbs and vegetables from smiling vendors whose overseas homelands were a distant cry from their new lifestyles. This market has become an institution with locals and some just couldn't survive a weekend without an injection of these unique smells, tastes and table gossip.

Many other markets, all with their own characteristics operate weekly and are part of the flavour and appeal of the Top End.

The claws on a full size muddie can bite through a broom handle, a toe or finger with ease. Take them out of the water and into a confined ring with dozens of half-intoxicated onlookers urging them on and they understandably get quite aggressive. The annual Northern Territory Crab Tying Championships are held at the Parap Tavern, just around the corner from the markets, and are open to anyone stupid enough to jump barefoot into the confines of the two-metre square ring with three of these combative creatures. Tying up the first one is the initial challenge, while at the same time, keeping the other two from doing some permanent damage to any exposed parts of the body. Blokes have been known to have their private parts attacked by these mobile crustaceans as they kneel down to complete their knotting. A total of 15 bravados in varying degrees of intoxication entered the challenge this year, some looking quite perplexed at what they had gotten themselves into. The only painful experience occurred when a big black islander had his toenail ripped off by a particularly agile crab, which took great objection to being tied up. It ended getting whacked by the other big black foot, before a double reef knot restricted any further movement. Through a process of elimination a mysterious Mr Frogg caught and tied up three of them in a record-breaking one minute, 45 seconds. The noisy crowd erupted once more as the agile winner held high his final 'tie' while a bit of money changed hands on this unexpected outsider. Mr Frogg indeed!

Marshall Perron was the No 1 man in the Territory for a long time, but politicians move on and he and his wife now operate a top little earner out of his back garden called Aquascene. They were smart enough to buy a lovely waterfront property in town at Doctors Gully and everyday around high tide, thousands of hungry fish thrash around in the water off their back garden, and fight for the never ending food that is thrown at them. Thousands of people every week queue up and pay six dollars a head for this pleasure. Bemused couples of all ages were sitting around on the cantilevered steps looking down on excited youngsters who were hand feeding and trying to stroke the multitude of milkfish, mullet, catfish and bream. When the tide recedes, the crowd disperses and the Perron household gets back to their normal daily activities. Marshall has a deal with local supermarkets and calls around early mornings to pick up any unsold loaves of bread, which must make a nice change from having to deal with a lot of back-stabbing mongrel pollies every day.

It was Darwin Show weekend and by the number of parked vehicles I reckoned that half of the city must have been there. There were a couple of items on the agenda that held some sort of fascination for us. Whoever came up with the old saying 'yes, and pigs can fly' obviously had not seen the 'Racing Pigs' outfit. Immaculately attired in colourful numbered racing silks, these cuddly three-month-old porkers obediently trotted down and lined up at the barrier, awaiting the starters whistle. The 36-metre dash is over before you blink, with the squealing winner breaking the five-second mark. They really do fly and all have names so the audience can cheer their preferred hog on to the victory. The first fab four to line up had been suitably christened Hambone, Miss Piggy, Porky Pig and BLT while Babe and other contenders snorted on the sideline.

Tony Vandeleur, who has been on the hoof around the shows of Australia with his little pets, hails from Adelaide, which he maintains has now reached the pinnacle of being named the pig racing capital of the world. It takes him about four weeks of concentrated work to train these specially selected little sows and after a couple of months on the road they are retired back to the business of making more little pigs. Tony spent a few years in the USA teaching the Yanks about Pig Racing, and it has now given the world leaders something else to shout about.

In addition to his eight racing pigs, Tony has two curly tailed wonders that climb up a ladder in their designer bikinis, teeter out on to a five-metre-high diving board and ungracefully plunge into the two metres of water below them. Achieving a pike and double backward flip apparently is well beyond their ability but we applauded their efforts anyway.

Cuddling the winner Miss Piggy after the final, proved a moving experience for Fay. Just like a household pet with its little pink eyes gazing in wonderment, she couldn't help giving the little porker a big' Rex Hunt' on her pristine little snout before we departed for the main arena..

I've always had a soft spot for those wonderful Clydesdales whose strength, patience and intelligence is a continual source of amazement. We watched these beautiful beasts going through a series of routines in the main arena pulling a reproduction 100 year old Carlton Ale wagon behind them. The precision of their movements in reversing, side stepping and weaving between obstacles reflected the silken touch of the handler and marvelous coordination of the team. Originally bred as a war-horse from Flemish stallions, the clip-clopping of their hooves heralding a beer delivery can still be remembered with fondness by some old timers. The Clydesdale epitomises the early days of Australian settlement and their gentle disposition and distinctive characteristics continue to provide enjoyment for young and old.

The Darwin Show offered hundreds of things to see and do and it was wonderful to see these annual events had lost none of their appeal for the thousands who look forward to them each year. It was here that we eventually caught up with the elusive Toe Sucking Cowgirls. We were fascinated by their name and after missing them by a day or so along the track, just had to see what this act was all about. Gleny and Tracey have been playing their mixture of Cajun, Bluegrass, Country and Celtic music for a couple of years and were just about to leave for a promotional trip to the UK and Ireland. I asked the girls about the background of the name, which apparently is a well-kept secret. The most plausible answer I got from them relates to a time before they took up their musical instruments and performed in the clubs as a contortionist act. Their encore consisted of a couple of energetic backward flips resulting in the sucking of each other's toes to the amusement and disbelief of the audience. The name stuck and with their first CD intriguingly titled 'Flaming Sheilas', they appear to be combining their fun and talent pretty well. Some frantic electric fiddle and accordion playing from Gleny and fine guitar work from Tracey got their audience going a treat, and as they write some pretty good material they could well find themselves climbing up the ladder of success real soon.

One thing that the capital is well known for is the genuine down to earth hospitality of the locals. We were parked one day and a friendly face put his receding hairline into the doorframe of our Sunliner and commended us on our lifestyle and our choice of transport. It turned out that Barry was thinking of converting his city lifestyle of running a big computer company to that of a wandering type, much the same as us. In return for a tour of Morrison, he and his lovely wife

Pauline, took us out on their super duper cruiser, showed us how not to catch crabs from their Cullen Bay mansion and made us feel at home in the members stand at the Darwin Derby. Barry confided that he was a real family man and had developed a 'bit of an attachment' for his mother in law. " It fits perfectly over her mouth" he chuckled, "but I couldn't get her to wear it to the races". He introduced me to his mates as his new found best friend, and I thought that's nice, as we had only met a few days earlier. We'll definitely cross paths when he gets around to buying his own Morrison and leaves behind the problems associated with running a stress-loaded computer company.

Our last night in town was spent on the cliffs, overlooking a motionless ocean, the deep red sun vanishing on our left and the beachside MGM Casino a few 100 metres away on our right. There was a $250 a head function taking place there, with 1200 guests enjoying fireworks, five hours of music, dancing and stand-up comedians. We saw the colourful pyrotechnics display exploding in front of us, heard the music, laughed at the jokes and did a bit of dancing, all for the price of a couple of steaks and our normal supply of liquid refreshment.

Long time friends Tony and Wendy had flown up from the miserable winter weather of Sydney to spend a week with us, and we were all keen to see as much of The Territory as possible in this short time. Litchfield National Park had been given the thumbs up by numerous fellow travellers so we all piled aboard Morrison and headed in that direction.

There is something quite exotic about swimming through a warm, pandanus-lined, spring-fed pool, sliding over smooth boulders and being totally immersed under the strong, massaging cascade of a thermal waterfall. The dappled sun filtering through tall palms combines with the beguiling sprays of water, teasing aching neck and back muscles, to create the perfect and purest of spas. What commercial city establishment could compete with this? We were at Berry Springs, a popular 'watering hole' less than an hour out of Darwin and just off the main road to Litchfield. We had previously paid several visits to this special place and could not wait to share it with our friends.

Right next door to the springs is a Wildlife Park, where the Territory Government has spent an absolute fortune in creating an area that sets the highest possible standards in flora and fauna preservation. Set on 1000 acres of bushland, it proved to be one of the most educational and rewarding days we have experienced for a long time. It is a blending of zoo, National Park, environmental educator, research centre and tourist attraction all wrapped in to one. All manner of Top End animals in their beautifully re-created habitats, birds by the hundreds in their wetlands and fish together with other aquatic life in billabongs and rock pools were just some of the visual treats. The largest domed walk-through aquarium in the Southern Hemisphere, designed to replicate an entire Top End river system, allowed us to eyeball fish and marine life at close range. The Birds of Prey demonstration was exhilarating with barking owls, wedge tailed and white bellied sea eagles showing off their instinctive hunting talents in a free flying display. There is also a series of nocturnal houses where in darkened surroundings we watched native species doing what they normally do at night. The girls were totally entranced and would have stayed the night but we were politely asked to leave well after the gates were shut.

Litchfield was calling and we were about to enjoy a few days of joyous romping with nature in its stunning waterfalls, rock pools, perennial spring fed streams and monsoon rainforests. It hasn't had the marketing fanfare that accompanies Kakadu but as the 'new kid on the block', it is a serious rival.

We entered the park and the first thing of interest that greeted us was – wait for it - Termite Mounds! Having been continually intrigued by these industrious critters along the way, we are a bit disinclined to mention them, but this lot are very smart little ants that build magnetic termite mounds. While reputable architects take the importance of the sun and wind into consideration, these two-metre high magnetic mounds are also built with an awareness of climatic changes. Their thin edges point in a north-south orientation while their broad backs and fronts face east west. This configuration is a sort of built-in temperature control mechanism, allowing only the least possible surface area to ever be exposed to the interminable heat of the sun. Now that's pretty smart and there are whole cities out there, with a boardwalk running through the middle so we mere humans can observe them at close quarters. After taking the mandatory photos, we decided that the lush green of Litchfield was more to our taste.

Florence Falls was spectacular and the hike down the few hundred steep steps made the refreshing waters a welcome relief. A pair of humungous black birds sat motionless on the nearby rocks, suspiciously eyeing us as we went through the painful process of that first immersion into the invigorating waters, seemingly unperturbed at the intrusion in to their haven.

Two exquisite falls plunge down from the high plateau into the broad pool, one delivering such force that the illusion of a fierce storm is created for those brave enough to swim out to its base. The screams that emanated from Wendy and Fay as they passed under the sleeting, crushing torrent of water was more than enough for the black birds who took off for the rainforest-garbed gorge. The sun eventually made its way over the rim to warm the pristine waters and provided us with warm rocks on which to thaw out.

Down the road, Wangi Falls was equally spectacular and quite popular due to its easy access. Rainbow bee-eaters, with their colourful plumage, entertained the many swimmers with their swooping antics giving the impression of miniature dive-bombers. We swam the 100 metres to the far side finding a natural rock bath tub, smoothed by time, full of warm water and only a short climb up the steep cliff face.

Camp was set up at the quieter Buley Rockhole, where a series of small waterfalls and rock holes gently cascaded into each other. Total strangers made new friendships drifting from one pool to another. At one point all four of us were in separate pools talking with entirely different people.

That night we sat around a roaring campfire and consumed far too much good red wine that our generous friends had brought with

them. However a mutual agreement was reached that wine indeed gets better with age – the older we get the better it tastes. The night called for a meal with a difference.
Dreamtime Smoked Chicken.

This is an innovative way of appreciating a chook with a difference. It is flavoured with tea leaves, the taste of which deliciously impregnates right through the flesh.
Earl Grey, Irish Breakfast, whatever takes your fancy. Spread the tea leaves,(tea bags definitely wont work) over the bottom of the camp oven about 1-2 centimetres deep. Upturn a couple of metal eggcups or any other tray-like support so the bird is not sitting on the smoking material.
Rub the chicken with sea salt, pepper and brush on some honey. Cook in oven for about 15 minutes then add some more honey. The bird should be well browned off in more ways than one in about 45 minutes and will smell and taste a treat. We served it with a big bowl of healthy salad and a crunchy damper straight out of the coals.

Sitting around the dying embers of the fire, with the night sounds all around us, we chatted about how different this was to the rush of city life. Tony asked if this was a typical camping scenario and we had to laugh when we thought of the diversity of interesting camping spots we had experienced since commencing our trip many months ago. Besides our preferred cliff-tops, beaches and river banks there has been a cemetery, racecourse, monastery, sporting oval, winery, jetty, orchard, pistol club, airport, golf club, rodeo ground, country church yard, luxury hillside housing development and boat harbour, not to forget outback-pub car parks and numerous lookouts. All these places we have called home; even if just for a night.

Mind you, we did come unstuck on one occasion when we were parked on the most idyllic beach imaginable. Contrary to our favoured spots of total seclusion, there was just one house that could glimpse us through the trees. After a lovely dinner, we were nicely settled down watching a movie when there was a loud banging on the door and a very rude and irate local informed us that we could not park there and in fact we were lowering the tone of the place. Morrison took great exception to that comment but he became even more upset when the deranged woman continuously walked round the van banging on his walls. In her mind, she obviously had visions of vagrant gypsy types that were not to be tolerated under any circumstances. She eventually tired of her banging activities and with discretion being the better part of valour, we finished our movie and moved a few kilometres down the beach.

'Kakadont' was a word on the tongues of certain ignoramus grey nomads who suggested that we would have our disappointments if we visited Kakadu National Park, a normally revered part of the Top End. We therefore headed towards this heritage-listed park with a degree of mixed feelings. After eventually spending over a week there it can only be described as a national treasure and I suggest those unappreciative sorts should get a new optometrist, make an appointment with a psycho or spend their holidays going to places like Dreamworld.

The most prized sights imaginable are to be found in this 20,000 square kilometre park and although reasonable distances have to be driven between the numerous highlights, the remarkable wild life, vast picturesque wetlands, exceptional rock art and unforgettable sunsets are rewards worth seeking.

Heritage listed means 'Outstanding Universal Value' and wherever we went, overseas visitors from far away countries, invariably outnumbering the local Aussies, were struck with awe at the sheer beauty.

Tony and Wendy were still with us and regretfully had pre booked at the rather bland crocodile shaped hotel in Jabiru. It somehow did not capture the magic of the park and the only way to determine that it is shaped like a crocodile is to take a helicopter ride over it or buy a postcard, and we had better things to spend our money on. It did though give us a central base making it easy to look around. We spent our nights on the banks of the nearby lake, watching the long files and phalanxes of cackling geese, the heavy flapping of their wings, passing so near and so low, seemingly oblivious to human presence. Whistling ducks in close formation, quacking with the joys of life, joined this orchestration of twilight noises. Sitting under the evening shade of a large coolibah tree, drink in hand, watching the reflections on the water, we felt very Australian and very much at peace with the world.

This proved to be our favourite spot for dinner and in keeping with our Aussie feeling a little bit of roo that had been marinating all afternoon seemed like a good idea.

Kakadu Kangaroo Kebabs

Marinate 1 kg of cubed kangaroo loin or fillet in a mixture of finely chopped onions and tomatoes, plus garlic, half a cup of oil, and a desert spoon of cumin & turmeric, for approximately two hours. Thread meat cubes on to skewers alternating with onion and capsicum pieces.
Pour over marinade and cook on barbecue, turning regularly for approximately 15 mins.
Served with rice and a green side salad it makes an enjoyable light meal.

It was easy to see why Jabiru had won various tidy town competitions. Unlike most towns in the Top End, not a single beer can, nor any rubbish or graffiti was evident, showing an unusual pride by the residents. However the fruit bats, wrapped in their dark capes, perpetually squealing and surrounded by an obnoxious odour, were the big offenders in town. When the smell and noise became intolerable, a line of trees around the police station was drastically chain-sawed in an effort to resolve the problem. The big mob of bats simply squealed with derision and moved on to the next line of trees.

Each evening in contrast to the bats, a million corellas screaming out of tune circle the town in a never-ending procession, slowly disappearing into the setting sun. Friendly Aborigines chatted us up in the street and humbugging wasn't even a consideration. We visited the Sportsman's Club, where the indigenous population congregates and it was difficult to imagine that this area was home to one of Australia's most impoverished communities.

There are two distinct drinking areas in this well-appointed club, which was generously built, like most of the town, specifically for the local community by mining giants Rio Tinto. The outdoor public bar, where most regulars lie around on the concrete floor, shouting and gesticulating with waving arms, was not our preferred choice. The comparatively 'up-market' saloon cum restaurant was quite different. The patrons were reserved and polite with black businessmen socialising in groups. Large-size TV screens, poker machines and a decent menu gave the place some credibility.

Half a dozen elderly black drinkers were having a great time in one corner and although well inebriated, they were not causing any concern at that stage.

Roger the barman was one of the few other white guys in the place, so I asked him whether the group was celebrating anything special, as they seemed to be on a monumental 'high'.

"You see the real old geezer wearing a funny hat and with no teeth. Well, he's nearly 90 and was up in court today accused of trying to rape a young girl in the village" Roger confided as he handed me another drink. "They think the whole episode is hilarious and are celebrating their friend's release." I asked him on what grounds was the case dismissed. "Dunno, suppose the evidence didn't stand up in court " he replied with a knowing smile on his face. This little black furphy, from a white guy with a cold green can, added additional colour to the already hilarious scene.

The nearby Ranger Uranium Mine had brought money and heartbreak, with over 50 million dollars being handed over to the black community in royalties over 20 years. Most of this had vanished and local news reports indicated that the vast majority had been spent on alcohol. Even if they were all really serious drinkers, that is a ton of VB for a community of only 300 members. Other reports suggested that unscrupulous actions of so called white experts and professional advisors had skimmed off many millions for personal gain. I suppose a realistic, unbiased view would be that the white man had his hand out for the greenback and the black fella's hand was on the counter for the green can. Royalties have caused more suffering than they have cured which is a pity as these friendly people deserve better.

There is always a high-spot to any particular area we visit and our foremost memory of Kakadu would have to be the early morning Yellow Waters wetlands cruise. It was advertised as the ultimate wilderness experience and the plethora of wildlife certainly made it just that. Within minutes of boarding our flat bottom boat, our guide pointed out a white bellied sea eagle only metres overhead, that was getting stuck into a substantially large black snake he had just caught. A gory start to an otherwise tranquil morning of closeness to nature. Cold-blooded salties that attack anything with a heartbeat glided past us or lay on nearby banks with unblinking eyes. Beautifully plumed jabarus, graceful brolgas, royal spoonbills and a myriad of other bird life went about their daily quest for survival. Delicate jacans, sometimes called Jesus birds as they appear to walk on water, lightly tread the large waterproof lotus leaves. Carpets of pure white water lilies float as far as the eye can see, contrasting with the bank-fringed clumps of bright pink lotus and the mirror-image tree reflections in the water. Gliding through these melaleuca swamps our guide informed us that this was just a small part of a ten square kilometre landlocked billabong, barely touched by mankind, where nature is raw and the crocodile rules.

Back in the 1950s a young lady was high kicking in the chorus line at the Empire Theatre in Liverpool, England. She got the travel bug and came to Australia to find excitement and a new life. She didn't think much of the southern part of the continent, but on her way home called in to Darwin and met a man who changed her life forever. Tom Opitz was a sort of an early day Crocodile Dundee who loved his showgirl Penny, as much as the unexplored Kakadu that he found so challenging.

They married and in 1964 opened the area's first tourist lodge. In those days, road access was minimal, life could be pretty intimidating, but the sheer beauty of the place was irresistible. Gagadju Cooinda Lodge, which is part of the Yellow Waters operation, was created and has been continually updated and extended since Penny and Tom's early days. Thanks to their pioneering achievements, the whole world can now appreciate this true Eden.

Up to ten years ago these vast wetlands had been desecrated by thousands of water buffalo, imported from Asia in the last century. A government tuberculosis eradication program saw the wisdom of halting the ruination of this eco system by killing 250,000 of these infected beasts along with 400,000 rogue cattle. Since then, flora and fauna have blossomed back to what it was in the days when the Aboriginal hunted with spear and white man was rarely seen. The first white explorer, back in the 1840s, one Ludwig Leichhardt, wrote in his diaries of seeing thousands of black people, spread over large plains and living well off the fruits of the land. How times have changed.

The Aborigines have controlled their land with fire for centuries and over a third of the park is patchwork-burnt annually. It is a burning question and some of those shortsighted greenies from southern states could well learn from these time-proven methods. This is a clear example of dichotomy between black and white men's views on the landscape where the former gets satisfaction and benefits from a recently burned country and the latter purely sees a barren scene of desolation. Fire, like earth, water, air and sunlight is an essential ingredient of Kakadu landscape.

Aboriginal history and culture is evident everywhere, with the various Visitors Centres offering movies and dramatic slides-shows, providing a year round insight into this much acclaimed area and its original people. It is hard to ignore the fact that they are the planets longest continuous culture.

Our last night was spent high on the rocks of Ubirr, watching the brilliant sunset behind the wetlands shimmering in a smoky haze. The smoke from the newly lit fires, drifted over the sweeping views of savannah woodlands and monsoon forests, turning water, sky and land into an interminable red glow. In the distance, the 500 kilometre long escarpment of mysterious Arnhem Land, once an ancient sea cliff, stood formidable. Ubirr is famous for its collection of rock art, which has been debated as the oldest form of human works. The avid rock art admirer can trace over 500 examples in Kakadu with the best selection being here at Ubirr.

Kakadu is a place that exudes peace and harmony with nature, a land of surrealistic strength and high energy, governed by the extremes of Mother Nature, with an overlay of gentleness.

We reluctantly tore ourselves away with Wendy & Tony heading back to Darwin for their flight home to the 'big smoke' and Morrison pointed south towards the historic township of Pine Creek.

This town did not seem to have all that much going for it except for the local Sporting and Golf Club, which was called Pussy Cat Flats. Having a penchant for unusual names, I was intrigued but no one seemed the slightest bit interested about the early-day pussycats of the area. Over a cooling drink in the local, the barman informed me that the name goes back to the 1870s when the first turf meeting in the Territory was held there. And that was it. I was really expecting a more interesting story than that and having little desire to exchange pussy cat jokes with him I bade farewell and we headed south.

There is only one road south out of the Top End and that is back through Katherine. Corroborees are held here on Monday and Wednesday nights and we were keen to witness one of these rarely seen traditional performances. My excited little wife and I joined the queue in anticipation of an evening's cultural awakening.

The sight of 20 lean black bodies, painted with traditional white daubings and dressed only in brief red loincloths and headbands, can be a little daunting as they charge towards you with spears in hand. A crackling fire in the arena centre, haunting didgi-inspired music and a dozen dance routines energetically carried out, proved a winning combination. The Black Cockatoo dancers from the Wugular Community presented traditional dances depicting animals, birds, fish, spirits and weather from their dreamtime stories. The men of the tribe threw themselves into their performance with much gusto and were only upstaged by their youngest member. Chappie was just 18 months old, and with his loincloth just covering his sparkling white nappy, caught everyone's eye and was the focus of the shutterbugs. His little leg and arm movements didn't quite have the energy of his older relatives but he's a quick learner, and once he gets out of those diapers, he'll be hard to hold back.

Spear-throwing demonstrations during the intermission encouraged members of the audience to get involved in this age-old hunting tradition. Needless to say most would have starved to death if they had to rely on their somewhat limited abilities with the long pointed stick.

The whole production was compered by a compelling personality who held everyone's attention like a magnet. This great-looking, charismatic individual with his big smile and flashing white teeth was like a ringmaster in a circus. Being the inquisitive sort of person that I am, a chat with him at the end of the show seemed like a good idea.

Tom E Lewis is a bit of a legend in these parts, partly because of his starring role in the 1970s acclaimed movie, 'The Chant of Jimmy Blacksmith' along with appearances in other productions such as 'We of the Never Never'. But in more recent times it is for his involvement in the awareness and appreciation of aboriginal folklore and customs that makes him the centre of attention.

His wife Fleur, a good sort by anyone's standards, whose translucent pale skin contrasted dramatically with his so dark, kindly invited us to 'pop over' for coffee at their place next day. 'Their place' was a community only 100 kilometres out of Katherine in the direction we were heading. "Just 50 down the highway, turn left and another 50 down a dirt road" she smiled as they shot off at a great pace in their nifty 4WD.

Beswick is about the size of a mossie dropping on the map and even before we left the highway, we had a gut feeling that our adventure was about to unfold into something quite special. A whole chapter could be appropriated to the events of the following five days, which would envelop this small, family-orientated, 300 strong community as never before.

On the approach to town, a roadside sign indicated that anyone carrying alcohol could end up in the slammer for six months.

How to conceal cartons of wine and beer in the comparatively limited space of a motorhome was our first challenge. The camouflaging efforts proved unnecessary, but enjoying an alcoholic drink was advisable only with discretion, in order not to flaunt the rules of the community.

This dusty little village held a few surprises. An interesting set of young white people, mainly from Melbourne drifted in and out of Tom and Fleur's house, while we sipped away at coffee that was well worth the 100-kilometre drive. An unusual display of musical instruments lay scattered everywhere while large signs and posters were being designed and painted.

Donald, who was Tom's father, was a wizened old elder whose two remaining teeth shone like beacons whenever he broke into one of his guttural laughing sessions. This happened often and for no apparent reason but certainly brought humour to the gathering. He was given a pot of black paint and started to draw images of fire-dogs on to wire netting squares.

It transpired that preparations were afoot for a very special occasion that we would be privileged to share.

Our one-day visit turned into five as Tom proudly showed us his land and talked about ancestral traditions. A 20 minute drive, at breakneck speed down a winding dirt road, brought us to a natural amphitheatre formed by a backdrop of beautifully coloured sandstone cliffs, dropping into a clear lake bounded by sandy beaches and dunes. At the far end a pretty waterfall tumbled down into a smaller pool before cascading into the main lake. This revered place where few outsiders have previously set foot, was to be the ethereal venue for Tom's long planned 'Walking with Spirits' production. Funding and support by the Australia Council for the Arts, Fred Hollows Foundation and Department of Arts and Museums had been acquired and it was to be part of the Festival of Darwin. Tom and Fleur had 18 months planning behind them to ensure the success of this very special project

Of all Tom's numerous acting parts over the years, his didgi playing days in classical and jazz venues around Europe, his greatest honour was being chosen to carry the Olympic torch around his beloved St

Kilda. But few achievements in Tom's life would compare with the cultural importance of this event.

Fleur had been the boss girl of a successful production company called Handspan in Melbourne for many years, and had discarded her corporate suits, nylons and high heels for a life in the outback. It was her contacts and dedication to the organisational side of this event that would help fulfill Tom's dream.

In the days preceding the occasion there was a hive of activity with dozens of black bodies carrying stages, lighting, equipment and the like across streams and sand, to prepare for the village's most significant event. Working for the dole, regardless of colour, creed or location was alive and well, even in outback whoop whoop, and these proud young fellas were enjoying every moment.

Dry, dusty Beswick is typical of many Aboriginal communities where, due to bureaucratical bungling over the last century, mobs of people from various tribes have been resettled together, without thought being given to their different cultures and way of life. These traditions that had been built up over the centuries are often poles apart and in many cases do not blend. Happily, the people of Beswick seem to have overcome these differences and live in relative harmony.

There is a shop, which opens for a few hours a day, an active school for the kids, council office, sporting ground and basic medical centre. And then there's the beer garden. Open for two hours a day, there are very strict rules here. Four cans for the ladies, six for the guys, ordered one at a time and that is the maximum per day. If they don't behave and fall about or argue then they are on the black list. Get themselves into a punch up and the committee has been known to hand out a life ban. Normally it's a week off the grog for first time offenders and a warning. We queued up with the locals and got our limited quota, handed through small openings in a grilled wall. Locals continually came up to us introducing themselves, asking our names and wanting to chat on about the basics of life. These were real down to earth nice people, accepting their lot in life, without wrath or retribution.

We saw peculiar looks in their faces as they asked why we had choosen to spend our nights out in an area that was wild buffalo country. " You's gotta be mad fella" said a crinkly faced octogenarian with white straggly hair and just the one middle tooth. " One charge and you guys gonna be gone" he confided, as though he had survived a 1000 experiences. The buffaloes didn't materialise, the braying feral donkeys were there each night and we felt sorry for the locals, whose gardens were regularly desecrated by feral pigs, rooting all about. Fay choked on her third warm VB of the night when the old fella told her the river we had been swimming in was crocodile infested. Now these guys had a good sense of humour and it took awhile before we realised that there is a special indigenous way to take the piss out of strangers.

The night everyone was waiting for finally arrived, with a cast of hundreds and an audience of just as many; 'Walking with the Spirits' was about to begin.

Hundreds of candles floated with divinity across the motionless lake, silhouetted figures mingled around campfires on the sand dunes, spotlights searched the crevices of high rocks and haunting didgi sounds emerged from the stage.

Tom E was rocking, introducing village talent, singing traditional and contemporary music with his Melbourne musician mates and welcoming the likes of 60 Minute's Jeff McMullen, who had quietly slipped in and was ensconced on the warm sand.

It was a theatrical journey, fusing dreamtime stories and modern history bringing together local performers in a rich and stirring production.

Spirit stories still abound in these villages but current ones are more believable than those from prehistoric times. Strange evening noises emitting from the surrounding forest alarmed some of the old folk a few years ago. As they lay in their beds at night, these previously unheard sounds were quite different to any living creature they had encountered. The Queensland Cane Toad had arrived for the first time and was beginning its journey of destruction. Now this was a long hop from the toad's original interstate base, but with the help of a few road trains, this little mongrel monster has created a new foothold in the Territory to spread his poison into the local wildlife.

We welcomed a surprising farewell gift of a superbly sculptured crocodile from the happy Donald, who had taken a bit of a shine to

Fay. Between his uncontrollable laughing bouts, he had taken a one and a half metre piece of kapok tree and shaved a beautiful crafted reptile for us. A donation to his favourite charity was duly provided. We left Beswick with a fondness for the people, and a far better understanding of their way of life.

The sign said Welcome to Mataranka home of ' We of the Never Never'. Besides being the location for the film of the same name, this past tidy town is only famous for a couple of other things. Meat Pies and Hot Springs, and it's not really good etiquette to appreciate the two at the same time.

Kelly's Pies are advertised as 'big enough to fill a bull', which is no bullshit as they stand about four inches high and are full of huge chunks of the best local beef. The pies are made in small batches in the back room of the service station and sell like proverbial 'hot cakes'. As the nearby heritage pub was unfortunately right out of pies when we ordered our beer, I had no choice but to slip down to the servo and ended up carrying them back along the main road. Perched on their plastic plates, they held together as the road trains thundered past.

Now the Hot Thermal Springs are a different ball game. Participating in something similar to a 'grey nomads' swimming carnival at a crowded municipal baths does not turn me on at all. It was shoulder to shoulder stuff at the well advertised Homestead Springs with plenty of chit chat for many, while others just stood quietly submerged in the warm waters in some sort of contrived spiritual ecstasy.

Unfortunately, I was trapped in conversation by a loud-mouthed southern belle from Kentucky, who was so boring she made me feel like I had wasted a whole day in only ten minutes. In our seemingly interminable conversation where I found it hard to get a word in at all, she appeared to have the answer to everything and the solution to nothing. Then the tour bus arrived and it was definitely time to move on. We departed leaving a small area for the coachload of enthusiastic, athletic looking-types who had been cooped up like chickens for the last few hours.

Just as we were thinking that the delights of hot springs were a waste of time, we remembered hearing about a less commercial situation on the other side of town. In contrast, the picturesque Bitter Springs, was a delight. Surrounded by bullrushes, pandanus, paperbarks and towering cabbage palms it exuded the tranquility we had been imagining. Thermal spring water combined with dissolved limestone created a crystal clear, translucent effect, which magically enhanced the colours of the green mosses and shiny pebbles underfoot.

We swam in a liquid heaven of warm 34 degree water, snaking through winding passageways, with not a living thing in sight, except the brilliantly coloured crimson finches that flirted on the water's edge.

It was Sunday and we had a few 'household' chores needing attention. Mataranka seemed to be suffering from a lack of interest, and it appeared that the whole town was either 'for sale', or not particularly keen to do business on The Sabbath. Given that tourism was one of the main sources of income, it was somewhat surprising.

It was, however, refreshing to sit down and sensibly converse with one local who appeared somewhat out of place here. He had spent a lifetime repairing ocean-going cruisers in Port Douglas, which was a far cry from running an art gallery and coffee shop in downtown Mataranka. Ian, who owns the Stockyard Gallery, travelled as far as he reasonably could, hoping his third wife wouldn't track him down here and settled in with his new partner, quickly adjusting to outback life.

I sympathised with his marital problems and told him about a friend of ours who had been divorced for many years, yet his ex-wife kept reappearing at the most inconvenient times, seemingly forgetting they had gone their separate ways. She had achieved the nickname of 'Thrush' as she proved to be quite irritating and hard to get rid of.

Wonderful aromatic smells wafted up from the plunger and we realised how much we needed a coffee hit. We were rewarded with one of the best brews we had tasted in months and were intrigued to find that it was in fact Byron Bay Coffee, produced only a few kilometres from our home. Appreciating the coincidence, Ian talked about some of the fascinating people that have passed through this quaint little town.

"The most interesting", he enthused, "Was a guy who was riding around Australia on a lawn mower". It appeared this old codger suddenly found himself a grieving widower with nothing to do. Wanting to raise money for charity, he jumped on a John Deere and was prepared to devote a couple of years of his life in helping those with problems greater than his. Now why can't more people have that attitude of adventure, instead of feeling sorry for themselves and rotting away like a couch potato in front of the TV every day.

Suddenly our host was in demand. A coach load of Europeans arrived wanting to be relieved of some currency in exchange for food, coffee and outback art. What better place could they have chosen in Mataranka?

The road heading south was repetitiously monotonous. There are legs and there are legs. The tanned, shapely one stretched out on the dashboard next to me was proving a minor distraction given there was nothing much else to look at. Its owner was fastidiously scrubbing, oiling and pampering it, just like a bird going through a preening process. It was hard to concentrate on the shimmering white line in front of me.

I was jolted back to full attention by the snake-like trails of zig zag tyre marks on the tarmac. Obviously caused by an overtired road-train driver, evading some impending disaster by seconds. Not wanting to be another statistic, I told myself to concentrate. Dry, parched fields screaming for water stretched as far as the eye could see. The effects of the drought were very obvious here and who knows how long it was since the last drop fell.

We pulled into Daly Waters for the night. The only reason to stop here is to visit the renowned pub for a drink and to enjoy the outrageous memorabilia covering the walls and ceiling. It really is a classic of its kind. There's an old ceramic bathtub full of muddy water on the footpath; a veritable trap for the unwary patron with too many drinks under his belt. The set of traffic lights on the road outside are constantly on red and the regulars love to have bets on how long the gullible newcomers will sit there waiting for them to turn green.

Characters drape themselves over the bar at night; sweat-stained

Akubras, shorts and singlets well overdue for a wash, and dust-covered boots typified these thirsty outback drinkers.

Looking at these prodigious imbibers I pondered upon the various preferred ales and the differing manners in which they are served from state to state. A 200ml (7oz), preferred by some ladies, is called a glass in Victoria and Queensland, a butcher in SA and a beer in WA and NSW. The most popular 285ml (10 oz) is a pot in Victoria and Queensland, a schooner in SA, a handle in the Territory and a middy in NSW and WA.. A 425ml (15oz) is a schooner in NSW & NT and a pint everywhere else. Must be rather confusing for overseas visitors who love their beer but are not quite sure what to order.

Which forces many to say "I'll have what he's having".

Sometimes its hard to work out a bloke until he's had a couple of schooners and the nice young chap on our right was a perfect example of that theory. We'll call him Frank for fear of retribution. Although he had a responsible government job in water management, he boasted to us that his main goal in life was to see every Aboriginal lined up and shot. Drinking companions like that I do not need and Fay was so incensed that she was starting to get a bit 'hot under the collar' so I dragged her off to bed before an unwelcome confrontation eventuated.

The ongoing road to Tennant Creek, was equally humdrum, much of it scrubby, stony, mongrel country. Imagine how much more challenging this tedious stretch would be with just two wheels and a pair of pedals.

It has always intrigued me when I see a cyclist, sweating it out under the midday sun, hundreds of kilometres from anywhere. Particularly if she is a top looking female. Jodie welcomed the break for a chat as we pulled up in front of her, and didn't have a bead of sweat on her tanned face. She was on the last few weeks of one mother of a marathon ride from London to her home in Melbourne. Both she and her boyfriend who we encountered a little further down the road had our total admiration. "When Michael and I first met a few years ago in the US, he asked me to go for a bit of a bike ride and that lasted seven months" she recalled.

On this marathon, they left the UK and have travelled about 30,000 kilometres through Europe and Asia with a million memories collected along the way. "We try to average 120 kilometres a day and prefer riding early morning and evening, but this headwind has slowed us right down, so we've taken to riding under a full moon at night and camping during the day". The amazing part of this story is the fact that their family homes are within a kilometre of each other back in Melbourne. So it will be a couple of very excited Mums waiting for them on a cold Victorian morning in September, when their bikes will be given a big rest and they can plan their next adventure.

Long distance cycling is a form of addiction that only the very disciplined can contemplate and accomplish. I'm in the vast majority of those who gaze in amazement at these dedicated achievers, preferring slightly less exerting challenges.

A good selection of CDs, talking books and tapes are high on the list of requirements for travellers in these outback areas. Radio reception is minimal and if you're lucky, one single channel might bring you a little light relief. It was Sunday afternoon, and guess what the locals look forward to every week. The bloody Goon Show. It was 30 or even 40years ago I regularly enjoyed the antics of Sellers, Seacombe, Milligan and the machinations of Colonel Bloodnock, Moriarty, Neddy Seagoon and company. But some things just haven't changed here in the Territory and the Goons are still the big drawcard on Sunday arvo radio.

What can I say about Tennant Creek? It is certainly not the sort of place where the astute buyer would want to consider investing in real estate. There is a sense of restlessness, mobs wandering aimlessly around town, empty forlorn looking shops and graffiti covered buildings, making the place a tad sorry for itself.

Our solitary evening was spent at a lookout, high over the town, offering 360-degree views and just one more stunning sunset, which was followed the next morning by an equally impressive sunrise.

We stocked up with food supplies and at the same time endevoured to buy a simple firelighter, the type used to ignite an emission of gas or even light a fire. Not normally a difficult item to purchase, but all the shops were right out of stock. The last shopkeeper, who had a permanent grin on his face, as though he knew something that I didn't, suggested that they were far more preferable to matches. "Some of the uncontrollable kids in town use them when they are burning houses down" he grinned, "and that's why there's a current shortage of stock". It appeared a few houses had, in fact, been razed to the ground recently, so he could well have been telling the truth.

July and August had been a wonderful point in time to be in The Territory. The flawless blue winter skies unfailingly delivered warm days designed for easy living, while the cool nights bedded us down to comfortable sleeps. The unparalleled wild life, diversely dramatic scenery and warmth of the people still make it one of Australia's best kept secrets.

As they say in their well worded advertising "If you never never go, you 'll never never know".

CHAPTER TWELVE

SUNSETS OVER SAVANNAH GRASSES

The Queensland border was fast approaching. On either side, interminable bleached pastureland, flat as a billiard table, vanished into the deep blue horizon. Nothing seemed to be alive except the thousands upon thousands of grazing cattle. Mobs of big brown healthy looking beasts, Santa Gertrudis and Droughtmasters were everywhere. The Barkly Tablelands, although seemingly dead to the ignorant eye, are among the best grazing pastures in Australia, the scrubby grasses providing all the trace elements to make any cow revel in its good fortune at being there.

We hadn't seen a drop of rain for months, water falling from the sky was about as unlikely as an English batsman getting his nose burnt, so the formidable bank of black clouds lined up along the state dividing line seemed to be a bit out of the ordinary.

The sun was about to retire for the day as we drove into the quaint historic township of Camooweal. An old bewhiskered chap, whose black shining features were overshadowed by his gleaming white ten-gallon hat, limped over towards us to chew the fat. 'Grey nomad' bush telegraph had suggested there was a nearby riverside camping place. He knew the exact spot, and with a beaming smile through his remaining couple of blackened teeth, he pointed a gnarled finger down the road from where we had driven.

We camped on the banks of this glass-like river just out of town, shaded by paperbarks, the site only needing our glowing fire to make it verging on perfection. In the following early morning light, dozens of graceful long legged brolgas strutted about the shallow waters like players in some dreamtime story. A myriad of other winged life was going about their daily business, gliding, swooping, flitting, making all sorts of bird noises. Around our site feral pigs had been silently rooting about during the night, leaving hog holes in the mud as big as the inquisitive calves that grazed by. As we took our morning constitutional along the riverbank, we congratulated ourselves on finding such a top spot in an otherwise fairly desolate quarter.

Camooweal is one of many towns we came across where most of the real estate, and some of the businesses have been bought up by the Aboriginal community. Locals we talked to just shrugged their shoulders, and with a veiled smile accepted these are changing times. Old timers, who built these towns in the days when horses were the main form of transport, now pay rent to the black community. Throughout the northern part of Australia, it was noticeable that very few Aborigines were seen to be working in the shops. We initially thought they might be unemployable, or simply just not interested in furthering themselves. However putting them behind a cash register can cause a few nightmares for the proprietor. Tribal customs are such that the employee is obligated to hand over, without payment, any goods that certain esteemed relatives may request. Refusal can have disastrous consequences. White owners of such places as supermarkets, gas stations and the like could have some glaring imbalances when they do their stock takes, with annual returns to the ATO verging on the farcical.

216

Huge road trains, up to 60 metres long, carriers of cattle, petroleum, and a range of produce thundered by as we headed to Mount Isa. These guys take no prisoners and hold their own on the often single-track highways, offering little alternative to oncoming motorists but to move off to the dirt shoulder. We regularly pulled over, slowed right down and held on for the buffeting wind and vibrations from these monsters, sweeping past with barely a metre to spare.

Low hills surrounded us, with snappy gums marching in formation over the scraggy country which opened up to vast grasslands, water holes and limestone caves.

Northwest Queensland is a vast panorama of pastoral and mineral wealth and the tide of tourism is slowly flowing into this most remote of Australian regions.

We increasingly noticed the almost indolent gestures of the finger wave from the steering wheels of passing vehicles. Equally laconic welcomes to the great Outback were repeatedly noticed in pubs, shops, in fact almost everywhere, showing a laid back friendliness that typifies this part of Oz.

A roadside sign proudly proclaimed 'You're not a true blue Aussie, till you've been to the Isa'. Although it's a city of just over 20,000 people it really is just a big friendly Queensland country town. It is somewhat of an oasis, standing among the ochre-red Selwyn Ranges and nestled along the banks of the Leichhardt River. Surrounded by desert, savannah and rich pastoral grasslands, the Isa is now a far cry from the raw frontier town of years past. It is certainly not what you would call typically Australian, but there again what is typical in this hugely diversified continent?

'Her Outdoors' has an alarming penchant for going underground whenever possible and went into a temporary state of depression when she was informed that tours of the mine had to be booked three days in advance. We had friends who were told it was booked out for weeks. This peculiar arrangement couldn't quite be explained properly by the sour young girl at the visitor centre who was obviously not having a good day. There must be a multitude of disappointed visitors who only stay for a day or two and are thwarted in their desires to 'go down'.

However, it was Fay's birthday, so as a very special treat, besides the multitudinous gifts and champagne that I showered her with in bed that morning, I suggested a visit to one of Isa's highly recommended clubs for lunch. I mean, what more could a girl ask for, especially as we had been bush for much of the last few months. Air-conditioned comfort, gaudy carpets, flashing lights everywhere and beaming bar girls. When asked for a Long Island Tea, one of my birthday girl's favourites, the young filly behind the bar grinned even more at this rare challenge to make a cocktail that virtually contains everything but the kitchen sink. Five different white spirits for starters. The locals downing their XXXX beers just looked on in awe.

After the comparatively high prices of the Top End, $50 for our various drinks, a good bottle of red, huge T-bones and all the accompaniments we could eat, seemed an exceptionally good deal.

It must have been a long time since I played the pokies. In fact I remember half the pleasure was exerting just enough pressure on the handle to pull an irregular supply of winnings. Imagine my surprise to see no handles at all, just bloody boring buttons to press, providing minimal interaction with these coin-sucking monstrosities. Changing technology can often defeat the pleasure in the way money is lost.

The mining industry is omnipresent in The Isa. Towering over the community like some huge phallic symbol, emitting thick grey vapour into the bright blue sky, is the 270-metre exhaust stack, reminding all and sundry that this is predominately a big industrial community. Being one of the world's top producers of silver, copper and zinc apparently hasn't changed the place over the years. Most people seemed to be pretty friendly and living in the 'small smoke' didn't seem to be a bad way of life to them.

This was the first place where we actually camped at a cemetery. Not exactly resting in peace next to the headstones, but right outside the entrance on a lovely grassy block of dirt, under the shade of cascading weeping willows. The Wall of Remembrance was metres away while the bright colours of the fresh flowers on the graves, a soft breeze blowing through the trees, and the subdued whistling of the birds, presented a quiet, serene setting.

The distinct difference about the feel of each state was more pronounced in Queensland than anywhere else. I'm not sure if it is the style of the buildings, with their combinations of timber and wriggly tin, often raised high from the ground and normally surrounded by wide verandahs, or the broad boulevard style streets of the country towns or the friendly disposition of the people. Probably a little of each. It was noticeable that the cost of petrol and general shopping items were mostly less expensive, compared with the Top End. Television and radio reception dramatically improved and there are many more Sunday afternoon alternatives to listening to the Goon Show. And most people drink nothing else but the locally brewed XXXX.

The vagaries of travelling were never more apparent than in Cloncurry where we pulled Morrison into the Mary Kathleen Park to the applause and incredulous laughter from Tony and Karen, a couple we first met early in the year just out of Perth. They then continued to mysteriously materialise in no fewer than half a dozen of the most unusual places during the following four months. Our travel routes were quite different, yet our paths continued to cross over half the continent.

Cloncurry has the dubious distinction of having the highest temperature ever recorded in Australia. It was a long time ago, just before the turn of last century, when the thermometer hit a blistering 54.1 degrees. "Last Xmas Day, wasn't too bad, it was only 46 degrees" smiled the lady from the Visitor Centre. At least she had air conditioning blasting away all day, which wasn't even on the inventor's agenda back in those early pioneering days.

But Cloncurry's main claim to fame, is its association with the Royal Flying Doctor Service, which was born here. The Reverend John Flynn first ventured into the desolate outback in 1912, primarily to preach and to help locals that had been stricken by illness or accident. Over the ensuing years, he had a burning desire to utilise the aeroplane to bring quick medical aid in times of trouble. His vision was to provide the outback with two desperately needed services, a doctor with wings and wireless communication.

Back in those days, airplanes were still a sideshow wonder, while small transmitters and receivers had not yet been manufactured. It took 20 years, a lot of faith in God and some assistance from the founder of Qantas, Hudson Fysh, before his dream was realised. In 1933,'The Victory', a single engine DH50 aircraft took off with a doctor on board, on its first mission.

"The single greatest achievement to the settlement of the outback" quoted Sir Robert Menzies. Today, 39 aircraft operate from 20 bases, flying over 11 million kilometres each year, serving the inhabitants of two thirds of the continent. Free medical attention is brought to 160,000 patients with over 17,000 transported to hospital annually. The memory of the much-revered John Flynn will remain in the hearts of outback people for an eternity.

The wry Queensland humour is never far away, even though the heat, flies and dust are ever present. I asked an old timer at the post office if this 'Dry' season was typical for this time of the year.

"Not on your life son" he drawled through ginger whiskers and a face so full of pitted lines I thought pieces might fall off. "I remember a time when it was so dry I had no choice but to staple the stamps on the envelopes". He looked at me with quizzically raised eyebrows but not a flicker of a smile, and I wondered if that's what could be termed as 'going troppo'. I was thinking of asking him if there was any truth in the rumour that due to the lack of rain, the dairy cows around here were squirting powdered milk, but thought better of the idea.

Properties in this part of the world can be pretty desolate and lonely, particularly when living alone. A well known farmer in his 50s, whose name I will not divulge, single handedly operates a huge spread about 100 kilometres out of town, his wife having tragically died a couple of years before. He was sitting on his verandah one night in the old family rocking chair, reminiscing about the past when a trail of dust appeared on the horizon. His next door neighbour who he had never met, had driven over from his own spread which was a fair distance away on the other side of the range.

" Having a party New Years Eve" the stranger called "There will be lots of drinking and eating, a bit of dancing and after all that, maybe a bit of sex; wanna come"? The widower gazed back, thought awhile, and slowly accepted the invitation asking his neighbour what he should bring with him. The thought of celebrating the dawning of an other year by himself did not appeal at all.

"Ah, don't worry too much" he shouted back across the fence, "there'll only be the two of us".

Such is life in the vast outback, but sometimes it is difficult to tell the degree of truth when listening to these stories from a stranger on a barstool.

We turned north in the general direction of The Gulf, along the Matilda Highway, named in honour of our national song, Waltzing Matilda. Back in the 1890s, A.B.'Banjo' Paterson passed along here and would never have dreamed that his writings would have continued their popularity into the following century.

Mobs of emus spread across the scrubby pasturelands. These big birds had been inquisitively watching us go by since we hit the outback months ago. Watching them in their wild habitat, it is hard to comprehend the amount of research that has been undertaken in assessing the value-added products these birds are capable of supplying. Ten kilograms of reduced fat makes seven litres of oil which is rich in vitamin E and oleic acid, while the 15 kilograms of dark red steak-like meat is gaining popularity as gourmet food. Two metres of leather are turned into a few handbags, belts and shoes. Emu feathers are becoming a fashion statement while egg painting and carving is a popular art form. The aborigines may not have been making emu omelettes and scrambled eggs, but they worked out that the remedial properties of the oil proved very useful when it came to resolving joint and muscle pains.

When is a town not a town? Answer. When it is a pub. I have heard of one-horse towns before, but little old Quamby with a total population of just five is nothing else but just a simple country watering hole. The Albert Hotel, which used to be the Customs house to a busy mining community is all that is left standing of what was once a prosperous gold mining and cattle fattening town. One blink and it was gone.

It is not uncommon to notice pre-loved cars, often deserted by their owners lying by the side of the road. In most cases, these vehicles have passed their use-by date and have given up the ghost and been left to rot. On some occasions though the occupants are still about, tinkering around with their mode of transport, wondering why it has suddenly decided to discontinue its journey. Some of these dusky characters are still a little confused about the necessity of petrol, oil and water in order to facilitate the functioning of the engine. These important ingredients are often poured into the wrong places with disastrous results. They go for long joy rides, oblivious to the details of the various dashboard gauges. The tank, radiator and sump are often found wanting and that's when the fun starts. After using all their concentrated efforts on resolving the problem without any degree of success, flagging down oncoming motorists is their only alternative.

Alarming thoughts race through the minds of the average motorist, as they approach these often excited occupants who stand in the middle of the road frantically waving their arms. Common sense says put your foot down and most travellers do.

Jill and Stewart were a young couple from Hobart, who were taking a year off to see the big outback and their emotions overcame reason when half a dozen fellas persuaded them to pull over. The open-backed truck was full of supplies for their community, and they were amazed to find the petrol tank was empty. Big smiles all round when our Tasmanian friends agreed to tow them along the highway to the next Roadhouse. After 120 kilometres the smiles had long disappeared from the faces of the good samaritans, although the guys being towed were having a bonza time. Downing a few green cans while they were being towed was all part of the fun.

Despite pleadings from the now intoxicated revelers, our young couple decided that another 100 kilometres of bushbashing across deserted scrub to a faraway community was asking too much. Amid protests the towrope was packed away and they drove off, leaving the disgruntled and inebriated figures lying next to empty VB cartons to contemplate their next move.

The tiny settlement of Gregory, or as some maps indicate Gregory Downs, consists of a pub, general store and a few assorted buildings. The sign on the gate to Billy Hangers General Store states 'You keep your pets out of my yard and I'll keep my bullets out of your pets'. Now that's a real nice country welcome and a clear warning to any inquisitive pooches in need of a leak or a few sniffs after a long journey.

Seems to be working, cause the mild mannered Murray, who owns the joint, hasn't grabbed his gun in years. Doesn't even look as if he has the temperament for anything more strenuous than taking your money and nodding g'day. But he has got a very dry sort of humour, and it took us several visits to the shop to realise that Billy Hangar is not an early pioneer nor even a person of particular note. It's a piece of equipment, which he just happens to sell in the shop, which supports a billy over a fire.

This place was one of the big surprises of the trip – we came for an overnight and stayed a week. Campers grab the dozens of dress-circle positions that hug the twisting banks of the fast moving Gregory River and we were fortunate enough to slip into one of these prized spots. The gurgling waters raced around the hairpin bends only metres from where we slept. Wild life in the trees and on the ground was ever-present. Smoke drifts from the campfires dotted along the banks at twilight time. The pristine beauty of this haven is the big drawcard, but it is the eclectic mix of visitors that creates the atmosphere that makes everyone 'linger longer'. It's a social gathering point and kindred souls that meet along the byways sparingly pass on its whereabouts. They were not what could be called a typical camping crowd, but in this magical place, new friendships were easily forged. An ever-changing mix of early-retired professionals, adventurous couples some with young kids at heel, solo eccentrics and colourful characters. All ages, different backgrounds and everyone interested in conversational interaction.

Tiah was just four years old, big brown eyes, cascading auburn locks and a beaming smile. Already a dab hand with the family video camera she was also a budding stalker, who loved following her daredevil dad through the bush in search of wildlife.

Father Lance recalled "Only last week, not far from here I came across some young feral piglets and pointing them out to Tiah, suggested she film me catching one". Worried about Mother Piggy's return while dad was wrestling with the little porkers, she forgot her filming duties and recorded nothing but a whole lot of soil and sky, while standing transfixed at dad chasing and wrestling in the dirt for their dinner.

Lance, his lovely wife Lee and two young siblings are not your average family. They have an amazing interaction with wildlife, which started when Lance was shearing sheep, cracking whips and working with dogs and horses in 'Australia's Wonderland' in Sydney's South Western suburbs. The family is on the road now in an old Bedford Bus, going round the country getting to know 'real people' and fine-tune their love of the outback.

The day we arrived, he had just shot a 50 kilogramme black boar with his bow and arrow after his two working dogs had cornered it. Like the Pied Piper, he was followed back to the killing field by 20 or more fellow campers, wanting to witness the gruesome gutting and quartering. That night everyone dined on roast pork around the campfire. It was an evening to remember, but we all had to 'sing for our supper' with everyone required to tell a yarn after dinner.

When one storyteller stood up and mentioned that Nike had recently introduced a new ladies running shoe called Dyke, which featured a six inch tongue and a one finger pull-on grip, a little old lady looked totally bewildered and shouted 'Please Explain'. This bought more laughter than the actual joke and the little old lady thought it time for her to go to bed.

An indulgent afternoon drink at the pub seemed like a good idea so we cycled up. The place deserted except for a female body lying behind the bar on a make shift bed. Her bleary eyes were glued to a ceiling television watching the footy. Thighs apart, arms outstretched, this18 stone lump of outback femininity was only interested in the rugby match and recovering from the previous night's hangover. A large blackboard on the adjacent wall indicated 'Only 35 days to go'. It transpired that the overworked manageress had an urgent desire to find greener pastures and this was the countdown. The last five years had seen Wendee dancing on the bar, sorting out the drunks, retrieving stolen produce and turning a run-down pub into one of the best drinking holes around. God only knows where she is today but she'll be having fun somewhere.

Apart from running the general store, Murray has a small canoeing business and dropped us 15 kilometres upstream to spend one of the most memorable days imaginable, canoeing down the tree fringed Gregory River.

Every Autumn over 200 entrants arrive for the Gregory River Canoeing Classic and paddle their way over 42 kilometres in under four hours. We were slightly less ambitious but still felt pretty daring up here all on our own. We got a thorough dunking on the first fast turn, which flipped the canoe right over as it slammed into thick undergrowth. Hurtling through swift moving rapids, we lost control on numerous occasions, spinning into clumps of prickly pandanus, and smacking into unyielding riverbanks.

Lack of coordination between front and back paddler can severely test the strength of any marriage or relationship. Particularly when my partner at the front was having difficulty differentiating between her left and right. Regaining composure after a rough start, we eventually drifted into interconnecting lakes of unspoiled beauty with the perfectly reproduced reflections of foliage and trees imposed on the motionless waters. Crimson finches, purple crowned wrens and azure kingfishers flitted from tree to tree. As the regular visitors rarely venture this far upstream, there was a feeling of trespassing into their private paradise. We skinny-dipped in the crystal clear waters remote from the outside world.

Six hours later, we emerged relatively unscathed but soaked to the skin, as the last rapid directed us straight to our riverbank where a rather concerned Morrison was waiting for us.

It had been one of our favourite camping spots but eventually we made the decision to drag ourselves away from this isolated paradise.

We were up at sparrows leaving with indelible memories saved in our mental computers. The early dawn is a quiet reflective time of the day. Time that gives space to contemplate on the simple things of life. The outback roads were deserted with wild life just awakening to a new day.

Large birds, bustards, emus and brolgas stood motionless as we sped by, gazing at us as though we were disturbing their solitude. Birds of prey were circling over a large black porker that had come off second best to a night vehicle. Mobs of droopy-eared cattle crossed in front of us, oblivious to our presence. Bleached yellow grasses stretched forever to the far horizons with the ever-present cities of fine sculptured termite hills peeping through.

Only a couple of rigs passed us before we arrived at the isolated Burke and Wills Roadhouse, where a lady who appeared to be of some importance, was busy padlocking and unpadlocking her pumps between each motorist's arrival and departure.

" Don't trust anyone" she growled, "'Specially after a couple of hoons filled up and pissed off without me getting their rego".

There wasn't the same sort of welcome when Burke & Wills and their ill-fated expedition stopped near here way back in 1861. And it was another 100 years before any thought was put into establishing a network of roads in the area. The subsequent Beef Road Scheme was built primarily to assist the transporting and exporting of cattle. The isolation, heat, monsoon rains, working conditions and lack of capital proved one hell of a challenge to those hard working Queenslanders. Thousands of kilometres of single-lane roads, peculiar to this State, are still waiting to be upgraded, making the network vastly inferior to any other road system in the country.

A big sign here proclaims 'Burke Shire an unchanged wilderness area, a forgotten land that still reverberates with the sound of loneliness, the drovers stock whip and the didgeridoo'. How apt a description.

Carpentaria Shire covers a vast area of mostly tedious savannah grasslands with only two dots on the map. The townships of Normanton and Karumba share this Shire but are like chalk and cheese.

I visited Normanton 12 years ago with a Variety Club Bash and about the only thing I could recall about the place was a garishly painted pub full of very inebriated revellers. Mind you, that could be said about most places where the bashers gathered after a hard day collecting monies for this very worthwhile charity.

The Purple Pub was still there and can't be missed, not because of its position on the main street, but for the outlandish paint job and the characters lolling around on the veranda. Rows of worn-out wide-brimmed bushman's hats lined the bar as though they were in a competition for the tattiest hat in town. Empty glasses were refilled within seconds of being emptied, and there appeared to be an air of urgency in the way they downed their drinks. Cattle skulls painted in purples and pinks hung from the bar, while mounted boars teeth, guns, boomerangs, turtle shells, dilapidated saddles and riding equipment adorned the peeling walls. Faded newspaper clippings told of times when punch-ups in the main street and 'men's talk' about wrestling with crocs, would not have raised an eyebrow. Country music blasts from screens on the walls. Blacks, whites and every colour between were lined up side by side on their barstools, in various states of intoxication.

DIPLOMACY IS THE ART OF TELLING SOMEONE TO GO TO HELL IN SUCH AWAY THEY ARE LOOKING FOWARD TO THE TRIP, was scrawled in purple crayon on a rough notice board. This place was jammed full of character and everyone wanted to have a chat with a stranger. Welcome to the Gulf Country.

Normanton also has some lovely old buildings, a gaol, museum, a couple of other interesting drinking spots, and an historical railway that is a big turn-on for train buffs. Of more interest to me were the pet brolgas in the station garden. Gregory and Mrs. Peck, how about that for innovative christening, strutted their pencil thin legs, and enjoyed being hand-fed. Their orange bonnets radiated around their inquisitive faces and combined with their silvery grey plumage, produced one of natures many wonders. For the princely sum of one dollar Fay bought herself a part ownership of this quite magnificent pair, with monies paid going to the local hospital.

A replica of the biggest croc ever killed, over 28 feet in old terminology, lies in the main street amid controversy as to whether it was actually shot or captured. Who cares? For some reason the council prefer the latter, while the lady captor, called Christine, who still lives in Mareeba on the Atherton Tableland, clearly remembers putting a bullet straight through its brain. Krys is awesome, he's got plenty of room inside him for a family of four and although only a replica, his monstrous jaws provided a clear reminder to be careful whenever approaching the rivers around here.

The dirty brown water of the Norman River flows alongside the town, with salties aplenty hiding under the mangroves. I pulled one or two good muddies in and with the eternal quest for a barra still unfulfilled, we took a local fisherman's advice and headed the extra few kilometres to Karumba.

Karumba is a sleepy little fishing village, a mecca for seafood lovers, and its population of 700 grows to thousands each winter with the onset of barramundi fishing. Most visitors head out to the Point, which embraces some of Australia's most beautiful sunsets.

"What time does the sun set'? seemed a simple question to the girl behind the bar at the Sunset Tavern, which is right on the water at Karumba Point.

"Don't know, never watch it go down, not interested in sunsets" she vacantly replied with a broad Lancashire accent and giving every appearance of just recovering from a recent brain transplant operation. "What's this $12.95 special for dinner tonight"? I patiently asked her, hoping to hear about something salivating to dine on.

"Some kinda soup, donnow what the pudding is, but I fink they're cooking up some kinda pig in the kitchen for the main course".

We decided to satisfy our appetites elsewhere, forget about the sunset and felt sorry for any business that might inadvertently end up employing this lady in a public relations position.

'The more you give, the more you get back', is a true adage on which Barry and Lorraine have based their success. Back in 1990, they came up from Dandenong and spent time in what was then a deserted backwater called Karumba Point. The sum of $60,000 bought a vacant one-acre block and they created Karumba Park Tourist Park, a winter destination that now brings thousands of friends together every year. Today it is five acres of shady trees, has a swimming pool, and is packed with keen fishing types who mostly spend four months of the year here.

Where would you find a camping ground that gives all residents a complimentary fish dinner twice a week? "Lorraine and I have given away over 8000 free fish dinners this season alone" Barry recalls " but it is worth the pleasure of seeing all our old friends and new visitors enjoying the show we put on for them". It all started when Barry and Lorraine offered to cook the excess fish that their campers brought in, but as the excess fish grew less, the scale of the event grew and they now buy-in fish for the occasion. The crowd is hooked on the entertainment. There's fishing competition winners, on-stage line dancing, a couple of country singers, Barry's continuous funny interjections and compering, and then there was old Joy.

She took an eternity to walk to the stage. Eventually standing erect behind the microphone, this matronly looking 80 year old held the attention of the fish-eating fraternity with her often smutty, occasionally crude, but always humorous repartee. She read from her 'Seriously Rude Joke Book', purchased for the pittance of $1.50 from the local second hand book shop. It was the best buy she has ever made.

Joy was just recovering from a mild stroke, and the deliberations and pregnant pauses between words and sentences, accentuated the emotions and jocosity of her performance. "I didn't give a hoot when a man of the cloth walked out on my performance last week, thinking it crude and unchristianlike." She recalled later.

" I've had a couple of old codgers commenting that I should be ashamed of myself, for telling smutty jokes at my age, but if it brings happiness to most people, then it's been worth the effort". It's a big change from being a schoolteacher for 30 odd years down Blair Athol way.

Out on the Gulf the fish were biting but nowhere near as plentiful as previous years.We pulled in a few salmon and other odds and ends while skipper Graham who has been fishing these waters for 30 years made the profound statement "If there's a drought on the land, there's a drought at sea". Where have I heard that before?

It would appear that in previous years, the fish were literally jumping into the boats. But this year the barramundi so far were about as elusive as the Holy Grail.

Fishing is a way of life for most of these people and they take it very seriously.

One couple who follow the sun and the fish, were very proud to let us know that the previous year in Streaky Bay on the Eyre Peninsular, they had caught exactly 1175 King George Whiting. And this in only a few weeks. Some readers may well think that is outrageously greedy. I can not help but agree. That is half as much again as Barry gives away to all his visitors each season. No wonder with people like that around, fishing grounds are slowly drying up.

Back in Normanton, my co driver had a sudden urge to experience a train ride, and it wasn't just the effects of a few drinks at the Purple Pub. The Gulflander train ride is not only for train buffs, it is a total outback experience. The most original railway line in the world, it has been running for over 110 years, the all weather track being built on special submersible steel sleepers. Hollow based, they are filled with mud, making ballast on the track unnecessary. This is also the mail train serving the numerous properties along the way, and guarantees delivery in the worst conditions. Savannah Guide and train driver Ken, is a mine of information and loves to share his knowledge with those that wish to immerse themselves in the history of the Gulf Country. Every Wednesday morning at eight-thirty prompt, a whistle blows at the very cute old world Normanton station and the diesel-engine train packed with excited 'traino's' in its two neatly refurbished carriages, pulls out on its five-hour trip to Croydon. I stood on the deserted platform as my little wife waved out of the carriage window, as if she was a five year old going to her first party. She was so excited it nearly brought tears to my eyes. As the train slowly disappeared in the distance, it only seemed reasonable to say my good-byes to Gregory and Mrs. Peck before Morrison and I left for the drive to Croydon.

It is short journeys like this, with absolutely nothing to look at or to concentrate on that makes for good contemplation. The isolation of these towns made me aware of the significant culture gap between the city and the bush. Technology is also slower to embrace the outback, due to the enormous distances, but tourism appeared to be partly responsible for closing that gap. Urban dwellers, that are 'going bush' and spending time with the locals, learn to appreciate the effort that goes into primary industry and the importance it has on our economy. Much of the wealth in this country comes from isolated areas where ingenuity has had to be utilised in order to survive. All a bit thought provoking, but I thought I would get it off my chest.

I arrived in Croydon in two hours compared with Fay's exhilarating five-hour train ride, which gave me plenty of time to discover the highlights of this historical little backwater.

The sign across the front stated, THE OLDEST STORE IN OZ. Another smaller hand written one offered, DINKY DI CAPPUCCINO which was just what I felt like after the morning drive.

It was like entering a time warp. With the exception of a few modern electrical gadgets, nothing much had changed since the place first opened in 1894. Even the owner Pat, looked like she was a turn of the century character actor as she busied herself around the dusty ramshackle place in her floral print dress and with a permanent broad smile on her face. She had her hands full with all manner of things. From stockfeed to fish and chips, tyres, batteries and car repairs to cold drinks and groceries, this woman was perpetual motion.

"All I need is a Cappuccino on the table outside" I meekly requested, and without dropping a millimetre of her smile, accordingly obliged. Sitting in front of my laptop at the sidewalk table, office open for business, I drew a few unusual looks from the locals. I doubt if some of them had seen a laptop before.

One young lady sat down at the adjacent table, intrigued at my workload, and turned around to flash her new 'T' shirt. Emblazoned across the front of her well-endowed chest were the numbers 96 and underneath the words SEXUALLY DYSLEXIC. With unseemly thoughts in mind, I totally lost all concentration and decided to look around the town.

Once again there was a recently constructed, but totally deserted grand swimming pool. It was 32 degrees, the sun was hot, yet not a single body was in the water. Another town full of wusses who thought the water a little cold for them.

There was a lovely Remembrance Garden with a number of exquisitely sculptured pieces in iron, dramatically rekindling the history of the place. Croydon was once a bustling gold mining town and legend has it that at one stage there were over 30,000 hopefuls digging away for their fortune in the area. All that fossicking around was thirsty work, and they were lucky to have had a choice of no less than 65 licensed drinking establishments where their thirst could be quenched. This had been a seriously busy place with a gold yield equivalent in today's money of $600 million. The gold stuff dwindled, prospectors left, and the town died. Historic buildings are reminders of those hectic years and today the locals are making every effort to capture the passing tourist dollar.

The weekly arrival of the Gulflander from Normanton is the big event in town, with buses and cars and generally inquisitive people with nothing better to do, all queuing up to watch the old girl clunk in to the ageing station.

And there was my little wife, half hanging out of a carriage window, waving as if she was trying to recirculate blood in her arm after falling asleep on it. She shared her excitement of the memorable journey with such enthusiasm, I decided to delay the news of my morning's illuminating activities until we drove off to Georgetown.

The countryside out here can best be described as a ginger ochre dusty straw coloured land of fragile beauty. Passing seasons have made little change to the stark beauty of the inhospitable terrain. Evenings bring sunsets of burnt orange as they fade into darkness behind the distant ranges.

It was twilight as we drove into Georgetown, and at the back of the town we came across an old cemetery, standing alongside the banks of a dry riverbed. Not your everyday resting-place, but it would suit us for the night. Fading old headstones going back to the 1870s, surrounded by wrought iron fencing were featured alongside more recent edifices; all surrounded by freshly mowed green grass.

Our camping spot provided a perfect little getaway, much to the intrigue of the herd of cattle who took great delight in dropping great poopats in our close vicinity during the night.

Back in Karumba we had frozen some of the Gulf's famous prawns and decided to give ourselves a cemetery-side treat, which is a simple but delicious way of appreciating a favourite seafood.

Prawns with a bite like a white pointer

*Crush 3 cloves of garlic, 1 red sliced chilli, and fry in heavy
base pan with olive oil until brown.*
*Remove and then briefly cook the peeled prawns in the now
flavoured oil and return chilli/garlic.*
*Squeeze lemon in final stages and garnish with parsley or
coriander*

It wasn't till the next day at the Visitors Centre that we were
informed that the big flood of a couple of years ago had washed
through the cemetery, taking bones, headstones and everything in
its path downstream. A very conscientious volunteer group spent
many working hours reestablishing this fine place of rest, although
small piles of stonework and iron railings reclaimed from the river
all looked a bit 'hit and miss'. I wondered who had the job of figuring
out which bones went with which grave.

I asked one such volunteer, a nice retired old soul with a perpetual
smile on his face,

"Do the fees for burials keep rising each year because they are
based on the cost of living". The smile quickly disappeared as he
pondered this thought-provoking question and slowly replied

"Are you taking the piss out of me"

Georgetown people like other communities on this long Savannah
Way were very proud of their town and realise the increasing
importance of passing tourists.

Mount Surprise was aptly named, but no one seemed to have a
sensible answer as to where the name of this tiny little settlement
originated. However, the place was full of surprises. The population
is just 65 and wherever we went, we kept on bumping into living
dynamos. They were all on extra large doses of happy pills and
determined to put Mount Surprise on the map. The hyped-up
Progress Association has done a deal and gained the services of a
local prisoner's workgroup to clean up the town regularly. The
fossicking museums, historic pub and food places have all got a
'you're welcome here' feel.

A rotund and rather excited sort of lady called Merle insisted we go take a look at the town's latest project which happened to be at the bottom of her back garden. Pride was an understatement as she opened the door to a newly constructed, state of the art, ridgy didge, recording studio, which no doubt would have cost an arm and a leg to build and fit out. " Mount Surprise could be a little Nashville in the making" she proudly declared. Husband John does the mixing and some writing and the local sergeant from the police station plays the drums. They've already made a few records there and its just another, but somewhat expensive way of getting the town on the map.

Good luck to them all we thought, as the road took us east. More townships should have that 'go get em' attitude, and the ones that do, will surely benefit.

We were in the heart of savannah country, which to many people typifies the romance of the legendary outback.

Lava Tubes may not be everyone's cup of tea but the Undara Experience can change that very quickly. Back in the early 1860s, two young pioneering brothers established themselves on untouched land called Springs Creek, and while enduring tough times, prospered and multiplied. Today the Collins family still own large tracts of this land, part of which is home to the world's longest, largest and most accessible lava tube system.

For the uninitiated reader, lava tubes were created around 190 thousand years ago, give or take a year or two. We are told that one day the earth trembled, the skies blackened and the Undara Crater erupted in flaming fountains, spewing out bubbling, boiling treacle-like lava, which incinerated everything in its path. The land was bathed in a fiery glow. This giant, scolding flood of magma filled the riverbeds, and while the top surface cooled and solidified, a fearsome flow of molten lava snaked its way down the river's course, creating rock pipes, which eventually became hollow tunnels.

Today things are a little more peaceful, with the fourth, fifth and sixth generations of the Collins family still there. The patriarch of the family, Gerry Collins is known as the 'gentleman of outback hospitality'.

"One of the high spots of my life" he recalled "was being given a fully endorsed appreciation of this project" by Sir David Attenborough. That set the seal of standards for this quintessential outback attraction.

Hospitality is a word often loosely used in tourism, but the staff at this place seemed to bend over backwards to satisfy everyone's needs. And they did it with such a genuine desire to please, it was a real pleasure to watch.

Just over 100 years after his pioneering ancestors found the place, Gerry Collins applied to the Queensland Government to gazette a National Park around the tubes which would protect and sustain the fragile eco system. These days, the tubes can only be viewed from the family owned Undara Lava Lodges, which was opened by Sir David Attenborough back in 1991. Experienced Savannah Guides provide rewarding interpretive tours, giving an insight into the diversified flora and fauna in the area. Birdos can get really excited, with over 120 species to be checked out though their binoculars. We had the rare privilege of watching a pair of wedge tailed eagles, with their eight-foot wing spans, swooping on to a female wallaroo, killed during the previous night by a couple of hungry dingoes. Nearby, the lush canopies of the rainforest seemed quite incongruous with the surrounding woodland

An authentic turn of the century touch was created by Gerry Collins when he came across eleven decommissioned railway carriages. Bought for a song and lovingly restored to their former glory, they now provide accommodation and restaurant seating around which the resort is built.

A lot has happened at Undara since nature carved her primeval foundations into this geological masterpiece. The original long gone Collins brothers who discovered this unique piece of Australia, in the shadow of the Newcastle Ranges, would be pretty contented in the knowledge that six generations of their family have continued to live here and have provided an enthralling destination that is still close to nature. This adventure playground which generations of young and old Collins family members have privately revelled in, is now shared with queues of admirers.

During the few weeks we spent around the Gulf Savannah country, a particular group of people caught our attention. Similarly dressed in their smart khaki outfits, they are a special breed who are sort of protectors of the local environment. The Savannah Guides, who impressed everyone with their knowledge, visit training schools twice a year where they pride themselves on learning the finer points of ecology, geology, land management and tourism. They recently won the world's best tourism organisation prize at the 'British Airways Tourism for Tomorrow Awards' in London. This says a hell of a lot for their dedication to interpretive tourism in this land of immense age and fragile beauty.

Spending time with some of these guys can be a rewarding experience. Tony Speedie had just finished an hour of entertaining around the campfire at Undara, enthralling the small crowd with his outback experiences. Little snips of very useful information such as how to catch a kangaroo without being mauled. "The secret is getting behind 'em real quick and then hanging on for dear life" he nonchalantly explained to his amused audience. Tony's laconic velvety Scottish accent had a touch of the Sean Connerys and along with his charming wife Helen enthralled the two of us over a drink or three long after everyone else had turned in.

After acquainting themselves with the hardships of the land through various arduous jobs, they earned their places as Savannah Guides and they have been happily at it since its inception. Prior to commencing at Undara they had a stint in an aqually controlled natural environment park where the motto was....wait for it! 'cage the people not the animals' "We had a ball until all the crocs went walkabout during a cyclone" Helen recalled. And so the stories rolled on well into the wee small hours.

We pulled out of Undara, and the three of us Morrison, The Co-Driver, and I felt the intoxicating draw of the coastal mountain ranges as they loomed ahead with the promise of a total change of scene.

CHAPTER THIRTEEN

THE TROPICS...
WILD, WET & WONDROUS

In a matter of only an hour, it seemed we had been transported into another world.

We had elevated ourselves to a tropical realm of rainforest-enshrouded waterfalls, lush rolling pastures, crystal clear lakes and charming rural hamlets.

Far North Queensland is as diverse in itself as the rest of the country put together. Our arrival on the Atherton Tableland provided a refreshing change, suggesting a very special course of events was about to unfold.

A considerable amount of time could easily be spent appreciating the vast array of natural beauty that takes on the appearance of a capacious roof top garden. The decision to spend a few days here proved to be more than justified.

Our journey was now some nine months old, covering nearly 30,000 kilometres and this was amongst the most alluring scenery we had experienced. Spread across an area between the Great Dividing Range and the Bellenden Ker Range this spectacular region sits heaven-high above sea level. The low humidity and temperate year round climate, provide continuous amenable weather which is pretty hard to beat.

We walked the five-kilometre boardwalk around Lake Barrine, created from a volcanic crater. This was Tarzan type country with massive hanging vines, remarkable buttressed root systems, and ancient trees growing in grotesque fashions with twisting, contorting strangler creepers vanishing into the upper foliage. A myriad of rainforest species is continually locked in battle, climbing over each other in a life and death struggle for sunlight and nutrients. Giant kauri trees, red cedars and figs have grown together for centuries giving a mediaeval mysterious feel. There are 760 species of bird life in Australia and around 360 of them live in the grand old forests of the Tableland, which are alive with a cacophony of relentless chattering, whistling and shrieking. And that's just the birds. It is also home to the rarely sighted tree-climbing kangaroos, sugar gliders, green possums, while platypus play in many of the creeks that snake their way across this fertile plateau.

Crystal clear streams rush over tumbling waterfalls, cleft by basalt outcrops, then continue their way over moss-covered rocks to disappear in a mosaic of ferns and lush vegetation. Bromfield Swamp, another superb crater-lake, has thousands of magpie geese, brolgas and sarus cranes. These, with their long legs extended behind them and their peculiar calls filling the air, make their annual migration from the Gulf Country to feed on the harvested paddocks of the tableland farms.

Tiny villages abound with quaint sounding names, inherited from early settler days, such as Milanda, Millaa Millaa, Mungalli, Tinaroo and Yungaburra. The latter is a really romantic mountain retreat with a touch of the Tyrolean about it and is full of history. The place has an abundance of heritage listed buildings, in fact more than any other Queensland town.

There are a few old timers here who find it hard to understand the changing times and get a little upset when things like bare breasts are part of a restaurant promotion.

'Nicks', is a multi award winning five-star Swiss-Italian restaurant and serves some of the best food imaginable. Nick is a success story in himself and his philosophy on life is to make people happy and to enjoy himself at the same time.

A few years ago on April 1, his large roadside sign indicated 'TOPLESS WAITRESSES...TODAY ONLY'. Now in a conservative place like Yungaburra, this caused quite a stir and a few old fuddy-duddies from the progress association reckoned it was their duty to ensure that titillation of that sort was not on the menu. Didn't they have egg all over their wizened old faces when Nick politely informed them it was just an April Fools Day stunt.

Short memories have some of these villagers, cause the next year these humourless busybodies noticed PLATYPUS STEW advertised on the same board. The very protected platypus are regularly sighted playing in the nearby creek and are respectfully treated as part of the village family. There were more smiles from Nick, loads of laughs from the customers and more embarrassment for the complaining locals when they realised they had been had again.

Last year he really tested their humour with the following advert. 'FOR SALE 6 TRAINED PLATYPUS'. That brought phone calls from the RSPCA, ABC and all sorts of media. The smile was on Nick's face for days until he got a weird call from somebody asking him questions about his advert.

"Yes, he'd sold them all for $12.95 each. Yes, they had been trained at Sea World on the Gold Coast", and ever the prankster, "Yes they just walked up my garden from the creek below".

Imagine his horror when the caller told him he was from The Wildlife Protection Society and there was a fine of $50,000 for selling protected and endangered species.

Days later he found that the tables had been turned and it was a prank call, but the preceding sleepless nights, worrying about supposed court proceedings, gave him plenty of food for thought. The irrepressible restauranteur had been 'hoist on his own petard', so to speak.

Many were the tales; all recorded in Nick's giant scrapbook, which is now getting bigger than the Bible

A hundred inspiring views and a thousand hairy bends is the road down to Gordonvale, which leads off the tableland to the Pacific Ocean. Twisting and turning down the Gillies Range, dropping to sea level in around half an hour was nothing short of exhilarating. Morrison's brakes worked overtime, while my nervous little passenger cum navigator clenched her toes on every turn.

It seemed a lifetime since we first attempted to pull an elusive barra out of the water, and an unexpected opportunity to test our limited skills, was hard to resist. In the shadows of the Gillies Range, we camped on the grassy banks of the Mulgrave River, in close proximity to our objective. Early next morning lines were cast and believe it or not, 'her outdoors' was the first to pull out a plate-size beauty, which put a smile on her face that lasted all day. With my help, one or two more were duly dispatched to the deep freeze and our day was made. I must admit that the source of this exhilarating few hours was a place called 'Catch a Barra', where a few dollars are paid per hour to cast a line in the well-stocked pond and another $10 for each fish taken away. Well I suppose its better than scouring the Territory and the Gulf and coming away empty handed.

The owner of this innovative little operation is a charming ex Cairns real estate chap called David. Tucked away in picturesque countryside he has created and built his novel hideaway where visitors can while away a few hours in the landscaped hothouse rock gardens, make friends with any one of the dozens of wallabies in his personal zoo, or just fish for barramundi. For those not in a hurry to go anywhere, there are barbecue facilities provided to cook the catch.

It's a bit like 'Faulty' fishing with fun never far away. Somewhat unusual these days for a lot of fishing fanatics who take their sport very seriously.

Sarah was a pretty little six-year-old with long blonde pigtails, freckly cherubic face and an infectious giggle. She had never been fishing previously and was taken totally by surprise when her first barra tugged the rod right out of her hands. Clattering along the bank and into the water, it went to the bottom where David said it could stay, possibly with a very confused fish still on the other end of the line.

Children and first time female fisherpersons often seem to have beginner's luck when it comes to pulling in a big one. While the rest of us were going though a spell of inactivity, a coffee-coloured youngster who was knee high to a grasshopper, was in all sorts of trouble at the end of one of the jetties. His line had fallen through a crack in the boards and that's right, he hooked one right under the decking. He was so taken aback with all the thrashing about underneath him, he froze in fright and screamed for his daddy.

Japanese visitors get quite agitated when the word crocodile is mentioned and the whites of their narrow eyes can totally vanish in terror. Ever the joker, David had affixed a sign that says BEWARE OF CROCODILES. Hideoki was from Osaka, and upon seeing a huge air bubble erupt in front of him dropped his rod in astonishment and did a runner. He was not interested in the fact that the eruption was caused by Davids 'oxygenation' process, and there was no way he could be enticed back to the wonderful world of fishing.

I was half expecting Manuel to arrive with some freshly caught kippers or Basil and Polly to emerge frantically in search of a drowned body.

David would be lost without his wwoofers and it is amazing how few people know what a wwoofer is. They are not fish, definitely not edible and certainly do not grow on trees. They are in fact human and normally come in the form of overseas backpackers or students who wander around this great continent with little money, but take the option to offer work in return for food and somewhere to sleep. The word 'wwoofers' was originally derived from the expression 'willing workers on organic farms' but these days the deal extends to any kind of place where a little extra help is needed. The wwoofers pay about $50 for membership and an introduction book, which includes hundreds of contact names. They happily travel the country enjoying a far greater understanding of our way of life than any normal tourist does.

Like hundreds of property owners, David relies on them to assist in general maintenance and to keep up with the many small jobs that constantly need attention. His wwoofers are often Japanese or Koreans who mostly have a very limited knowledge of our language and customs.

Koya was newly arrived from Tokyo and had an amazed look of surprise on his face when David asked him if he had brought his snakebite survival kit with him. The dry humour often goes straight over their little Asian heads, especially when it came to crocodile signs and snake jokes. Luckily for Koya, there was an 'old hand' from his hometown who happily guided him through those first few confusing days.

Full of the joys of our successful fishing expedition, we decided to spend another night at our riverside camp. The steep mountains thrusting out of lush fjord-like green valleys towered above us. The river gurgled and babbled, surging over small rapids, its dark waters reflecting the surrounding landscape. Near the rapids, a shiny black darter spread his wings to dry after securing his dinner. The nightlife became active as we sat in the still twilight. A mixture of animals hopped around suspiciously eyeing us, while the bird noises in the surrounding trees slowly subsided.

We wandered up to the nearby River View Pub for a celebratory drink and a chat with the locals. The menu did look appetising but the thought of our recently caught barra, waiting in the fridge was sufficient to spur us on to empty our glasses and return to camp.

Barramundi can vary tremendously, depending on whether they are caught wild or are farm grown. The latter is a growth industry and is becoming increasingly popular with restaurateurs who are guaranteed of year round supply. Grown to a large plate-size the mild -tasting fillets always appear to have a regular shape and texture.

The ones we caught at 'Catch a Barra' were originally bought as fingerlings and after a few months had grown to a size that was perfect for two portions and which we were about to enjoy.

Bonza Barramundi - Tropical Style

My preferred way of cooking barra is virtually the same as found in many Chinese restaurants. Finely sliced ginger, a little oil, a dash of soy sauce and preferably steam it.for about 20 to 25 minutes
To add that tropical feel and a sweet and sour taste, lightly poach some mango cheeks and place around the fish before serving. Finally sprinkle some coriander leaves on top to complete this colourful fusion of tastes.
If steaming presents a problem, wrap fish in a foil 'boat' and cook slowly over a hot plate for the same amount of time.

With the gurgling river only metres away and too many stars to count, it was the perfect finale to a great day.

Heading into Cairns through its increasingly busy suburbs and shopping centres was just a temporary detour before we headed further north. Fay and I had been here a couple of times before, and as previously experienced, were in awe of the magnificent backdrop of mountains that stretch along this coastline. This is a city with a country atmosphere and a tropical feel all in one, but we were back in the world of traffic lights, queues and urban living which was not our cup of tea for more than a day or two.

The day was perfect, and the 34 four foot Mustang was purring at the marina waiting to take us out to the blue yonder. Our pals John and Louise were temporarily living on 'Pretty Woman', which was a perfect description for this spunky looking petrol guzzler. Our destination was Upolu Cay, on the Arlington Reef about 15 kilometres out from Cairns and seemingly in the middle of nowhere.

Our hosts and long time friends were up from the Gold Coast, overseeing some building developments along this tropical coastline and were itching to get out on the water after a week of dealing with builders and tradespeople. Upolu Cay is simply a small, dazzling white sand dune rising out of incredibly clear aquamarine waters. Before mid morning and after three it is the epitome of the classic deserted island, but in between it is like the A1 Highway at peak hour. Commercial boats discard dozens of sightseers anxious to view a bit of the reef and a few of the brightly coloured tropical fish that were swimming everywhere. A group of Japanese tourists wearing flippers, snorkels and masks for the first time, splashed past in a tightly knit group looking like some churning oil slick drifting determinedly to their destination.

Watching all this activity from Pretty Woman's stern, eating our freshly cooked Asian style prawns, and knocking back the odd glass of Sauvignon Blanc, we felt quite hedonistic.

A large bullet-shaped boat dropped anchor a few metres away, metal music blasting from the speakers and a hive of activity emanating from the cockpit. The peace of the afternoon was quickly shattered as kids screamed and dive-bombed in the water while their peroxide blonde Mum staggered about in a bikini four sizes too small for her, arguing with hubby and abusing her offspring in loud slurred tones.

It was like having front row seats for a stage performance. Her morning's lubrications had set the scene, and throughout many vocal outbursts, her 'loved one' just sat behind the steering wheel, minding his own business and not saying a word. 'Copping it on the chin' could well be the preferred analogy.

The whole performance reminded me of an old facetious observation: Marriage has a beneficial side to it - it teaches obedience, tolerance, loyalty and other commendable qualities that a man wouldn't need if he was single. The show was finally over as the 'Sylvania Waters' type family drew anchor and speeded off allowing peace and tranquility to be restored.

In the twilight of the evening, the lights of Cairns were turned on like a faraway Christmas tree. We sped through the balmy night air on auto cruise, the black waters flashing by and city lights growing in size In the middle of this sublimity we were suddenly attacked by a band of caped crusaders. An army of seemingly suicidal fruit bats incessantly dived bombed us, missing PrettyWoman's speeding hull by centimetres.

Above us a panorama of glittering stars studded the unclouded sky as we pulled in to the marina, and yet another magical day was behind us.

Dennis and Suzie our champagne-donating friends from Byron Bay were on holiday in the boutique hideaway resort of Palm Cove.

"Come and spend a few days with us" they enthused, which we thought an excellent suggestion.

Just a short drive from the city and we entered a whole new world of cosmopolitan glamour. The beautifully manicured strip is home to a long line of stylish, colorful buildings that exude the image of indulgence. Plans for more resorts and investment apartments abound, making Palm Cove the perfect up-market target for international tourists.

Local architect Leigh Ratcliffe has been the main driving force in maintaining controlled building development and he is convinced that the intimacy, tranquility and harmonious surrounds make it the ideal antithesis to city living.

The morning we arrived, a bit of a gale blew up churning the normally calm blue ocean into a frenzy. The well-dressed set appeared unconcerned as they sipped their lattes and cappuccinos, hidden behind their morning papers and magazines in the stylish coffee and cake places dotted along the picturesque esplanade.

Only 200 metres away, a man was fighting for survival in the turbulent sea that was now an ugly pea green. The rather overweight local fisherman, who hadn't seen the inside of a gymnasium in 20 years, had cottoned on to a very large catfish. A combination of the wind, the size of his catch and near fatal misjudgment on his part, saw him topple in to the heavy seas.

The strong current quickly pulled him out towards a far off island, while his mates summoned a tinnie to rescue him. The seas were so rough that even after being located and towed towards shore, the little rescue boat could not beach. Our bedraggled fisherman was swept out once again, only to be rescued a second time by a courageous lifesaver. Now throughout this entire ordeal, which I estimate would have taken a good half-hour, our totally exhausted survivor never let go of his fishing rod. He proudly held it high as he was beached by the teenage lifeguard, and was astonished to find that the catfish was no longer there.

He lived to tell the story which no doubt will be embellished in time, as most fishermen's stories are.

About the only other memorable event I can recall from our time in Palm Cove was on the nearby golf course. My mate Dennis had just hit a lovely drive down the fourth fairway only to find his ball lying less than a metre from a boobook owl. This lovable, normally nocturnal bird of prey stood his ground, stared at the ball, then at Dennis and then at the hole. Not wanting to take a drop, or move the bird, my ever-conscientious playing partner had to virtually stand over our unblinking friend to play his shot. Legs splayed wide, he struck the ball perfectly with his nine iron, only to see it fall just short into the deep sand of the bunker. And guess whoo whoo he blamed for this error of judgment. That's right. The fucking owl, who had followed the flight of the ball with an all knowing look. We left the little fella unblinking and unmoved on the fairway waiting for the group behind, who happened to be four Japanese ladies. God help the owl.

Port Douglas is just a short drive north along the coast. This dramatic winding road would have to be one of Queenslands most picturesque coastal drives. Tree covered steep sided mountain ranges flank the left, while coconut-fringed small white beaches, lapped by the most azure waters imaginable, regularly appear with every twist of the road.

Cane Toad Racing has been popular with visitors for years up here, and people still pay money to watch these obnoxious little critters hop for their lives, amongst the bedlam of party excitement and inebriated screams.

There is a fascinating drinking spot on the main drag in Port Douglas that looks as though it has been around since the year dot. In fact it was only erected mid 94 and that's the last century, not the one before. The Iron Bar is all wriggly tin mixed with interesting timbers, successfully taking on the appearance of an old outback pub. It sits on the site of the towns first Post Office and stands out like white balls on a black dog amongst all the upmarket, chic buildings.

Frog lovers and haters and those quite indifferent, pay small amounts of money to see these warty, clumsy, amphibious creatures, race each other, all in the name of selling beer.

Clancy is a local musician who probably makes more money providing fresh toads three nights a week than playing guitar. He collects them from the local golf course while they are hypnotising themselves under the sprinklers, and arrives with a bag full of these grotesque creatures in time for their evening performances.

No money is supposed to change hands and while we did not see it happening, I'm sure there were a few private wagers being made on the side. These little uglies are all given names and after a few beers, it was easy to let go with a few screams for 'Prince Charming', 'Fat Bastard', 'Forrest Jump' or Freddo the Frog'. We cheered on 'The Prince', with his bright pink elastic hair bunchie round his fat tummy, who romped home a winner. Devotees of this sport and those who became decidedly un-sober were enthusiastically urging on their favourites by merrily blowing away on gaily-coloured party poppers. A couple of two-pot screamers looked as though they might well have been attending their first kindergarten birthday party.

Cane Toad Races are 'Queensland all over' so let's hope that nobody croaks with excitement and the sport doesn't end the same way as 'two up', which is now only legally enjoyed on Anzac Day, at posh casinos or the Back of Bourke.

Port Douglas is 'same same, but different' to many sophisticated tropical resorts that offer everything on a plate for the discerning jetsetter. Apart from being decidedly hip, it also has the advantage of being the closest town to the Great Barrier Reef.

Back in the 1980s, Christopher Skase spent lots of other people's money making his resort 'just right' and there is a certain 'je ne sais quoi' feel about the place. Spending unlimited amounts of easily accessible money can often bring wonderful results, but to some, the memory of the man would not be quite so wonderful.

Today Port, as it is known locally, is an international Mecca where heads of state, film celebrities and sporting greats mix with holidaymakers from around the world. The little fishing village of earlier days has come of age. Despite its development and up-market tendencies, there are still no traffic lights, zebra crossings or parking meters which is an added bonus and maintains the casual feel of the place.

A visit to the weekend markets is a must. Dozens of stalls were erected along the shady riverbanks of the Dickson Inlet. No better location could be imaginable, with a refreshing breeze blowing off the sparkling waters. An amazing colourful array of locally grown or crafted products, many at bargain basement prices were on offer. Whether it was painted, sculptured, created, manufactured, sewn or whatever, the infectious atmosphere pervading the place, gave the impression to the thronging crowds that 'made locally' was well worth supporting.

On the superb Four-Mile Beach, the rolling waves of the Coral Sea challenged our limited body surfing talents, mainly due to the sloppy conditions. Above us, Flagstaff Hill looked across the isthmus of Port and the surrounding aquamarine waters, providing gobstopping views for the multi million dollar real estate properties that straddled its steep sides.

Anyone that visits this neck of the woods is out of their mind if they don't spend some time visiting the Daintree and Cape Tribulation areas. We don't normally choose to spend a day on organised tours but we needed a break from driving and the name of the company, 'Billy Tea Bush Safaris' had a certain ring about it. We had seen their little vans around the traps and they always seemed to be having such a good time. This was one occasion when having a naturalist guide with us, explaining the history, flora, fauna and environment would be well worth while.

The Billy Tea people are a family operation and have got to know the Daintree intimately over the last few decades. Marilyn & Berrick have won all sorts of tourism awards for their high standards in providing wonderfully informative tours. Their guides are all well trained - you throw a question and you get an answer, often with a touch of humour.

We set off bright and early and it was not far to the day's first attraction, which was an hour on the MV Matilda that transported us slowly down the Daintree River. Behind the wheel, Captain Bill, who looked as though he had just got out of bed after a very heavy night, was a mine of information. Interwoven with dry humour, he picked out anything of interest that flew, grew or swam in the waterway which winds its way through 120 kilometres of mangrove fringed banks. Bill told me that this whole area is part of the oldest continually surviving rainforest on earth.

"It is one hundred million and three years old" he pointed out. I questioned him on his pinpoint accuracy and was gratified that mathematics was high on his curriculum. "Three years ago some archeologists were out here and estimated that the plant and animal life had been around for a hundred million years" he replied with a glint in his red eyes.

This huge tropical rainforest area is a blanket of raw beauty covering over 900,000 hectares from Townsville in the south to Cooktown in the north. Queensland has the most diverse rainforest system in the world, from the mist-shrouded lichen-covered forests of the border ranges to the semi deciduous scrubs of the Cape York Peninsular. In this, the world's driest inhabited continent, every rainforest type from temperate to tropical can be found. The World Heritage listed Daintree area, a living museum, has remained undisturbed since time immemorial. Lush green jungles have remained relatively stable and undisturbed, while the rest of the world is experiencing dramatic climatic changes.

Exhilarating views from the top of The Alexandra Range across the Coral Sea were breathtaking. 'The Reef and Rainforest Coast' a spectacular 200 kilometre sweep of coastline, is certainly one of the true wonders of the world.

Our barbecue lunch was appreciatively devoured whilst perched on large river rocks. The water from a pristine creek was gurgling and tumbling only metres away as our guide amused us by swinging a large billy can of tea in a full circle over his head. Dappled sunlight filtered through ancient trees down on our small party and tropical birds hovered in anticipation of a feed. A small, furry, chocolate brown animal was searching for fallen fruits across the stream. The shy Musky-rat, the smallest and most primitive of kangaroos scampered away between king ferns and bowenia cycads, living relics from over 100 million years ago. .

Four million litres of rain falls in this World Heritage listed rainforest annually, providing a perfect haven for the teaming birdlife, reptiles,green tree frogs and butterflies of extraordinary colours.

The publicity people at the local tourism office call this area 'Nature'sTheme Park'. As we headed out towards Mossman we came across a themed resort which was significantly different.

Nudist Camps are places where people that are so disposed can shed their garments and relax without being stared at by all and sundry. I must admit I just never got around to spending time at one of these establishments, but believe that there is certainly a place in society for people who feel more comfortable without the restriction of clothes. I rarely wear anything in the privacy of our home so I have a certain understanding for these social gatherings so long as they are not upsetting anyone.

It was therefore intriguing to find that a motel in working class, cane-growing Mossman has opened up as a Nudist Resort. What a great name, The White Cockatoo, as plenty can be seen strolling around the gardens, corridors and eating areas. It's not one of those clothes-optional places where pervs can get a thrill, while any overt sexual activity will be treated with immediate eviction.

Owners Tony and Leonore Fox are a handsome young couple who should be congratulated for dreaming up the concept. The White Cockatoo respects people's privacy and the unethical use of cameras and videos can also see the offender out on the street with their clothes quickly following. Swim, play pool, sizzle your sausages or sip a cocktail at the bar, are simple ways of passing a clothes free day. Tony, who has been a dedicated nudie from way back, has set aside five of the 23 chalets for guests who are a little shy.

"There's no hard feelings" he maintains towards people who want to cover up, "but after a while it comes quite naturally and most guests eventually realise the pleasures of not having to get dressed every morning.

Thursday is a good day to get out of Mossman, clothes or no clothes, as the Social Security cheques are exchanged for copious quantities of the liquid amber with the inevitable results.

It is a four hour drive to Cooktown and the steep, exhilarating, snaking road, with its dozens of nerve racking hairpin bends to the top of the range, presents unforgettable views. Morrison came through the challenge with flying colours but appreciated the breathing space at the various lookout points, which made us realise the enormous task of constructing this highway back in the early 1900s. The last section over a still unfinished dirt road was pretty forgettable until a road sign indicated an historic watering hole only a few kilometres off the track, which appealed to our now rather dry throats.

Tucked away in the shadow of the Black Mountains is the Lions Den, which has been serving grog since 1875. It is the first pub I have ever visited that has signs everywhere stating, 'NO CAMERAS..NO VIDEOS ALLOWED. I was half expecting a strip search, as the no-frills lady behind the bar looked as though she could handle just about any kind of problem.

"Locals don't like their photo being taken" she replied to my simple enquiry. She had that sort of exasperated look on her weather-beaten face that gave the impression I was the 20th person that morning that had asked the same question. Looking at the line up of suspect locals downing their morning schooners, I could only imagine that the glorified tin shed had a few mysterious secrets to hide. The place is certainly very photographic with every conceivable wall and ceiling space covered with graffiti, an assortment of undergarments, paraphernalia and nostalgic items from past eras.

It just reeks of good times and hard drinking.

Apparently it got its name from the nearby tin mine, which was found by a stowaway called Daniel. He emerged one day from this hole in the mountainside and a local landowner, who was an avid reader of the good book, aptly called it The Lions Den. For over 120 years, the only licensees have been women, six in all, including the current owner Suzanne, who lobbed in a few years ago from Mission Beach and decided to stay.

Now that's a bit of a record in itself, particularly as the place has a reputation for a seeing a drop of blood on the floor. Locals around here haven't much else to do except while away their hours tippling, and they're known not to take a backward step when it comes to an argument.

Four wheel drivers coming down the Bloomfield Track normally pull over for a cool one as it's the only place to quench a thirst. Unfortunately there is no tap beer, just bottles and cans, which along with the banning of cameras and videos all appeared a bit unusual for a supposed pub of renown.

I enquired of an old bearded codger, who was lolling on the balcony in a decrepit rocking chair

"Many crocs in the creeks around here mate?"

He stared at me as though I had broken some unwritten rule

"A bloke from here lost both his legs when a big fella caught 'im by surprise while he was fishing." He unemotionally replied, distinctly looking like he was 'ten cents short of a dollar'.

"How long ago was that" I inquisitively enquired.

"Ah lets see…..'bout two years ago,……….. and he's been bumming around here ever since". He stared at me to see if I was on his same level of thinking.

I asked him about his bandaged fingers that looked like he might have been in an accident.

"Just walking home last night, after a day's heavy boozing and some fella trod on them" he replied with a vacant stare.

I think he was having a quiet little go at me. We decided that a change of scenery was needed.

We immediately fell in love with Cooktown not just for its appealing frontier town atmosphere but also for the ever-present sense of history. There was much talk about when the 50 kilometres of dirt highway into the town would see a cover of bitumen on it. Real estate prices are soaring with the completion of this considerable undertaking being promised by the government before 2005. The end result will no doubt be a vast improvement on some of the single-track outback Queensland roads that we have barely survived.

The extra-wide streets of the town are flanked by historic buildings, many of them dating back to the gold rush days of the 1880s. The place was quickly transformed from a deserted wilderness into a sizeable community of over 30,000, seeking their fortune at the nearby Palmer River site. A myriad of tents were erected overnight on the grassy riverbanks creating an instant busy little seaport. At one stage it was one of the wealthiest places in Australia. Each year 360 overseas vessels called in and the main street, a blaze of lights, was three kilometres long.

Still standing proud amongst the old pubs, railway station, post office and public buildings is the town bank. This majestic building with its beautiful red cedar fittings, teller cages and elaborate cornice work is now open to the public again. For the princely sum of just two dollars we sauntered around the immaculate Victorian style building with its Old World charm reminding us of yesteryear banking days. Diggers and miners, straight in from weeks or often months in the outback, handed over their bags of gold, the sizes varying dramatically depending on their success.

At the height of all these transactions, the bank manager unexplainably decided to lock himself in the vault one night and hang himself with not a word of warning. Peter was found next morning, his shiny black shoes dangling two feet above the ground. Needless to say he was a bit on the nose after spending his last night swinging around in the claustrophobic surroundings of the vault. His suicide was never explained, the vault left untouched, but his ghost is ever present according to the nice old couple who collected our $2.

The place abounds with 'Cookisms' and what better place for the good Captain's crew to have a bit of R & R than on the banks of the meandering Endeavour River. He experienced a bit of a confrontation with a reef down the coast and pulled in here with a big chunk of coral stuck in his hull. It was back in 1770, and due to the seven weeks it took to repair the Endeavor, Cooktown lays claim to be the first established white Australian settlement. Cook's legend will never diminish and he was known to embrace his pioneering expeditions wholeheartedly. His life was dedicated to exploration and the expansion of scientific and geographical knowledge.

Indigenous animals, birds and plant life were first seen and sketched on this visit. Previously unseen by Europeans, the kangaroo was first sighted and christened here. The local Aborigines called them 'Gangaro' and our national animal has continued to intrigue and provide worldwide enjoyment ever since.

Like any frontier town, and that is exactly what it is, the place abounds in characters and history.

Dutch Len as he is vaguely known in these parts is a hard man to find. Mainly cause he likes it that way. Hidden away under his tarpaulin, lolling on his hammock he was surprised that we had found his secret hideaway. Overlooking a virtually deserted moonshaped beach, he whiles away his days, fishing, walking, contemplating and appreciating his solitude. He has had a couple of decades spent in the 'University of Life' and has no desire to return to the world of people and their problems.

Len certainly doesn't look in his 70s, with his deeply tanned body, far-reaching muscular legs and flowing flaxen hair. His only clothes, a pair of faded blue Y fronts, floppy hat and sunnies. Faithful dog his ever-present companion, he maintained he was just a bushman at heart. "An extraordinary bushman though", he unabashedly drawled in his guttural Dutch accent.

"I used to work for a big corporation years ago, but retired and found living outside of suburbia was my life. From outback cattle stations, the Flinders Ranges to Far North Queensland, I have loved every minute of my bush days". He quietly recalled as he loped in front of us along his virtually private beach.

Comparisons could easily be made with Robinson Crusoe's Man Friday, even though Len can leave his hermit-like existence and hop over to Cooktown for supplies and emergencies. When we asked if he ever tired of his hermit lifestyle, he made a statement that summed him up perfectly " Life is life, wherever it may be lived."

Our return walk from Len's hideaway via the top of Grassy Hill, followed the footsteps of Captain Cook, who made frequent visitations here to work out how he was to escape the myriad of reefs that surround this haven. The summit of the steep climb offered stunning panoramic 360-degree views, the vast blue waters of the ocean contrasting with the snake-like river twisting its way to a distant chain of steep tree covered mountain ranges.

Linda has been known for many years as the 'Croc Lady', not only because she runs the 'Croc Shop' in the main street, but also for the years she spent on the isolated Cape York Peninsular. Linda has put to print a sort of biographical adventure story of her life under canvass, getting to know crocs, man-eating snakes and learning how to survive in isolation. The book is called 'Paradise Found' and a string bikini'd Linda is on the front cover, 303 shotgun at the ready, standing over a huge croc. Jaws apart, the stuffed replica really looked what some might call ' Ridgy Didge'. The first thing I thought was 'what an unusual outfit to go croc hunting in'. But the book tells a good story and so did Linda when she autographed my copy.

She initially reminded me of a white version of the GollyWog on a Robertson's Jam Jar label. A halo of tight black curls surmounted a widely smiling and contented pale face; this lady had found peace with the world after all her days of hardship in the bush.

"One of the most traumatic moments of my life was when a huge brown snake sank its fangs into my ankle" she recalled. "My husband, Ken, and I were filled with fear and foreboding when we calculated that it was a five hour drive to the nearest station. We arrived at midnight and by this time I was hysterical with pain."

"I really thought I was going to die and put on a bit of a show; screaming, contorting and clawing at the bandages on my quickly swelling foot" she quietly recalled in her easy-going manner.

The Flying Doctor Service was contacted but couldn't land at the station till first light next morning. The doctor on duty reluctantly informed the concerned group that "as it was now five hours into the ordeal, there was little they could do and the young lady would either make it through the night or she would not"

"I made it, and the FDS were saved the trouble of flying over a body bag" she laughed. This proved to be a tough lesson on the foolhardiness of tramping around at night wearing thongs and without a torch.

Apparently only one in ten snakes are poisonous, and of those only one in ten are seriously venomous. But as Linda knows, it only takes the one to cut your life short.

There was another experience with a slightly larger snake and one which she obviously relished telling. "A group of bikies camped upstream from our bush shop under some mango trees and about midnight, bloodcurdling screams rent the air. I thought someone was being murdered until we raced out to find an eight-metre amethystine python, which lived in the tree above, devouring one of the bikies. The long- bearded one was sleeping with his hands under his head leaving an elbow as an attractive starting point for the snake. It quickly started engorging its prey but got to a bit of an obstruction when the shoulder and torso arrived. It was at this point that the inebriated bikie woke up to find the face of the monster only centimetres away from his.

Black and blue and still petrified with fear, he mounted his silver and black Harley and roared out of the place at early light".

Linda would still be out on the banks of the Wenlock River today, but after all those years she was approached by the elders of the local New Mapoon tribe who told her they were going to run the shop themselves.

" You're lease pretty good dead fella," they said, " best get out".

"Who the hell would want to set up a business out here with no electricity, no water, no facilities, no house and no TV" she justified her disappointment in having to leave.

A great lifestyle disappeared overnight and the black fellas never did want to run the shop, just wanted to get rid of the mad white woman.

Linda's Croc shop suddenly got busy, so those were the only stories she had time to recall. The book is a nice read and you've got to admire a woman who has got the balls to live out her dream in such primitive conditions for all those years.

The social life in Cooktown starts on the jetty around five-thirty each morning.

It's all pretty busy with locals jostling with visitors for enough space to cast their lines. Only live bait is used so extra consideration is required when the nets are thrown in. On my three mornings there I didn't see a single fish caught with the exception of the character next to me.

He was a lovely old Irish guy with one of those warm syrupy brogues from Killarney or somewhere like that. He wore a flat little ratters hat which looked a bit incongruous in this tropical setting but loved a chat like any Irishman does.

"Last year I would be pulling in ten nice ones every morning and go home to the missus for me breakfast" he enthused.

"My oh my, where oh where have they all gone this year" he lamented as a mackerel struck his line for the first time and he pulled it in without the slightest hint of emotion.

I had heard it before and it was getting a little monotonous.

"When there is a drought on the land be Jesus, you'll be getting a drought at sea, son" old Paddy mumbled as he trundled off for breakfast.

At eight-thirty there was a mass evacuation as everyone disappeared in various directions. I enjoyed two big runs before the bastards broke my line, but at least the boredom had been broken.

There was much more excitement when some large fibreglass tanks were unloaded that morning full of hundreds of freshly caught coral trout. Gazing through their porthole windows, colourful reds and blues reflecting in the sunlight, they had no idea of their forthcoming travels. Each one was line- caught, local fishermen getting paid $9 for each one pulled in. Meanwhile the perfect plate-size fellas, so the gossip goes, get sold for $140 per kilo over in Japan, where they are shipped live.

The quite wonderful James Cook Museum, which a very young and attractive Queen Elizabeth opened back in 1970, is a treasure trove of historical items, which most visitors would find absorbing. Cooks original cannon and anchor are among the many displays in this well presented exhibition, which is undoubtedly the pride of Cooktown. There are reminders of two catastrophic cyclones which ripped this picturesque town apart, ensuring visitors realise the challenges of living in the tropics.

It gets so windy at times that there is a saying in surrounding towns when it blows up a bit - 'It'll be blowing the dogs off their chains in Cooktown'

Reading the local papers, I noticed an article confirming that people had been feeding crocs in a nearby river with road kills and leftover food. The idea being that salties would associate people 'with food' instead of 'for food', although it's too early to tell where their preferences lie.

A well-known character around the drinking spots in town called Simmo, wrote a half page editorial on how his life had changed since he gave up the demon drink.

"I was the second best drunk in town, lying in the gutter, falling off me bike and generally making a nuisance of meself. But now I have seen the light, I am walking the path of righteousness, overjoyed and happy am I".

I am told he used to be the towns undertaker, so his final quote of "Its not the cough that carries you off, but the coffin that they carry you off in" seemed quite appropriate for this born again non-imbiber.

We left town with a heap of good memories and headed off for our regular dose of 'getting back to nature' at nearby Archers Point, where our virtually isolated beachside camping spot overlooked the tranquil Coral Sea. Pyramid-like mountains fell straight into the aquamarine waters conjuring images of Hawaii or Tahiti.

Bali Hi was almost calling when we noticed an unloved Ford sedan at the far end of the beach. It was a perfect day but its owner seemed to be spending an inordinate amount of time inside. He rarely made an appearance during the time we were there, except for occasional but necessary moments of relief when he disappeared into the bush. He had no chairs, no cooking equipment, no tent, and no swag and just stayed inside his grubby vehicle, minding his own business.

Fay was feeling a little unnerved by his presence and suggested I wander over for a chat and see what his problem was. He informed me that he travels from one free camping spot to another, just calling into the nearest town for his dole cheque and a few basic supplies. t Staring through his windscreen, day after day contemplating God only knows what would indicate some sort of depressive or mental problem. At least he had a degree of sense to choose million dollar real estate from which to work out his problems.

The second night at Archer Point was one of those special full moon occasions that we wait for each month. Its silvery reflection shimmered across the broad waters of the bay surrounding us with a fantasyland of light and shadows.

Something special on the menu was warranted and I came up with a simple but effective way of cooking lamb.

'She'll be right' Leg of Lamb

Anyone can cook this simple meal - it's as easy as ABC. If it's underdone or overcooked there will always be the right slice for everyone. In other words 'she'll be right'

If the butcher can't bone the leg for you, I suggest you get a new butcher. Being on the road, we don't have that problem. However, it only takes a few minutes with a sharp knife to take the bone out and when completed open up the joint and flatten out by slicing into meat. Cover this side with a mixture of olive oil, garlic, cracked black pepper, salt and lots of rosemary. (Fresh is far preferable).

Cook on a hot barbecue, with the outside of the joint being cooked first. Regularly turn meat so it doesn't get too black. You'll end up with a variety of cuts, charred, pink and in-between. Serve with potato/onion mash and seasonal vegetables.

Delicious and one of my favourites, and dont forget to keep the bone for the crab pots.

Cooked over an open campfire that we kept burning well into the night, and accompanied by a brave little red that we found tucked away in the bin, the night was certainly one to remember.

Cooktown was a turning point as this would be as far north as we were to venture on the Queensland Coast. From here on it would all be southbound, with a few deviations to the west. We were into our second month of spring and the weather was still glorious with no hint at this stage of the heat and humidity that comes with summer.

It was late Saturday afternoon and the trip from Cooktown took us through the picture postcard village of Kuranda, which lies high above Cairns near the Barron Falls, and is famous for its award winning railway station. The last time we had been here was on a Sunday when the teeming markets that were one of the tablelands big attractions were in full swing and there were people everywhere. This visit was a little different. It was like a ghost town with not a soul to be seen, except a young black couple who were endeavouring to engage in deep conversation while lying in the gutter. The place reminded me of a Hollywood film location where the crew was having the day off. The shop fronts were like set pieces while the train station, Skyrail, pub, shops and service station were all deserted. 'Saturday Night Fever' was not happening in Kuranda unless they all had a fever of a less desirous kind and were recovering in bed.

Having fallen in love with the Atherton Tablelands on the trip north, a return visit for a few days proved to be irresistible. There were many sights still to see on this rich rolling plateau, which covers an area greater than the Island State of Tasmania. Sitting at an average of 700 metres above sea level, it is a true mountain retreat, climatically refreshing and invigorating.

The rich red volcanic soil is a perfect growing environment for just about anything that comes out of the earth. Believe it or not, there are more types of exotic and tropical fruits grown here than anywhere else in the world. Little roadside stalls, most with honesty boxes, offer recently picked foodstuffs at throwaway prices. The World Heritage rainforests are laced with sparkling mountain streams and mist-shrouded waterfalls.

As we returned across the gentle rolling hills, herds of fat healthy cows munched the greenest of grass with very contented looks on their faces.

Lake Tinaroo is three-quarters the size of Sydney Harbour and was created in the 1950s by damming the Barron River. Life-giving water has now been provided for vast surrounding areas of agricultural farmland, which produce all manner of fruit and vegetables. There are 200 kilometres of shoreline surrounding this huge reservoir, with dozens of waterfront camping spots. Fishing, bushwalking and water skiing for relevant enthusiasts were actively being pursued by our fellow campers.

The worlds largest recorded barramundi was caught here by a bloke called Dave Powell back in 1999. He pulled in a whopper weighing nearly 40 kg and measuring 124 centimetres. That's one hell of a fish yet the Fisheries Department reckon there are even bigger ones out there to be caught. Unless you throw, you'll never never know.

Brett Thompson comes up here regularly and has the uncanny knack of being able to cast his lure precisely to any chosen spot. Hitting a soft drink can from 20 metres is a bit of an art, but when you are the state lure-casting champion you would expect nothing less. He had just returned from a morning on the water and told me that he flicked a lure near some weed and pulled in the nice looking 15-kilo barra in his ice chest.

"After that, a few one-metre fellas drifted under the boat but none were hungry" he recalled. That's fishing, but at least he would be feeding on fresh fish that night.

We were as much in love with Nicks Restaurant at Yungaburra as we were with the Tablelands. Not to make another visit would have been unthinkable. Nick was his usual jovial self and had another good story for us.

On the first Saturday in August each year, Swiss National Independence Day is celebrated at the restaurant with dancing and yodelling and all those things that Swiss people do on their special day. The staff dress in national costume and guests could well believe that they were ensconced in some mountain chalet in Europe. An attractive young waitress who actually hails from the hills of Scotland left home in her car, all dressed up in a borrowed Tyrolean outfit. She looked a real little Heidi with her blonde plaits, short skirt and long boots. Unfortunately her car ran out of petrol on a country lane, so she walked to the nearest cottage for help. The 20 bikies inside had booked a French stripper for the night and weren't they delighted when little Heidi appeared.

" We booked French and we got Swiss" screamed an inebriated bearded one, with a belly like a sumo wrestler.

With a bit of Scottish cunning she talked herself out of a somewhat compromising situation and conned one of the more sober members of the gang to give her a lift on the back of his Harley. She roared up to the front of Nicks with plaits and skirts flying but her honour intact. Nick was most amused and felt she was in urgent need of a few mouthfulls of grappa before she joined her other Edelweiss friends in the evening's festivities.

Annual Rock Throwing Competitions, Oktoberfest, St Patrick's Day, Salami Making Competitions, Italian Nights, Jazz Weekends, Frog Festivals - you name it, Nick will be in anything that gives the restaurant a bit of publicity and his guests a bit of fun. No wonder he continually wins such awards as QueenslandsBest Themed Restaurant.

He is 'Mr. Perpetual Motion', cooking, playing his accordion, singing and fooling around at night while during the day he is busy organising his new wedding chapel, giving a bit of staff training or planning the next of his extravaganzas. Along with his lifelong partner and lovely wife Gina, he deserves all the accolades heaped upon them since arriving here with nothing but a suitcase many years ago.

We love success stories, particularly about people whose accomplishments haven't changed their basic outlook on life. Nick and I had shared lots of good chats about cooking and recipes and as he waved us off with his twinkling eyes and mischievous smile, he called,

"Eh, Mr. Ian, why you not come back 'ere as guest chef some time". Good thought, I might just do that.

Yungaburra has a bit of a reputation for platypus spotting. A local volunteer group has cleaned up the banks of the dainty, winding creek on the outskirts of town, and there are paths with lots of places to sit and watch these cute amphibious animals. We were told by Gina that early morning or late evening were preferred times and as Fay has long wanted to add these fascinating little egg-laying mammals to her growing list of 'sightings' much time was spent here, motionlessly staring into the still, dark waters. Apparently they can stay under water for up to ten minutes and with their eyes and ears closed, their soft, rubbery-like bill forages away for food.

They seemed as elusive as the bloody barra that we had spent months searching for and they had either decided to stay at home or we were just in the wrong place at the wrong time. At least we actually spoke with other avid platypus watchers, who had seen them with their very eyes, playing along these banks so we knew for certain it wasn't just a myth. But sadly we had to leave the Tablelands without actually seeing one for ourselves.

The back road out of Innisfail is all banana plantations and vast fields of sugar cane. The fresh verdant shoots of recently planted cane were vibrant in the morning sun, contrasting sharply with surrounding fields of tired old crops of browns and faded greens still waiting their turn for the harvester. Cane cockies and farmers toiled in the heat, as they have done for years, dwarfed by the imposing grandeur of the mountain ranges.

Another 20 minutes south of this country town of Innisfail a fascinating story unfolds, that is based around two men that came from different eras. Their lives inextricably intertwined, even though they never met and lived decades apart.

Today's story evolves around Mark Evans, who with his wife Judy found a derelict castle complex distorted with the rigours of time. The winning of tourism awards for Heritage and Cultural significance only a few years later, shows the enthusiasm and dedication of the man.

Lets go back to 1913 when an itinerant penniless worker arrived from Spain in search of his fortune. Jose Paronella left his betrothed back in Catalonia, and had a dream to build a castle for his future wife. He worked like a maniac in the cane fields, initially cutting and subsequently buying and selling farms until he made a heap of money. In those days 20,000 pounds was serious cash. After 11 years he returned home to claim his bride, who after not hearing a word from him in all those years had decided to marry elsewhere. How long can a young senorita wait for the odd letter. She had a younger sister, Margarita; he took a shine to her, got married and brought her back to Mena Creek, just south of Innisfail. For the mere sum of 120 pounds they bought 13 acres, with a substantial waterfall cascading into a large lake and fresh mountain streams flowing through magnificent forests. They settled down to build his dream castle and pleasure gardens for the appreciation of visitors.

They worked from dawn till dusk, seven days a week for seven years with unswerving determination. With his own hands, using sand and clay from the property, disused railway tracks and imported cement he constructed a series of buildings in the finest European tradition. Finally Paronella Park was opened to an amazed public in 1935.

They were romantic days, tennis was played on the courts, orchestras serenaded, small boats were rowed on the lake and movies were shown in the ballroom. Jose built a 138-foot tunnel of love for his Margarita. He planted 7000 trees, creating mystical walkways through forests of bamboo and kauri leading to acres of gardens.

He built Queensland's first hydroelectric plant, which provided all the power to the estate.

Lets face it, this was one hell of an achievement for someone who couldn't read or write, had no building or architectural experience but just worked bloody hard and lived for his dreams.

He was a complex mix of dreamer, businessman, and romantic, yet a little bit of a rogue. He certainly nailed the fallacy that his fellow countrymen were indolent. He died a lingering death from cancer, in his wife's arms in 1948 after seeing disaster strike his stucco palace from floods the previous year.

Fire, neglect, and Mother Nature took their toll and this amazing edifice, carved out of raw jungle, became derelict, moss covered and forgotten for 16 years.

Mark is an ex-corporate type who was taking his family round Australia on an extended holiday when he heard about the ramshackle ruins hidden under years of forest growth at Mena Creek.

The place has been reinvented; this year 150,000 people will gape in awe at the vast project that was undertaken by one very entrepreneurial man all those years ago.

Mark has ensured that Jose's legacy to tourism remains.

His enthusiasm is defined by his spruiker-type attitude in greeting every visitor personally in the car park. He is there most times of the day, welcoming, gesticulating, and organising groups with a level of high professionalism.

It has even been suggested that Mark is Jose reincarnated, and watching the man in action makes the theory quite believable

A very short drive south, overlooking Dunk Island is the pretty township of Mission Beach which also happens to be home to a strange, three-toed flightless bird that is a tourist attraction in its own right.

The cassowary is a very special Queenslander and quite unlike their human counterparts, is slowly becoming extinct. Some bureaucratic body did a head count, and apparently there are only about 1000 of these quite magnificent birds still living. I'm not sure how they realistically achieve these figures when these elusive creatures are extremely talented at camouflaging themselves. They come from the same family as the emu, New Zealand kiwi and South America's rhea, although the tall helmet or casque perched on their heads, and brilliant red and blue neck and wattles make them quite distinctive.

Just out of town there is a one-hour walking track through the Tam O'Shanter Forest, meandering around the quite enchantingLacey Creek that is supposed to house the highest concentrated population of these near-invisible birds. We found beautiful clear water holes with turtles and fish a-plenty while gurgling streams wound their way through luxuriant foliage. The paths showed piles of nice fresh cassowary poo indicating they were around, but these solitary birds were just as hard to find as the platypus and barra that had been the target of our fruitless searches.

Heading further south, the dramatic mountain scenery along the 'Great Green Way' is nothing short of stunning. They call it the 'Natural Jewel of the Tropics' and when it rains here, it really pours down. Tully is know to be the wettest town in Australia and the clouds drop over four metres in an average 'wet' season.

Black clouds roared in over the ocean, providing an almost pleasant change after the months of perpetually blue skies that we had been enjoying to the utmost. The normally luminous aqua seas of the Hinchinbrook Channel had turned into muddy brown soup. The precipitous pinnacles of the mountains on the offshore islands, shaded black in the afternoon storm looked ominous. We sat on the beach near our camping spot in the Edmond Kennedy National Park and watched this drama of nature unfold before us.

Cardwell is building a reputation as a top fishing town. There are stories of some highly credentialed catches out of the Hinchinbrook Channel but local fishing guide Michael told me that life on the water often has its challenges

"I had four blokes out for a day's fishing who had just flown in from Melbourne and were definitely a bit worse for wear.

Each holding a cold can in their hand they stumbled aboard the boat and continued to take the drinking more seriously than the fishing. After an hour or so, they were so pissed they could hardly cast their lines. Inebriation aside they still caught a few good-sized ones, which proves it doesn't matter what condition you're in, there's always a chance off beautiful Hinchinbrook" he recalled, hardly taking a breath.

To add insult to injury, it also appears that the most lubricated of this quartet, pulled in three fish on the one line, and that is not a fisherman's story.

At this point I thought his fishy tale a little far fetched, but as they say in the classics, 'Never let the truth get in the way of a good story'.

It was well into October, yet the place was humming with March Flies. Why is it that these annoying little bastards, who often give a nasty sting, are named after a month which never sees them around? As soon as you kill one, half a dozen of his mates attack you in some sort of suicidal revenge. At least they are slow movers and easy to knock off with a quick slap of the hand so some satisfaction is gained.

The wet tropics of North Queensland are one of the state's greatest environmental assets and a huge tourist attraction. As we left this lush area and headed towards Townsville, which is the driest town on the East Coast, there was a serious change of scenery, which reflected the long-time absence of rain.

This region is known as the 'dry tropics' which to us seemed like a contradiction of terms. As we drove into Townsville, we felt a little flat and wondered if the best of the trip was behind us.

CHAPTER FOURTEEN

BUT WAIT...
THERE'S MUCH MUCH MORE

The busy city of Townsville was a big surprise. It had a great feel about it and had seen some monumental improvements since we were last there. Councils throughout the country are often berated for wasting ratepayer's money, or for spending millions of dollars without long-term thought to resident's needs. The mob who run this big city have spent wisely and with foresight. The end result of their big budget improvements to the waterfront esplanade, The Strand, and its facilities, has proved to be world class.

Our computer was having a nervous breakdown, so while it was in for treatment we spent a pleasurable 24 hours parked on the Strand. A leisurely lunch was enjoyed at one of the excellent waterfront restaurants and we watched the locals at play. The pathways were a hive of activity with joggers, rollerbladers, bike riders, dog walkers and pedestrians just out for a stroll, all appreciating the views across Cleveland Bay to Magnetic Island.

Next morning as we soaked up a bit of sun while having our morning cuppa we were entertained by the continuing passing parade. Waves and nods were exchanged and everyone seemed super friendly and not at all surprised to see a rather large motorhome parked on their 'bit of turf'.

One skinny young thing who looked as though she was straight off a catwalk, niftily dressed in brief shorts and not much else, was being towed along at top speed on her roller blades by two hyperventilating balls of energy. Her Jack Russells weaved in and out of the more placid walkers, missing some by centimetres, obviously as excited as their mistress at this new game. Not often are dogs spotted taking their owner out for their morning exercise, and it was a sight to behold, attesting her complete faith in her 'best friends'.

Morrison was also in need of attention – his ball joints had to be replaced. As we had the weekend to fill in while waiting for his Monday appointment, a jaunt out to Charters Towers just 135 kilometres inland seemed a good idea and besides we were about ready for another bit of 'country'. We had heard that there were big festivities planned in conjunction with the 'Year of the Outback' so the nice and easy two hour drive for a bit of fun and action wasn't even a consideration as we headed up into the desolate hills.

This big country town does have two zebra crossings, so it didn't exactly fulfil our criteria on preferred places to stay, but it has got so much history and character, it would have been a shame not to enjoy the atmosphere. Pride in this old gold mining town was obvious wherever we looked, and it wasn't just the weekend's activities that put a smile on just about everyone's face.

It used to be Queensland's second biggest town surrounded by the richest gold field in Eastern Australia. Magnificent historic buildings line the streets, reminding us of a time when the earth yielded nuggets to some of the lucky diggers and brought extraordinary wealth to the town. After a backbreaking day under the relentless sun, the miners had a choice of no less than 92 pubs in which to satisfy their thirsts.

That's a lot of grog, and didn't they celebrate when a bloke called Tom Hoy came home with a huge 143-ounce nugget. The biggest ever found. The ghosts of the past, although not immediately evident, are there to be discovered along with the stories they have left behind.

Cattle are now the big money earner and the area boasts the highest number of beasts of any local authority in Australia. Times have certainly changed over the 140 years since the shire was first surveyed and stories abound of characters from bygone days and the bizarre situations that surrounded them.

One such story only goes back a few decades, to the 80s, when it was not an uncommon sight to see a horse enjoying a couple of coldies in one of the local pubs. A local doctor was the perpetrator of this unusual happening. He had had his license taken away for drink-driving and after visiting his ever decreasing list of patients in the mornings on horseback, then rode straight to his favourite watering hole at lunchtime. Slobbering straight from bottles of XXXX, his four-legged nag made a real mess on the tiles, but it amused the locals and was good for business. The landlord of the day was more than aware that an old tavern licensing law allowed a man to water his horse, so there was certainly no comeback if the beast preferred the local brew. The daily problem was getting the good doctor back in the saddle after an afternoon's drinking binge.

Local gossip has it, that he 'saw the light', changed his ways and went on to become a neuro-surgeon in Brisbane. For an imbiber of renown, that's an interesting career change, especially after years of 'having the shakes'.

Like a lot of outback towns, Charters Towers has its fair share of flying fox problems. In a certain area where they have decided to take up permanent residence, the smell is quite nauseating and the destruction of the trees disturbing. Scenarios such as these can be a topic of conversation often heard when sitting on top of a barstool at the local.

One of the numerous prodigious tipplers came up with his solution to get rid of these troublesome little critters. "Us mere white people aren't supposed to harm the little bastards" my new friend loudly declared to his fellow drinkers. "But what if we persuaded the local

Murri tribe to kill them all off with their catapults and stones and spears. Black people are allowed to catch and kill anything they want and wouldn't that solve a big problem" he rambled on, trying to enthuse his audience with his exciting new solution.

We moved round the bar to where the conversation was less provocative and noticed a large sign on the back wall, 'BEER ...HELPING UGLY PEOPLE TO HAVE SEX SINCE 1864'.

Old Harry just loves his barbwire stubbies, downing copious quantities of the stuff nightly and truly epitomised the image of a professional imbiber who 'drinks with both hands'.

Intoxication was in control, but amazingly and with remarkable clarity, he occasionally broke out into some profound observations. One of his favourite offerings was

"Beauty is often in the eye of the Beerholder", which he repeated twice to ensure I had correctly heard. It was difficult to ascertain his level of sobriety but then he stared me in the eye and proudly declared "I tried sniffing coke once, but the ice cubes kept getting stuck up me nostrils"

There is something I like about sitting next to strangers in these character-filled country pubs, listening to the world's problems being resolved in such a succinct manner.

We had come to see the much publicized outback celebrations and it was to be the biggest weekend in the town's history. There was a Grand Parade, camel races, an historic aircraft fly-in, rugby matches and a dozen events at the local showground including sheep shearing, camp drafting, branding, line dancing, entertainment, bush poets and working dogs. You name it, they had it and the crowds responded accordingly.

I've never actually seen camels racing, and presumed that there would be some sort of resemblance between these ruminant long-necked dromedaries and their faster, sleeker counterparts that compete in 'The Sport of Kings'. I was correct, there is a vague similarity.

These haughty looking beasts initially take an eternity to plod out to the starting line. Due to their unpredictability, they then may have a change of heart about even starting the race, decide they don't like their jockey and endeavour to dislodge him, or not take the race at all seriously. With these problems in mind, serious punting is limited.

The form guide in the racebook does though offer some enlightening advice to those gamblers wanting to throw their money around. ' Could be the Dark Camel of the Field', 'Very Smart Camel', ' Wouldn't come all this way if he couldn't gallop', 'Seen More Tracks than Burke & Wills', 'Is Known to be Erratic', were just some of the fascinating background highlights on the day's contestants.

They have some interesting names like Eunuch, Barbed Wire Jack, Aladin and King Solomon and all had their respective numbers roughly painted on their necks. But it was the slobbery foam emitted from a few mouths after each race that gave the clear impression that some determined jockeys take to their mounts quite aggressively.

Sharing a couple of cold ones after the final event with Australia's leading camel jockey, I gained an interesting insight into this increasingly popular sport.

Paul Grieg has been hanging on to the hump of the country's fastest camel, Eunuch for a couple of years now. His career-highlight was winning at Randwick against the countries fastest 16 dromedaries prior to the Sydney Olympics. Paul certainly looked the part with a head covered in curly brown dreadlocks, a wispy foot-long beard and baby-blue eyes flashing behind his wrap-around sunnies.

"Since the advent of bigger cash purses, there has been a lot more professionalism brought into the sport, and it is now being taken a lot more seriously" he told me. "This year I will ride at about a dozen camel race meetings around the southern half of the country and am lucky to have a camel like Eunuch, who just refuses to be beaten".

Back at the showground another rider grabbed our attention for a completely different reason. Young Bill was deftly guiding his huge 15-hand mare around the big mob of calves waiting to be branded. Now this wouldn't normally create much attention, except that the confident young rider was just five years old and ankle high to a bull ant. With a new Akubra perched nonchalantly on his head he really looked like a miniature version of his more experienced elders.

"The young fella has been riding since he was 18 months old," said his very proud father Clayton, who watched admiringly as Bill, who was not long out of nappies, circled and calmed the agitated beasts.

"Hasn't got a nerve in his body. We recently had a feral cat under our house in Longreach making some real wild noises. No way the dog would go in after it. Young Bill grabbed the slug gun, wriggled his way under the floorboards and shot the bloody thing dead" dad recalled with some measure of pride.

" I really wanna be a famous bronco rider when I grow up" confided sweet William as he munched away at a huge hamburger after his morning's duties. We felt sure that whatever he did, it would be from the back of a horse.

Across the arena, a mob of scruffy looking sheep was causing some problems for the working dogs. Normally in complete control of such situations, the clever canines had come unstuck when a couple of woolly wallies disappeared into the midst of a line of axe-wielding woodchoppers. The dogs gave it away in disgust. The scoreboard showed Sheep 1, Dogs 0.

The Akubra seemed to be the accepted headgear around these parts, compared with the leather stockman and bushie hats found up in the Territory. Akubra is an Aboriginal word meaning head-covering and has today become the Australian colloquial term for hat. Each one of these quality fur-felt pieces goes through 250 procedures over six weeks before they are ready for sale. High or tapered crowns, broad or narrow brims, these custom-made styles are made for different people in different conditions. Through their iconoclastic roots with the outback, the Akubra is the accepted symbol of outback living.

Saturday night at the Showground and the place is packed to the rafters. Everyone in town is there for the big 'under the stars' spectacular. Backstage there are bullock teams, a few dozen riders on horseback, Aborigines all painted up, dancers, singers and an anchorman cum compere who was only given the job and his script a few hours earlier. Nobody worried too much about a rehearsal, which made things pretty challenging for the stage manager, who had to work with strange people and agitated animals in the dark of the night. With a fair amount of talent and a dash of good luck, bush poet, joke teller and narrator, Bob Miller held the show together. There were a few worrying moments, such as when a totally inebriated indigenous gentleman caught security off-guard and staggered onto the arena looking for an argument. However, everything somehow ran to plan. What the hell, this was Charters Towers on a Saturday night and everyone was having a good time.

It was a nice easy drive back to Townsville for Morrison's appointment with the repair people but due to unanticipated screw-ups that can often happen with busy organisations, the parts had not been ordered as promised. This small oversight subsequently meant that we had to extend our stay. In hindsight I must thank those inefficient buggers, otherwise we would not have had the opportunity to visit Townsville's Reef HQ and The Museum of Tropical Queensland. Both are quite remarkable in their individual ways.

I find it quite a fascinating experience coming face to face with predators of the deep that appear to be totally oblivious to my presence, particularly if I am only centimetres away from them. Sharks, rays, sea snakes, lovable turtles and over a 100 species of brilliantly coloured tropical fish elegantly drift by looking very much at home in their superbly recreated surrounds. Feeding time is when they all come out of their self-hypnotised state and provide an absorbing highlight of the day. Frustrated fishermen like me can only imagine the results of dangling a baited line from above.

Engrossing information provided by the guides is educational and humorous, providing a wonderful insight into the fascinating world below the surface.

Right next door is the recently opened and highly acclaimed Museum of Tropical Queensland. It's not your everyday museum, some of which can bore the pants off a lot of people.

Around 200 years ago, The HMS Pandora sank off the Far North Queensland coast while on a voyage from England. The instructions to her captain had been to capture the mutineers from the Bounty and return them to the Motherland. The stricken vessel was not found until the early 1900s, and the museum is now home to an amazing collection of artifacts, belongings and equipment collected by divers from the ocean bed.

A whole floor is given to the re-creation of these events, with a life-size model of the front-end of the ship, and its beautifully carved bowsprit staring down at us as we entered. Lifelike characteratures and innovative maritime scenes creatively depict the moment of the sinking, the hardships of life on board and the subsequent tragic events. Haunting voices from the past tell their grueome stories, while films on recovery and shipwreck exploring make the hours pass very quickly. And of course we were made aware of the original Pandora's Box, a claustrophobic confinement area for the prisoners, affixed to the top of the deck.

Visitors are enlightened as to the instigation of a number of colloquialisms regularly used in our language today.

I learned that the word 'grog' is attributed to the actions of an Admiral Vernon, who sailed the high seas in the 18th century. This infamous seafaring tyrant was given the name 'Old Grog' because his coat was made out of a material called grogram. He was intent on curbing drunkenness on board his ships by watering down the liquor provided to the crew, thus giving birth to the slang expression 'grog'. Those were the days when sailors were rationed four litres of beer a day, which is nothing compared to some serious two-handed drinkers that I have the pleasure of knowing.

'Chewing the Fat' came from the same era, when sailors talked and grumbled deep down in the bowels of the ship, about the toughened salt meat that was forced on them throughout their entire voyage

The upstairs floors of the complex provide the most detailed information on coral, tropical species of animals, fish, computerised science games, and interactive exhibitions. Those who conceived and coordinated the building of this quite remarkable museum, should be congratulated on achieving a world class presentation.

We spent the balmy nights overlooking the Marina, tucked away on the water's edge with the outline of Magnetic Island across the bay. The traffic and activity of the city a blur in the distance. Watching the sun go down, and the reflection of the twinkling city lights across the bay, it did occur to us that anyone with a desire to live in a tropical city, would find the friendly lifestyle up here an acceptable proposition. Like a number of other Northern Queensland towns,

Townsville has numerous elegant old buildings but it was unfortunate to notice the excessive number of empty shops with 'To Lease' signs in their windows.

Morrison had his new ball joints fitted, which was surprising for one so young, but Ford had recommended him being recalled for this important task. Unlike our Sunliner the laptop had not been enjoying it's long journey and had been showing an increasing propensity to annoy the living daylights out of us by not wanting to perform certain tasks on certain days. The little bastard was now ready to go back to work after having his brain tumours removed and a new main board installed. The prognosis being that his nervous exhaustion was caused by nine months of being totally overworked on beaches and bush roads.

Enough of this city life, we've had our quota for the moment and with our jobs all done, it's off south in search of more unplugged places and entertaining characters that haven't been tarnished with changing times.

No one can figure out how Alligator Creek, which is just south of Townsville got its name, particularly as this member of the crocodile family has never been sighted in Australian waters. Winding its way down under the shadow of the towering granite mass of Mount Elliot, its cooling streams and rock pools are often visited by Townsvilleites en mass during the hot months of summer. Much safer here than the stinger-infested waters on their front doorstep. It's all part of the Bowling Green Bay National Park and a dream for hikers and bushies.

Most places where we have spent any length of time can be remembered for a particular view, event, meeting or occasion. Alligator Creek will always have fond memories for the particularly friendly rock wallaby, which decided to invite himself inside Morrison and get to know us. He was of course after a bit of tucker, but his curiosity in checking out all corners and edifices of the van, entertained us for a good hour. He then decided to stay for dinner. No way was he leaving without partaking of some tasty morsel, so the potato peelings were a highlight for him, particularly as the water-hungry forests were devoid of much nourishment.

Our friend Jiff mobiled us from Sydney during this wonderful interactive occasion. On learning of our uninvited guest, he caustically commented that we should dining on, and not with, this tasty treat from the bush. His dry sense of humour wasn't exactly appreciated especially when he came up with a delicious sounding recipe for stewed wallaby with quandongs.

His response to Fay's horror was predicable "Well, I've never known Ian to miss a good opportunity before!".

The suggested accompanying 1996 Tyrell's Shiraz wasn't even worth a consideration.

The ranger commented next morning that the last time such dry conditions were recorded was back in 1915, and if there was another month without rain, all water life in the creek would cease to exist.

Just a short drive south and there she was in total contrast, the mighty, bountiful Burdekin, the lifeblood of this area. Ayr is the major commercial centre for the rich farmlands and canefields of the Burdekin Valley, and there is an abundance of water here which doesn't necessarily come from the heavens or the river.

Back in the late 1880s, a wee guy from Scotland called John Drysdale figured out that there was a substantial underground water source flowing only a few metres below the surface. The brainy Scot, famous for his gaudy tam-o'-shanter, was a civil engineer and smart enough to work out how to tap and subsequently pump this life-giving resource. Introducing the then innovative spear system for irrigation, a whole new farming enterprise was created, which still successfully flourishes today. Being given the 'keys to the city' would have been small reward for these endeavours, although the town clock was erected in his memory as some sot of gratuitous offering, 40 years after his brainchild was born.

Vast areas of irrigated land now provide many varieties of fruit and vegetables that end up on tables around the country. It's also the country's richest sugar growing area, supplying enough to put one million tonnes in to our tea, coffee and cakes. That's worth around $400 million to the local economy, so take a bow John Drysdale. This forward thinker became known as the 'Father of the Sugar Cane Industry'.

The 'Silver Link' crosses the mighty 'B' and you need all your concentration traversing this unique structure which took 10 years to build. It's the biggest bridge on the East Coast and as there was no rock-bed to drill into, the engineers did the smart thing by making it a floating bridge.

We were about half an hour south of Ayr and looking for somewhere interesting to set up camp. Suddenly there was a small blue and white sign at the side of the road, proclaiming 'Township of Wunjunga', and pointing towards a desolate stretch of country. None of the maps we scanned indicated that such a place even existed, but the idea of 'hanging out' in another Aboriginal settlement had a certain appeal.

The ten kilometre dirt road to get to this coastal outpost was like something from a 'Mad Max' movie, with desolate saltpans and a demoralising plain of nothingness. Thousands of stark dead trees, scrubbed clean with the ravages of time, were sticking out of the dried-up mangrove swamps. The first sign of any life was a lonely seagull, forlornly standing on the welcoming sand dunes. The long curving bone-white beach suddenly came into view, raising our hopes that we might well be rewarded for our efforts.

Our images of shanty beach shacks, Aborigines hanging around the street corners, roaming dogs and unloved gardens did not materialise. Instead Wunjunga is a tidy seaside hamlet, consisting of about 50 buildings of no particular character. Nestled around a headland and with Mount Beachmount as a backdrop, the mostly besser block houses spill down to the deserted beach, some being lucky enough to actually have their back gardens right in the sand. 'Absolute Beach Front' at its best. Across the wind-blown bay, Cape Upstart looked dramatically imposing in the late afternoon sun. A block of dirt here with ocean views can still be bought for a mere $45,000 with all the advantages of being well away from bureaucracy and the restrictions of normal urban living.

Apparently back in 1989, the soul destroying Cyclone Ibu paid a brief but hostile visit and the whole settlement consisting of 60 beach shacks was bowled over like a pack of playing cards. Today the township has been rebuilt of firmer stuff; no more squatters, and now all the mod cons like power, telephone, garbage collection and street lighting. I called in for a cuppa with the unofficial Mayor who has been 'sort of' elected to represent the handful of full-time homeowners. I found the idea of having a Mayor for such a one-eyed backwater place sort of amusing, but Helen takes her position very seriously.

As one of the very few residents, she informed me that Wunjunga is an Aboriginal name for 'restful place near the water'. Restful it was certainly was. It was like a ghost town, without a sign of life or movement anywhere.

Down the road the locals have set up a free camping spot, which is still in its embryonic stage, with willing volunteers planting lines of young trees which will provide much needed shade in the future. It bears the unusual name of 'The Funny Dunny Park'. I sat there for a while using this quaint facility, which was the centrepiece of the park, doing what comes naturally in such a place, and couldn't for the life of me think of the slightest thing humorous about it. Certainly the couple of car owners who misjudged the treacherous sand at the ocean front section of the park and ended up leaving their vehicles to rust away in the ocean, would not have seen the funny aspect of this location. We parked Morrison well back from the soft stuff.

Adam was a young guy who regularly drove in at evening time, from nearby Home Hill, to try his luck at a spot of fishing. A likeable, knockabout sort of bloke, he towed along his two excitable dogs to give them a bit of exercise. This energetic pair of scruffs were perpetual motion and enjoyed the fishing game as much as their owner.

"I feel a bit safer when they're around, just in case a hungry saltie swims around from the estuary" he confided. "I reckon Spot or Bluey would get snapped up before me". This enlightening theory made me feel a whole lot more relaxed as I cast into the darkening waters of the late afternoon, edging just a little bit closer to the dogs.

Adam's fishing efforts were much more successful than mine and as we shared a beer back at camp he confided that his wife apparently has a few peculiarities. She forbids him to take his catch home as she can not bear the sight and smell of dead fish, although she just loves battered fish and chips if they're wrapped up in butcher's paper.

"What do you do with them", I lamely asked, looking at a mangrove jack and some sort of large cod with glazed eyes, staring at me from his bucket.

"I normally give them away to me mates" he inquisitively looked at me.

Wasn't I happy when he decided that I was his new mate and his catch quickly changed hands in exchange for a couple of cold ones. The freezer was full again and we dined on the freshest of fish. The night was spent only metres from high tide, the camp fire blazing away, fed with bleached driftwood scattered along the all but deserted foreshore.

The land on each side of the highway heading south was parched and as dry as old dog's bones. It appeared the barren land was good for nothing. Yet dotted amongst this desolation were rich verdant fields of irrigated crops. Rock Melons, tomatoes and the like, the fields busy with workers on tractors toiling away in the most perfect day.

A big faded sign on the roadside welcomed visitors and proclaimed 'BOWEN ......CLIMATE CAPITAL OF AUSTRALIA'.

What the hell is a climate capital? There is nowhere on this earth that hasn't got a climate, so what's with the capital bit? The mind boggles as to which overpaid advertising genius came up with that one.

Bowen is not on most travellers' holiday agendas, but tucked away along the southern beachfront are a couple of the most delightful bays imaginable. Horseshoe Bay is sublime and even though the Victorians take it over en masse for the winter months, they had recently departed and it was a drop of heaven when we arrived.

The brown mucky soup that we had experienced further north suddenly changed into an ocean of sparkling clear aquamarine water. It became apparent that the world famous Whitsunday Islands were just around the corner.

The view from the Flagstaff Lookout, which overlooks the vast harbour, winding river and surrounding mountain ranges was spectacular. Views of 360 degrees, which is the name of the café just being completed there, gives an extraordinary perspective of the surrounding countryside. .

Back in town and through the suburbs, Bowen can be pretty forgettable with the council needing some lessons on how to beautify the scruffy foreshore areas. Their dozens of large signs condemning camping seemed more important than making the place appealing enough to come there in the first place. Fair enough, the whole area was as dry as camel dung, that liquid stuff from the heavens was a distant memory for most.

The magic of the Whitsundays just came at us out of the blue. A total of 74 tropical islands lying out there in the aquamarine yonder, begging to be explored and appreciated. Airlie Beach is the Gateway to the Whitsunday Islands and it is a real pot pouri of life, where the bars and nightspots rage through till just before sunup. The whole town revolves around tourism right from the backpacker scene to diverse loads of boaties and various other tourists making a stopover on the way to the reef. Despite its name, Airlie does not have a decent beach, but in recent years has acquired an enormous and attractive lagoon right on the foreshore which offers year round swimming 24 hours a day. The combination of the lagoon and a developing restaurant scene is a great encouragement for visitors to linger longer.

How does the 'Whitsaturdays' sound? Well that's what they should really be called, as Cook screwed up on his dates and forgot to take into consideration his crossing of the International Date Line. Whitsaturday hasn't quite got that touristy ring about it, has it? He had other things on his mind at the time, like becoming a Captain, so it was probably just an oversight for the then Lieutenant.

It is all part of The Great Barrier Reef, which is the largest structure on Planet Earth that has been created by living organisms. There are 3000 reefs and 350 coral islands which stretch over 2000 kilometres, making it one hell of a big structure. The sheer size of the reef gives it an aura of majesty, and it is easily the biggest Marine Park in the world; a pulsating, living ecosystem with 400 species of coral, 1500 species of mainly exotic fish, 4000 types of molluscs and 215 types of birds. The teeming citizenship of the reef is endlessly diverse, continually amazing and often quite unbelievable.

Today, five-star travellers coexist with backpackers, families, everyday couples and adventurers, all enjoying the numerous island resorts and a large variety of activities.

Queensland quite rightly tags itself as the Sunshine State, epitomised by its laid back lifestyle, its emphasis on outdoor activity and a quickly expanding population. Lying back in the warming sun my mind was filled with images of all things Queensland; XXXX and Bundy Rum, Allan Langer and Hansonisms, Flo's Scones and Jo's Peanuts, The White Shoe Brigade and Brown Paper Bags, Cane Toads and Potholes, The Barrier Reef and Stingers, Akubras and Blowflies, Lamingtons and Cockroaches. This state certainly has its own inimitable flavour.

The hazy, sugarcane-lined country road toward Mackay had an enigmatic feel as the lowering sun filtered through in the late afternoon. Fields of cane in contrasting shades of greens and browns spread as far as the eye could see, while 'Thomas the Tank Engine' type trains busily pulled their loads over a myriad of mini train lines. Amongst this tranquillity, a mystical glow hung over the distant burning fields as black smoke drifted to the heavens.

'Her-outdoors' has a nose like a daschund when it comes to sniffing out 'stay overs', that could often be construed as prodigious. We camped right on a deserted beach near the tip of a peninsular and with drinks in hand, watching the finality of the sun's disappearance, shaded briefly by drifting faraway cane smoke.

Mackay to Yeppoon, which is just out of Rockhampton, is around 350 kilometres. It was difficult to refuse an offer to spend a few days on our friend's cruiser idling around the Keppel Islands, so we pointed Morrison in a southerly direction and made the trip in four hours.

Richard and Lynn hail from the Gold Coast but spend much of their time sailing the Queensland Coast in their comfortable and commodious 36-foot cruiser called 'Lollipop'. Getting a sensible answer from them as to why the 'good ship' had been christened with such a frivolous name proved difficult, but that became totally inconsequential as we left Rosslyn Bay Marina for a bit of R&R round the islands.

Richard is known for his dry sense of humour. Reminiscing on days gone by, and well before his marriage, he recalled his philosophy on single life.

"Every man should have a female companion for sex, sympathy and culinary delights. Of course the preference was to have them at three different addresses" he laconically drawled with a smirk on his face, narrowly avoiding a friendly backhander from Lynn, as he altered course for a new island.

We crossed the Tropic of Capricorn at ten in the morning which provided a vague excuse to have our first tipple of the day and quickly realised that there is little else to do at sea but relax and indulge ourselves in life's excesses. The days of slicing through the blue beyond were bliss, but exercise was minimal and mostly horizontal. The occasional chance to explore a deserted island, where footprints in the bleached sand are rare, provided the opportunity for a much needed work out.

Richard is an experimental foodie who loves to dabble in his galley, so the meals proved to be of a creatively high standard with each of us trying to outdo the other with innovative ideas. This recipe is an adaptation of one given to us by Fay's friend Terri, who fed us well with it on our last trip to the Harbour Bridge city.

Capricorn Cous Cous with Spicy Salmon

So titled due to the final mix being completed within sight of the Tropic of Capricorn.

I haven't met anyone who hasn't raved about this interesting hot and delectable combination of tastes, and we have certainly surprised a few.

Wrap one salmon fillet per person in buttered foil and cook over barbecue or hot plate until only just cooked through. Set aside to cool and start working on the cous cous.

Heat a tablespoon of olive oil in a wok or deep saucepan until smoking; add ¼ cup of couscous per person and stir well until brown. Stir in a tablespoon of harissa sauce, 1/2 cup of stock, preferably fish but chicken will suffice, season & keep stirring until stock has been absorbed. Set aside & fluff up cous cous to loosen after five minutes.

Cube a good sized peeled cucumber, mix with some preserved lemon pieces, ½ cup of chopped cashew nuts & add a cup of yoghurt with a squirt of lime juice.

Place couscous in a bowl, and mix with some chopped rocket, flake the salmon pieces over, then top with the cucumber/lemon and pour over remainder of yoghurt mix.

An easy dish to eat while sunning ourselves on the deck, leaving one free hand for a chilled crisp white.

On our last day we plunged into the seductively inviting waters of Fisherman's Beach, right outside the Great Keppel Island Resort. It took my mind back to less than a year ago when my oldest son Scotty nearly died in exactly the same spot.

It was a hot January afternoon and within minutes of his dive into the briny, the deadly Irukandji jellyfish had claimed its first victim in these parts. There were people of all ages swimming in the vicinity, yet he was the unfortunate one to get stung.

Scotty recalled "Within a short period of time I was delirious, breathing became restricted, my heart rate soared and I had cramps. Spasms followed with nausea and vomiting and I experienced this mounting sense of dread and doom. I was drifting in and out of consciousness, with each mounting wave of pain becoming worse. I was rushed to Rockhampton Hospital and awoke two days later surrounded by white-coated doctors".

He still shivers at the thought of the pain, and like many of those stung by this peanut-sized translucent killer blob, has spent time researching some history on the little critter.

Before the time of the white man, the Irukandji people were tormented by this tropical timebomb, which has now claimed a number of lives and is currently a serious threat to the multi billion North Queensland tourist industry. Last year 1800 specimens were caught by dragnet in just one week, with the hope of creating much needed antivenoms. Government research monies are virtually non-existent, which is a bit of a worry as very little is known about this phenomenon.

Other victims have rated the pain as 15-20 on a scale of 1-10, some saying that they would have preferred to end their lives to escape it.

Scotty's compelling gripe was that this busy internationally recognised resort did not display warning signs and gave no information to guests of the possible presence of these little bastards. Amazingly no medical facilities were available on the island, making his ordeal even worse, with the only management comment, " Sorry pal, but we haven't seen 'them' around here before". It is good to see that the new owners Contiki have at least created a first aid room, to provide much needed assistance should there be more Irukandji victims in the future.

All good things must come to an end and it was nice to find our land legs still working after our idyllic days spent on the water. Morrison waiting patiently at the Marina and was happy to have us back on board and was all ready to tackle the homeward stretch.

As we passed the Yeppoon Tourist Park, I noticed a most unusual rig, which made me stop and take a look. Sitting on a trailer and standing out like shag on a rock amongst caravans all lined up like sardines, was a houseboat. What a marvellous innovative idea to pull an amphibious home behind their 4WD and launch it down the nearest ramp for a few days on the water whenever the opportunity presented itself. An upturned tinnie lay on the roof of the oversized ute while the houseboat had all the facilities of any normal mobile home. Whoever thought that one up should be on to a winner.

We had intentions of heading inland, continuing down through central Queensland and reacquainting ourselves with the outback. Massive dust storms were devastating large tracts of the state at the time, while humidity was creeping up to the uncomfortable level. Full-on summer was with us. The refreshing breezes of the coast eventually proved a better option.

Emu Park, Kinka, Keppel Sands and Mulambin are a string of pretty little beachside villages, set along some glorious stretches of coastline. They could well become fashionable retreats one day, with real estate prices already on the rise and a feeling in the shopping centres that something was about to happen.

Bustling Rockhampton, 'Rockie' to all and sundry, proudly maintains it is Australias beef capital, and visitors are welcomed by a life-size statue of a bull at the entrance to the city. Sadly, the most imperative parts of the animal's anatomy are rarely hanging in place. There really are some 'desperates' around who think it is hilarious to nick such tacky souvenirs. After spending so much time in the quieter parts of the country, we were well and truly back in a world where wankers seem to reign supreme.

I have always harboured some sort of subconscious desire to visit the Town of 1770, a place I had read about with great interest.

Many years ago, I was travelling around the good old U.S of.A and spent some time in New Orleans. A brief affair eventuated with a

284

charming young lady from middle America, who happened to be a third generation regressionist. A world of past lives surrounded her and I believe that she later became somewhat of a celebrity through these fascinating talents that she had inherited from her mother. Mary Jo knew nothing of the world outside her own country and in fact had never even heard of 'the land of the kangaroo'. After a sensational meal of seafood gumbo one evening, she asked me if I would like her to practice her skills by doing a reading on my past life.

Holding a personal item of jewellery in her left hand and my right in hers, followed by much deep concentration, she proceeded to inform me that I was an old soul who had been on this earth many times before. One particular 'visitation' had been in the 18th century when as a seafarer and adventurer I had discovered lands far overseas. When I asked my name, she looked me deeply in the eyes and said Cook, you were a Captain Cook. I took all this with a grain of sea salt until she gave me the sordid details of my death on a beach at the hands of a bunch of overexcited Polynesians.

So it was with a certain degree of trepidation that I steered Morrison into 1770, the place where Cook first stood in Queensland, the birthplace of the State. We drove with a sense of anticipation to the marked spot of this momentous occasion. Standing in his footsteps I was hoping for some divine intervention or even a cold flush, but absolutely nothing eventuated. My little wife meekly suggested that Captain Hook might have been a more likely prediction.

Disillusioned, but not exactly distraught, after all those years of believing the good Captain and I were sort of family, I suggested we retired to the only drinking spot in town, where a cool refreshing drink can be taken overlooking the exhilarating coastline and estuary.

Steve Foster looks like a reincarnation of an 18th century seafaring rascal. This character who looked like a bit of a scallywag, with tousled hair and laughing eyes, had articulate and rapid vocalisations which somehow reminded me of those yesteryear days. He annually dons an original officer's uniform and plays the good Captain in a reenactment of when white feet first trod these soils.

Steve's been around here for 'donkeys' as he succinctly puts it, and used to run the camping park down by the water.

"About the only strenuous part of the job" he recalls " was sawing up lovely old logs for the campfires. Really gave me the shits when I used to regularly catch Victorians bundling the wood into their car to take back home with them. How desperate can you get?"

Steve is a true environmentalist and recently dedicated his rural property to the 'Land for Wildlife' programme.

"Clearing land, eradicates wildlife and flora, so I'm doing my bit" he proudly declared over another cooling ale at this quaint old bar overlooking Bustard Bay. His comments reminded me of a statement made by another environmentalist in the local rag, which I thought quite relevant

'The birdsong has given way to the dogbark, the rustle of birds has been replaced with the silence of the cats.' Few city folk, if any, give much concern to our changing and deteriorating world.

Today 1770 is still an idyllically beautiful sleepy hollow, but the talk in the pub was all about real estate prices.

"More expensive than Byron Bay and Noosa" some commented, with council rates of $3000 a year for a small block.

"Retiring here, means a lot more than just picking up your dole cheque" another drinker commented.

Celebrities have quietly bought in here along a small millionaire's row, the whole area being environmentally protected by the extensive Sir Joseph Banks Conservation Park. Back in the 40s when simple fishermen's shacks first went up, basic timber ones with magnificent river and ocean views, were going begging for around 200 pounds. Today the same shacks, probably untouched in all those years except for a rare coat of paint, are being snapped up for three-quarters of a million dollars.

Down the road in Agnes Water, the sort of twin town to 1770, there are two shopping centres, super chic real estate developments and a distinctive feel that the place is on the move. The new estates are a bit like lotto land, with an amazing array of colours and textures featured on the futuristic homes that are going up like mushrooms. And it is not the baby boomers buying here, but 30 to 50 year old successful corporate types who feel they have found their bit of paradise and are moving north in droves.

Wayne runs the incredibly well-stocked surf shop in town and has been coming to this outback place for nearly 30 years.

"Used to be just a few shacks mate, dirt road, no shops, no facilities, no nuffing" he beamed.

He's an old surfing fanatic and at 40 years or so, is still one of the many characters around town. Nicknamed Grommet by his mates, his waist-long curly flaxen hair would be the envy of any beach babe. A few grey strands may well be forthcoming due to his efforts in ensuring that the town is heading in the right direction.

"We're virtually crime free here mate," he proudly stated, just as a young sheila screams from the car park "My cars been stolen". He looked pretty disconcerted for a moment until it transpired that her boyfriend had taken it for a refill to the gas station. The crime level remained intact.

"Surfing the reefs mate is the big adrenaline rush around here" Grommet continued, unfazed by the car park activity. Old time surfers from all over the place get the charter boat out 50 k's or so and spend days out there in absolute surfie 'eaven"

But Grommet is more concerned about changes in the town. "Council doesn't seem to have a town plan, no infrastructure, yet they're trying to get the population up to 10,000 people in the next few years. Bloody marvelous eh".

Known as Queensland's marijuana capital up to a few years ago, the place doesn't seem to have a heart. There's no main drag to walk down, no beach side activity, a total lack of quality eating spots and no 'green' recreation areas. It does though boast the fifth best climate in the world, which is comparable with Hawaii. The distinct lack of tourists, particularly American ones, seems to suit the locals just fine.

We body surfed each day in what Grommet described as a 'gentlemen's surf'. Suited us perfectly. The warm translucent water was so inviting we just 'chilled out' and enjoyed every moment of it.

Let me tell you that camping on a narcotically beautiful beach with the water lapping the shore only metres away can be quite hedonistic, but when you find that the friendly couple next door, brew their own grog, then the playing field rises to a new level.

We were invited over for happy hour or two. Imagine our surprise when large bottles of Johnny Walker, Jim Beam and Bundaberg Rum were lined up next to Baileys, Butterscotch Schnapps and other such delights. Rick has been playing around with his alcoholic still and fine-tuning his methods to produce some bloody good drops, which he just loves to test on new found camping friends. Merrily mixing his pre dinner cocktails, his highly recommended 'Cocksucking Cowboy' was a real ball-tearer whose effects lingered on well in to the next morning.

"Once you've made the alcohol, it is all pretty easy after that" he confided.

After the copious liquid offerings of Rick's moonlighting talents, it seemed only fair to invite him and his charming wife to join us in our evening repast.

The mellow coals of the open fire had been quietly bringing the contents of the camp oven to fruition and hey presto we have

Camp Oven Pastrami

This is just a posh way of saying Silverside, which is so easy to cook. Buy it corned which is available just about anywhere and is good value, as you can get a few meals out of it.
Soak the meat in water for at least half an hour and in the meantime make a marinade consisting of mustard, Lea and Perrins and HP sauce. Mix into a fine paste and coat the Silverside. Sprinkle lots of cracked black pepper all over and place into hot camp oven, add a glass of red wine and a couple of bay leaves and cook for about 45 minutes.
Set aside to cool and slice thinly. It is great as a main course with salad and boiled potatoes and keep the rest for open sandwiches.

Our initial few days here had extended to a week and it was time for a change of scenery, something that the folks of Agnes Waters will be seeing plenty of in the years to come.

We breezed through Bundaberg, having brief thoughts of a visit to the rum distillery, but even though we go through a bottle or two of the stuff most months, the making of it didn't appeal nearly as much as the imbibing of it.

Fay and I had previously driven straight through the lovely historic town of Childers. The recent tragic event now causes more people to stop and look around, and we increased those statistics by two.

Only a couple of days before we arrived, dignitaries, political leaders and the like were part of a service commemorating the opening of a $1.75 million building, which replaced the burned-out Palace Backpackers Hostel to become a memorial to the lives lost. We slowly walked the 20 steps leading to the commemorative room where an eight-metre glass wall featured pictorial cameos of the young lives that tragically ended in the fire of 2000. It provided one of the most moving moments imaginable, standing and gazing with teary-eyed visitors from around the world, wondering why these terrible deeds take innocent young lives.

Bill Trevor, a big bearded burly man is the town mayor, and was the face of Childers during those distressing times. His warm humane approach guided the people of this farming community through one of its most trying times.

Childers, a National Trust Town with numerous heritage buildings, has had its fair share of tragedy over the years. Back in 1902 another fire swept through the town with disastrous effect, destroying many of the wonderful buildings. Lets hope that these hard working decent Queenslanders can put their grief behind them and are allowed to get on with their lives.

As we drove out of town, it was difficult to ignore the endless fields of rich red volcanic dirt, which grow just about everything. The countryside exudes an air of abundance, a feeling of prosperity, with the backpacker brigade slowly returning to work in the fields.

The tree-lined, winding, country roads around the back of Gympie are an absolute joy. A part of Australia that rarely sees the tourist vehicle, mainly because there's nowhere really popular to come from or, for that matter, to go to. The scenery is magnificent, green, mountainous cattle-grazing country with the occasional farmhouse or hamlet nestled into the valleys.

The appearance of long straight rows of stately pines and huge dark green bunya trees, lining each side of the road, indicating that civilisation may well be ahead.

Kin Kin consists of a telephone box, a country store, an art studio, a couple of nice timber homes and the 100-year-old pub. The only movement in the street when we arrived was a solitary dog yawning. However, there was a small degree of activity inside the historic Country Life pub, where they have a most unusual menu. That is, of course, when the restaurant decides to open. As the owners have a weird sense of humour, it is best to see if you can actually obtain a reservation before making a decision to dine. Fortunately they were closed the day we were there, else we would have had to make a serious decision between the Witchety Grubs or Wombat Wantons for an entrée. Fay reckoned she would have definitely plumped for the salivating sounding Pickled Possums for a main, while I would have been somewhat conservative and tried the Battered Etna Bats. Blowfly Sponge Cake was an obvious dessert, or pudding as they still like to call it out here.

It appears business had been rather slow and we couldn't figure out why.

There were a couple of lost souls at the bar, staring aimlessly at nothing, and one particular fella hitting his prime years wanted to chew the fat.

"Had a killer storm here 'bout 30 years ago, leaving a few dead and injured" he slowly drawled, as if this was about the only event that had ever happened to the place. "There were two churches side by side, top of the hill, an Anglican and a Catholic one" he rambled as though he had our undivided attention. "Storm blew the Catholic one away…. all gone but didn't touch the other". We waited for the conclusion to this long winded story with baited breath.

"Catholics pulled out of town so I bought the land for a $1000. So what do you think of all that?" I was only vaguely interested in the demise of the Catholic population and why the Anglicans were so blessed but more concerned in finding out about the discontinuation of the annual Kin Kin Races.

Our newfound friend didn't seem to be forthcoming on this subject but was far more set on continuing the story of his God-sent good fortune and the fact that he was giving serious consideration to erecting a dwelling on his 'religious historical site' after all these years.

The famous Kin Kin Racs were the the town's big attraction and advertised as Australia's toughest horse race. Man and beast threw themselves around a torturous four kilometre mountain course much to the delight of crowds. This strenuous event has been part of the folklore in this backwater hamlet for the past decade or two and has suddenly come to an abrupt end. The lady who runs the local rag maintains it's all due to the insurance companies. Public indemnity insurance premiums are not what they used to be, and the ridiculous increases have put many non-profit organisations and private people out of business.

It appears that the insurance hike was the straw that broke the camel's (or should we say horse's) back as the races had been in a state of decline, with the number of entrants dropping each year.

It appears that thoroughbreds were slowly replacing the stockman's horses, which takes away the excitement for the local farmer who likes to see the local nags succeed. A new annual attraction, the Valley Event, scheduled to happen each October hopes to give the place a new lease of life.

Kin Kin which is Aboriginal for 'Many Black Ants', started out at the turn of the century as a service centre for the local timber and dairy industries. There is an independent spirit amongst the 100 or so self-sufficient locals, created by the fact that there is no railway line or main road passing within cooee. It's got a hippie frontier town feel about it, which we both quite liked and enjoyed during the short time we spent there.

Tucked away in the hills, well to the south of Maryborough, is a picturesque 120 acre property called Curtis Park, which is operated by some ex Gold Coast friends of ours, Peter and Anne. Peter has spent a lifetime in that somewhat demanding profession of legally representing clients and helping them sort out whatever trouble they may have got themselves into. A few years ago he saw the light, unplugged the proverbial plug on the corporate world, along with the restrictions of suburban living and found his piece of Utopia. Now he's doing what he loves best, living on the land, working with his horses and providing courses for overseas visitors who seek basic training in the skills of outback work. Anne goes along with it all, providing great country fare for the in house guests and even gives lessons in English to those who require it.

There were a happy group of young English and Asian visitors there over the few days we stayed. The dinner conversation was lively and diversified and we thoroughly enjoyed being 'at home in the country', which provided another perspective of our already diversified journey.

Proudly framed and hung on a living room wall, is a certificate indicating that Peter is 'Proficient in Pregnancy Testing'. This simple document, as one would expect, has brought all manner of curious comments and questions. An English girl thought it amazing that we colonials hadn't got around to learning of the benefits of the pill. And there were numerous other weird and wonderful observations to this diploma. The document of course doesn't qualify what or whom he is testing, which in fact are horses and not his female visitors.

Horse whispering is certainly an art that takes not only a fair degree of talent, but also a mental insight into the simple mind of this normally uncomplicated beast. Contrary to popular belief Peter has a simple but persuasive argument that horses are quite the silliest animals on this planet and to successfully train them, it has to be with gee gee logic.

"Think, talk and act as though you were a horse and the chances of achieving your goals will improve considerably" he confided.

As somebody who only occasionally saddles-up, who am I to question his philosophies, but the interaction between himself and his dozen four-legged friends seemed to be working well. Winning the veterans division of the challenging Booubyjan Run a couple of years ago proved he knew how far to push his favourite nag.

Horses aside, his motley mob of cattle were lined up alongside a fence admiring the grass on the other side, which was certainly greener. Peter had finished a fencing job, with a little help from yours truly, and had opened the gate to let them into this green piece of heaven. They just stood their ground, staring at us both and waiting distrustfully to see which one of them would make the first move. I thought the moment right to enquire of my host if he had heard of the question 'are laughing stock, cattle with a sense of humour?'. His dismissive look at my sorry sense of humour was lost in a cloud of dust, as the mob suddenly had a change of heart and stampeded past us.

Fraser Island is a gigantic sand bar measuring over 120 kilometres long and I read somewhere that sand from along the entire East Coast of Australia eventually lands here, on what is now classified as The Great Sandy National Park. We had previously experienced memorable visits to this magnificent island so decided to give it a miss on this occasion, particularly as Morrison does not adept well to such sandy conditions

Instead, we found an idyllic camping spot right on the waters edge at Inskip Point, just opposite the southern tip of the Island, not far from where 4WD's lined up on the beach waiting to be ferried across the narrow channel to the island. Along the approach road which runs out from Rainbow Beach, there is a myriad of places to set up camp, hidden away under shady trees or next to a protective sand dune. Ocean facing or looking across the protected still waters leading to Tin Can Bay, either choice is a winner.

An army of soldier crabs was marching along the wet sand, laid bare by the receding tide while several turtles slowly cruised by. Boats lay at anchor on the mirror-like waters as the distant mountain ranges framed a glowing setting sun. A couple of bush turkeys, red and yellow neck bands glistening in the twilight, scurried through the bush while a cacophony of bird noises heralded the end of another day.

Yet this was not just another day, much as we found it hard to believe, it was our last day. This 'au natural' setting personified the type of place where we felt perfectly comfortable and we were content to sit back, take in every second, every sound and pull a cork on a cool refreshing drink.

As always, conversation came easily as we lazed under a picturesque star-studded sky and as a farewell gift, Mother Nature who had been so kind to us throughout our journey, sent us a perfect full moon.

We reminisced on the fact that although Morrison had carried us over 30,000 kilometres in just under 12 months, we had still only visited an infintesimal part of our great country. Two weeks of substandard weather during that entire period had given us excellent travelling conditions, albeit in a year when the word 'drought' had brought unimaginable heartbreak to many.

Our final leg through the urban sprawl of South Queensland back to our home base in Byron Bay was a day's drive. Morrison, sensing the finishing post was in sight, like a racehorse in the final strides before a spell, literally chewed up the kilometres.

Our large map of Australia, looking down on us from the ceiling of the cab was highlighted by 120 coloured map pins, each one indicating the various camping spots that had been our temporary home for one night or more.

It had been without any doubt one of the most exhilarating years of our lives.

The famous American author John Steinbeck once said "A journey is sometimes over, well before you return home".

Our journey remained the adventure we had hoped it would be right until the very last moment.

We had been away nearly 12 months, it had seemed like 12 years yet we hadn't aged a single day